the Communist Challenge in the Caribbean and Central America

the Communist Challenge in the Caribbean and Central America

Howard J. Wiarda and
Mark Falcoff
*with Ernest Evans and
Jiri and Virginia Valenta*

American Enterprise Institute for Public Policy Research
Washington, D.C.

Acknowledgments are given at back of book.

Distributed by arrangement with

UPA, Inc.
4720 Boston Way
Lanham, MD 20706
3 Henrietta Street
London WC2E 8LU England

Library of Congress Cataloging-in-Publication Data

Wiarda, Howard J., 1939–
 The communist challenge in the Caribbean and Central America.

 Bibliography: p.
 1. Caribbean Area—Relations—Soviet Union.
 2. Soviet Union—Relations—Caribbean Area. 3. Soviet Union—Foreign relations—1945– . 4. Communism—Caribbean Area—History—20th century. 5. Geopolitics—Caribbean Area. I. Falcoff, Mark. II. Title.
 F2178.S65.W52   1987   327.729047   87-14032
 ISBN 0-8447-3627-9
 ISBN 0-8447-3628-7 (pbk.)

AEI Studies 458

© 1987 by the American Enterprise Institute for Public Policy Research, Washington, D.C. All rights reserved. No part of this publication may be used or reproduced in any manner whatsoever without permission in writing from the American Enterprise Institute except in the case of brief quotations embodied in news articles, critical articles, or reviews. The views expressed in the publications of the American Enterprise Institute are those of the authors and do not necessarily reflect the views of the staff, advisory panels, officers, or trustees of AEI.

"American Enterprise Institute" and are registered service marks of the American Enterprise Institute for Public Policy Research.

Printed in the United States of America

Contents

	FOREWORD *Christopher C. DeMuth*	ix
	PREFACE *Howard J. Wiarda*	xi
	CONTRIBUTORS	xiii
1	INTRODUCTION *Howard J. Wiarda* The Debate over the Soviet Presence in Latin America 1 Proxies, Partisans, and Satellites: Aspects of the Soviet Presence in Latin America 3 The Book: A Look Ahead 10	1
2	COMMUNISM IN CENTRAL AMERICA AND THE CARIBBEAN *Mark Falcoff* The Caribbean in Soviet Strategic Planning 16 The Political Environment in the Caribbean Basin 17 Cuba 20 Nicaragua 30 Grenada 43	13
3	SOVIET POLICY IN THE CARIBBEAN AND CENTRAL AMERICA: OPPORTUNITIES AND CONSTRAINTS *Howard J. Wiarda* Sovietologists and Latin Americanists: A Meeting of the Minds? 51 The U.S.S.R. and Latin America: New Capabilities and Tactics 55 The Soviet Union and Latin American Realities 62 Conclusions and Implications 70 Bibliography 76	51

4 SOVIET STRATEGIES AND POLICIES IN THE CARIBBEAN BASIN
  Jiri Valenta and Virginia Valenta 79
   Shifts in Soviet Policies, 1960–1986 81
   Soviet Strategic Objectives 85
   Soviet Policies toward Revolutionary Regimes: Cuba, Nicaragua, and Grenada 92
   Soviet Policies toward "Progressive" Regimes: Mexico and Panama 109
   Soviet Policies toward "Bourgeois-Liberal" Regimes: Venezuela, Costa Rica, and Colombia 113
   Soviet Policies toward "Reactionary" Regimes: El Salvador, Guatemala, and Honduras 118
   Regional Conflict in the Caribbean Basin 123
   Future Soviet-Cuban Strategy in the Caribbean Basin 126

5 CUBA'S STRATEGY IN EXPORTING REVOLUTION
  Mark Falcoff 144
   Theories of Revolution: Conflict and Convergence 145
   Cuban-Soviet Military Links 147
   Cuban Contributions to Soviet Expansionism: Methodologies 149
   Cuban Contributions to Soviet Expansionism: Resources 151
   Cuba's Role: The Case of Nicaragua 154
   Cuba's Role: The Case of Grenada 155
   Cuba's Role: Nonrevolutionary States 156
   Future Prospects 156

6 REVOLUTIONARY MOVEMENTS IN CENTRAL AMERICA: THE DEVELOPMENT OF A NEW STRATEGY
  Ernest Evans 160
   The Earlier Generation of Revolutionary Movements 161
   Contemporary Revolutionary Movements in Latin America 168
   Patterns of Violence 177
   Conclusion: Implications for U.S. Foreign Policy 179

7	**BISHOP'S CUBA, CASTRO'S GRENADA: NOTES TOWARD AN INNER HISTORY** *Mark Falcoff* Cuba's Revolutionary Foreign Policy 187 Cuba and the New Jewel Revolution 188 Implications for Future Cuban Policy 193 Implications for Future U.S. Policy 194	187
8	**THE IMPACT OF GRENADA IN CENTRAL AMERICA** *Howard J. Wiarda* The Rising Soviet-Cuban Presence in Central America and the Caribbean Basin 199 What the Grenada Documents Reveal 199 The U.S. Intervention and Its Effects 205 Conclusions and Implications 212	198
9	**NICARAGUAN HARVEST** *Mark Falcoff* Nicaragua's Revolution 218 Nicaragua's Problems 220 Rising Totalitarianism 226 The Opposition and the Future 231	218
10	**AFTERWORD** *Mark Falcoff*	234
	ACKNOWLEDGMENTS	240
	INDEX	243

The American Enterprise Institute for Public Policy Research

A nonpartisan, nonprofit research and educational organization established in 1943, AEI is supported by foundations, corporations, and the public at large. Its purpose is to assist policy makers, scholars, business men and women, the press, and the public by providing objective analysis of national and international issues. Views expressed in AEI publications are those of the authors and do not necessarily reflect the views of the staff, advisory panels, officers, or trustees of AEI.

Executive Committee

Willard C. Butcher, *Chairman*
The Chase Manhattan Bank, N.A.

Paul F. Oreffice, *Vice Chairman*
The Dow Chemical Company

Christopher C. DeMuth
President, AEI

John J. Creedon
Metropolitan Life Insurance Co.

Richard B. Madden
Potlatch Corporation

Robert H. Malott
FMC Corporation

Richard M. Morrow
Amoco Corporation

Richard D. Wood
Eli Lilly and Company

James F. Hicks
Vice President, Finance and Administration, Treasurer, Secretary

Patrick Ford
Vice President, Development and Public Relations

Council of Academic Advisers

D. Gale Johnson, *Chairman*
University of Chicago

Donald C. Hellmann
University of Washington

Robert A. Nisbet
Albert Schweitzer Professor of Humanities Emeritus at Columbia University

Herbert Stein
A. Willis Robertson Professor of Economics Emeritus at University of Virginia

Murray L. Weidenbaum
Washington University

James Q. Wilson
James Collins Professor of Management at University of California at Los Angeles

---

Gerald R. Ford
Distinguished Fellow

Arthur F. Burns
Distinguished Scholar

Jeane J. Kirkpatrick
Senior Fellow
Counselor to the President for Foreign Policy Studies

Irving Kristol
Senior Fellow

Herbert Stein
Senior Fellow
Editor, *AEI Economist*

Ben J. Wattenberg
Senior Fellow

Claude E. Barfield
Resident Fellow
Director, Science and Technology

Douglas J. Besharov
Resident Scholar
Director, Social Responsibility Project

Phillip Cagan
Adjunct Scholar
Director, Contemporary Economic Problems

Marvin L. Esch
Director, Seminars and Programs

Robert A. Goldwin
Resident Scholar
Co-Director, Constitution Project

Gottfried Haberler
Resident Scholar
Economic Policy

William S. Haraf
J.E. Lundy Visiting Scholar

Karlyn H. Keene
Resident Fellow
Editor, *Public Opinion*

Evron Kirkpatrick
Resident Scholar

Marvin H. Kosters
Resident Scholar
Director, Economic Policy Studies

David Michael Lampton
Adjunct Scholar
Director, China Project

Marion Ein Lewin
Director, Center for Health Policy Research

S. Robert Lichter
DeWitt Wallace Fellow

John H. Makin
Resident Scholar
Director, Fiscal Policy Studies

Michael Novak
George F. Jewett Scholar
Director, Social and Political Studies

Norman J. Ornstein
Resident Scholar

William A. Schambra
Resident Fellow
Co-Director, Constitution Project

William Schneider
Resident Fellow

C. Eugene Steuerle
Resident Scholar

Edward Styles
Director, Publications

John C. Weicher
F. K. Weyerhaeuser Scholar

Howard J. Wiarda
Resident Scholar
Director, Hemispheric Studies

Foreword

AEI has long been in the forefront of strategic and foreign policy studies, with extensive publications on Asia, the Middle East, Europe and NATO, Latin America, and the U.S.-Soviet relationship. Over the years we have analyzed such diverse topics as SALT, detente, the Atlantic alliance, terrorism, the defense buildup, and U.S. strategic policy and made policy recommendations on them.

In this volume we turn our attention to the role of the Soviet Union, Cuba, and Nicaragua in the Caribbean and Central America. Two main arguments have dominated the debate: one, that the Soviet Union and Cuba are the cause of all the trouble in the region; and, two, that the Communist issue is a red herring, a bogus issue without basis in fact.

This book sets the record straight. It outlines the rising Soviet military, cultural, diplomatic, economic, and political influence in the region. It also traces the growing sophistication of Soviet strategies and tactics, as well as the limits on the Soviets in the area. It shows how the Soviet Union, while not the instigator of most Latin American instability, has learned how to play on the heightened nationalism, anti-Americanism, and desire for change in the region and to profit from them. In taking advantage of the shaky insitutions of the area, the Soviet Union is able to expand its influence, embarrass the United States, and turn the existing instability to its own purposes. We hope this book will encourage discussion on these critical issues.

This book was completed with financial support from the Mellon Foundation, Citicorp, the Pew Memorial Trust, and another major foundation, which wishes to remain anonymous. We thank them for their generous support; the book that follows, however, expresses the views of the scholars involved in the project and not necessarily those of the sponsors.

CHRISTOPHER C. DEMUTH
President
American Enterprise Institute

Preface

The debate over the Soviet role in Latin America has waxed hot and cold; only occasionally has it been factual and enlightening. On the one side are ranged those who believe that all Latin America's troubles, including every signal of rebellion and upheaval in that often tumultuous region, can be blamed on the machinations of the Soviet Union. On the other side are ranged those who believe that every charge of "Communist-inspired troubles" is another red herring, a false charge without substance, and probably designed as a smoke screen for U.S. intervention. Surely somewhere in the midst of all this heat there is room for a little light as well.

That, in any case, is the assumption on which the present volume is based. The Soviet Union *is* a rising presence in Latin America, and one would be foolhardy to deny this fact. Our book helps trace, document, and substantiate this new Soviet presence and activity in Central America and the Caribbean and to provide the factual bases on which informed judgments and policy decisions about the new role and influence can be based. For one of the main problems for policy in this whole area is that Soviet activities, strategies, and tactics are little known, either by the general public or by Latin America specialists.

At the same time one would be equally foolhardy to overstate the Soviet role and threat or to blame all of Latin America's troubles on the Soviet Union. The fact is that while the Soviets are a rising and serious influence, they also face severe limits and constraints on what they can do in Latin America. The Soviet Union can exacerbate troubles that already exist in Latin America and turn them to its own advantage to embarrass the United States; but it is still the case that the United States remains overwhelmingly dominant in the Western Hemisphere, while the Soviets consider the area of secondary importance. These dynamics and their implications are explored in the book.

This volume is the result of a considerable collaboration among several persons of distinct backgrounds and specializations. Mark Falcoff and I were both at AEI while this book was planned and written; over the past five years we have collaborated on projects too numerous to list, and our points of view and academic backgrounds (history and political science, respectively) have provided a nice complementarity. Ernest Evans has written extensively on terrorism, guerrilla movements, and ideology and in the past six years has increasingly turned his attention to Latin America. Jiri Valenta is a Soviet and East European specialist, adding a further dimension to our understanding; his wife Virginia Valenta is a Latin America specialist; and their joint efforts help bridge the yawning gap between these two academic and policy areas of specialization. The five of us have collaborated on various scholarly ventures in the past, and we look foward to working together again in the future.

Some of the chapters contained in the book have been presented or published previously in other forms and formats but in such diverse and scattered places that they deserve to be brought together here in a single coherent and readily available book. The chapters by Ernest Evans and by Jiri Valenta and Virginia Valenta were first published in another AEI volume *(Rift and Revolution: The Central American Imbroglio)* and received such favorable acclaim in the reviews that we asked them to prepare revised and updated versions for the present study.

We wish to thank Janine Perfit, our loyal research assistant for these several years, and Louise Skillings, secretary *extraordinaire*, for their assistance in the preparation of this volume. The AEI staff was, as always, helpful, skillful, professional, and supportive. The book was made possible by generous grants to AEI's Center for Hemispheric Studies by funding agencies and by several major foundations acknowledged in the foreword and by one foundation that wishes to remain anonymous. Such reticence is exceedingly rare in this day and age, so that while respecting the foundation's wish for anonymity, we as authors would also like to express our gratitude. With or without anonymity, of course, the foundation bears no responsibility for the product; that rests solely with ourselves.

HOWARD J. WIARDA

Contributors

ERNEST EVANS, a guerrilla warfare expert, is a professor of political science at the University of Missouri and has taught at MIT and the Catholic University of America. He has written on terrorism, Latin American politics, international relations, and revolutionary movements. He is the author of *Calling a Truce to Terror; The American Response to International Terrorism*.

MARK FALCOFF is an international affairs fellow at the Council on Foreign Relations completing a book on Chile. He received his Ph.D. from Princeton University and has taught at the Universities of Illinois, Oregon, and California (Los Angeles). A specialist in Latin America, he was a senior consultant to the Kissinger Commission and served as a professional staff member of the Senate Foreign Relations Committee during the Ninety-ninth Congress. He is the author of numerous articles and books on Latin American history, politics, and international affairs.

JIRI VALENTA is professor of political science and director of the Center for Soviet and East European Studies at the University of Miami. Previously he was professor of national security affairs and coordinator of Soviet and East European Studies at the Naval Postgraduate School, Monterey, California, and a fellow at the Woodrow Wilson International Center for Scholars, Washington, D.C. He has written many studies on Soviet foreign policy, Eastern Europe, and Soviet-Cuban involvement in the third world.

VIRGINIA VALENTA has analyzed Soviet and Cuban policies in Latin America and is coauthor of articles on Soviet-Cuban involvement in the third world.

HOWARD J. WIARDA is a resident scholar at the American Enterprise Institute and director of its Center for Hemispheric Studies. He is professor of political science at the University of Massachusetts,

Amherst, where he was the director of the Center for Latin American Studies. He has published extensively on Latin America, southern Europe, the third world, and U.S. foreign policy and is the author most recently of *Finding Our Way? Toward Maturity in U.S.–Latin American Relations*.

1
Introduction

Howard J. Wiarda

The Debate over the Soviet Presence in Latin America

The Soviet Union is a rising presence in Latin America—politically, culturally, economically, diplomatically, and militarily. Moreover, the Soviet strategy and tactics in Latin America in recent years have become far more sophisticated, nuanced, and effective. But that presence and the challenge it poses both to Latin America and to U.S. interests in the area must be understood and dealt with realistically.

It will do little good either to deny this rising Soviet presence in Latin America or to wish it away, as a number of scholars, journalists, and professional Latin Americanists are inclined to do. Their image of the Soviet role in Latin America is often still shaped by ideas that go back to the 1950s. Then, the Soviet presence in Latin America was minuscule indeed, and, although there was significant Communist participation in the revolutionary government of Jacobo Arbenz in Guatemala in the early 1950s, the idea that Stalinist legions were about to take over Latin America seemed ludicrous—as in fact it was.[1]

The disparagement of Soviet possibilities in Latin America by professional scholars of the area was further reinforced by knowledge about local Communist parties. These parties, in country after country, were minor "pocket parties," often in the pay of the reigning men-on-horseback, thinly organized, without strong support among the trade unions, peasants, or the general population, weakly led, and consisting, in the words of an often-cited report, of "old and tired bureaucracies."[2] The Latin American Communist parties seemed to constitute no threat to anyone and certainly not to the existing governments of the region, let alone to the United States.

In addition, the "Communist infiltration" charge had been used so often as a red herring or as a smoke screen for U.S. intervention and other misguided activities in Latin America that it was almost totally discredited. Hence, when someone brings up the Communist issue nowadays, or suggests a rising Soviet presence, the immediate reaction among scholars and professional students of the area, shaped by this earlier tradition, is disbelief. The Communist issue has been so misused, so often exaggerated and blown out of proportion that it lacks credibility today. The cry "wolf, wolf" has been heard far too often—whether the wolf was actually there or not—so that when the same warning is issued now, disbelief and skepticism are the typical reactions. Hence currently, when there are indeed a rising Communist and Soviet presence and problem in Latin America, the first reaction among those who know the region is to scoff. Moreover, the bitter aftertaste of McCarthyism and reaction against it remain sufficiently strong that even if the evidence of Communist involvement is presented, no one wishes to raise the issue for fear of being labeled a McCarthyite or of having used the now discredited technique of guilt by association.

While blindness to the rising Soviet presence in Latin America or unwillingness to credit it is prevalent in the academic, artistic, and journalistic communities, there is an opposite, and related, problem that is equally problematic for policy. That is the tendency among some to overstate and exaggerate the Communist problem in Latin America. In the first case the problem is one of underreaction to the emerging Soviet and Communist problem; in this case it is overreaction. The fact is that while the Soviet Union is a rising presence in Latin America, its influence is still quite limited and nowhere equal to that of the United States. Further, it is definitely not the case that the Soviet Union is *the* cause of all the problems in Latin America, that all revolutions in Latin America are *ipso facto* Communist revolutions, or that the main issues in Latin America can be understood in terms of the East-West axis.

On the other hand, while the Soviet Union is not the one cause of all the problems in Latin America, it is a contributing cause, able to exacerbate and take advantage of already existing problems; and it is obviously the cause that does, and must, most concern U.S. foreign policy makers. The primary concern of any U.S. policy maker must be the defense of U.S. security and strategic interests. That is a fact, a reality that those who study Latin America professionally or who are genuinely interested in its history and culture must understand and come to grips with. It is a reality that will not change soon, if ever; and if the facts are taken into account, this prevailing posture and preoccupation with strategic concerns should explain a great deal of U.S. policy toward the area. Such a view is probably the proper one, however much Latin Americanists may feel uncomfortable at times with some of its implications.

In addition, it needs to be said that although not all revolutions in Latin America are Communist revolutions, since Cuba and Nicaragua the possibility has become strong that what begins as a largely indigenous revolution with broad-based popular support may be manipulated by the Communist elements within it—or be taken over later by Marxist-Leninists after first having disguised both their goals and their degree of participation in the revolution. Politically as well as strategically, no American administration can afford to take a chance that a Latin American revolution might go in a Communist direction. And further, while the main issues in Latin America should not be understood exclusively as an element of the East-West conflict, that is—for good or ill—the dimension that the U.S. government and the U.S. public are preoccupied with—and moreover, the situation is likely to remain that way.

These considerations add nuance and complexity to the issue of the Communist role and presence in Latin America. Further, they suggest that American perceptions, including those of policy makers and the general public about the Soviet Union and the Communist role, may be as important as what is objectively the case. These comments also hint that domestic political considerations may play a significant role in the government's framing of these issues, or in the opposition to its policy.

Above all, these comments suggest—and the analysis is further broadened in the subsequent chapters—that the Soviet Union *is* a rising presence in Latin America, which cannot be ignored and which must be dealt with concretely and realistically. At the same time, the Soviet role and capacity should not be blown up and so exaggerated as to make the argument ludicrous and incredible and therefore productive not of an effective policy response but simply of further divisiveness, polarization, and policy paralysis.

In this book we seek to achieve some degree of balance and realism among these contending viewpoints, to trace and assess in a serious way the growing Soviet and Communist presence in Latin America without unduly exaggerating it; to analyze changing Soviet strategy and tactics in the area as well as those of its proxies; to offer assessments of the Cuban, Nicaraguan, and Grenadan revolutions; and to evaluate the U.S. policy response in the region and offer suggestions for its improvement.

Proxies, Partisans, and Satellites: Aspects of the Soviet Presence in Latin America

The Soviet Union has not been a significant actor in Latin America in the past. There have been Communist parties, trade unions, and student groups in most of the countries since the 1920s and 1930s, but these were not major actors and certainly constituted no threat to the status quo. Nor has the Soviet Union itself been strongly interested in the region until recently: Latin America is far away, the logistics are difficult, Soviet vital interests are not affected, the Soviets lacked the naval and marine forces to extend themselves so far from the homeland, and the area was viewed as lying within the U.S. sphere of influence. Through the 1950s the Soviet Union provided some limited aid to the local Communist forces and was supportive of local Communist activities, but its commitments, activities, and enthusiasm for Latin America were not very great.[3]

That attitude changed significantly in the late 1950s with the Cuban revolution and the falling of the Cuban plum into the Soviet lap. The Soviets had done practically nothing to aid the revolution, and to the end the Cuban Communist party had applied that worst of all possible epithets to Fidel Castro: a "petty bourgeois reformer." But the Soviets certainly did not turn down this gift, and thereafter their activities in Latin America began to increase. The Soviet Union broadened its diplomatic relations in the area and in various countries aided and abetted insurgent movements aiming to topple existing governments. This phase ended in considerable disillusionment, however, with the numerous failures of the Cuban revolution, the lack of success of the several Soviet-supported insurrections, and the death of Che Guevara in Bolivia.[4]

It was also during this period that the U.S. response and position with regard to the new Communist presence in Latin America were established. That position quite simply was "no second Cubas"—hence, the Alliance for Progress, the Peace Corps, and other programs that presumably would help prevent "second Cubas" from occurring in Latin America. But it is important to ask what the policy of "no second Cubas" meant. The usual interpretation has been that it meant the United States would tolerate no more Castro-style revolutions from coming to power. That is true, but it is only part of the story. That stance has enabled critics of the United States to assert that the United States was a reactionary country, that we would always defend the status quo, and that we would permit no change in Latin America—all charges that are patently false but that have enough glimmers of truth to give the critics' arguments some plausibility, particularly among the uninformed. In fact, the United States has often been in the forefront of change, usually within carefully prescribed bounds to be sure and not always enlightened or informed about the sometimes unintended consequences of the changes it introduced. Indisputably, however, since the early 1960s the United States has helped lead, stimulate, and initiate the change process in Latin America.

For policy makers who were in government in the early 1960s (such as Lyndon Johnson), however, "no second Cubas" meant not just a prevention of Castro-style revolutions inimical to our goals and interests, but also an overwhelming desire not to allow the Cuban missile crisis of 1962 to be repeated. That is what is really meant by the "no second Cubas" strategy, and it accords with our earlier analysis of the overriding importance to U.S. policy makers of security and strategic interests. For not only was Cuba a revolutionary and Marxist-Leninist state, a Soviet satellite aimed at subverting its neighbors, which the United States would clearly resist, but it had also become a base for the implantation of Soviet missiles aimed at the United States. For those who know how close we came to a major, even nuclear, confrontation with the Soviet Union in 1962, that was an experience never to be repeated. Hence the "no second Cubas" policy should be looked at as double-edged: no Cuba-style regimes dedicated to subversion and Marxism-Leninism and never again the possibility of the use of such a Soviet satellite for the implantation of missiles or a military capacity that threatened, even potentially, the United States. That is clearly a major preoccupation for U.S. policy makers in dealing with Nicaragua. The policy was antirevolutionary, but the motives grew as much from basic, fundamental security and strategic considerations (a direct threat to the United States) as from political and ideological ones.

Following Guevara's failure in Bolivia, meanwhile, the Soviet Union again changed its strategy. These changes are detailed in the contributions by Ernest Evans and by Jiri Valenta and Virginia Valenta in this book. Instead of concentrating all its efforts on aiding guerrilla movements that had not proved successful, the Soviets turned to a long-term strategy of strengthening their diplomatic representation in as many of the countries of the area as possible, building up their bilateral economic relations, quietly increasing their military presence in Cuba, establishing good relations with as many governments as possible, strengthening cultural ties, and using Latin America's rising nationalism and anti-Americanism to its own advantage to construct broader anti-American coalitions. This strategy was both quieter and much more sophisticated than that used by the Soviets in the past. It was aimed at building legitimacy for Soviet activities and policies, in Latin America as well as globally. It also corresponded, during virtually the entire decade of the 1970s, to a decline in the U.S. presence and interest in the region, to a period of "benign neglect" of Latin America by the United States, and to a period when the United States was perceived in Latin America to be a declining and weakening world power. Hence, it was viewed as prudent by the Latin American countries to, in the phrase of the times, "diversify their dependence" by opening up stronger ties with the Soviet Union and Eastern Europe.[5]

It is this newer and more sophisticated strategy, and the increasing Soviet presence that goes with it, that has been largely ignored by professional Latin Americanists. To a considerable degree they are still prisoners of that earlier epoch when the Soviet Union was an insignificant actor in Latin America and, with the exception of Cuba, its attempts at sowing subversion and revolution were largely failures. Moreover, given the frequent use of the Communist bogyman as a red herring and as a cover for other and sometimes less noble U.S. activities, many U.S. Latin Americanists are simply unwilling to credit the facts of an increased and increasing Soviet presence. The overwhelming majority are themselves not Communists, but because of this history they are often unwilling to criticize the Sandinistas, for example, and, in the absence of incontrovertible evidence, to believe the charges of a Marxist-Leninist takeover of the revolution or of assistance to guerrilla forces in other nations. Part of our purpose in this book is to speak to these issues and to provide information on the emergence of the Soviet Union as a significant and growing, if still secondary, presence in Latin America.

When the Nicaraguan revolution succeeded in 1979, and when that same year the New Jewel Movement came to power in Grenada, the Soviet Union once more reassessed its position. Latin America now again looked ripe for revolution—hence the stepped-up Soviet aid to the Salvadoran guerrillas and similar groups. These changes and new Soviet opportunities and strategies are also addressed in our chapters.

Most recently, since the U.S. invasion of Grenada, the wheel appears to have turned again. The information we have is incomplete, but it appears that in the wake of Grenada the Soviets have once more reassessed. The U.S. buildup in Central America and the Caribbean has been so immense, and the stakes there for the Soviets sufficiently modest, that from their point of view the costs of challenging the United States in its own backyard—where the United States enjoys overwhelming local advantage—may not be worth it. Hence, there are indications that the Soviet Union may again be deemphasizing Latin America and concentrating its efforts in countries or regions where it enjoys local advantage: in Afghanistan, for example, or in its relations with India or the pressure it is currently putting on Pakistan. The Soviets are clearly not pulling out of Latin America, but they are certainly reevaluating their prospects there, as against other global priorities and regions of influence.

The history of the Soviet role in Latin America, therefore, is a limited one, modest in the past but increasing considerably in the past two and a half decades. Moreover, the policy and strategy followed by the Soviet Union have become more and more complex and sophisticated. This enlarged presence of the Soviet Union in Latin America needs to be recognized, understood, and dealt with realistically.

The rising Soviet presence is also related, we have said, to a certain diminishment of the U.S. role in Latin America in the 1970s and to a more assertive, nationalistic, and independent Latin America seeking to diversify its international connections and relations. Up until Castro's successful revolution in the late 1950s, the United States had had Latin America almost exclusively to itself. Now, with a variety of new outside actors, that is no longer the case. Latin America's international relations, connections, and interdependence have become much more complex. Besides the United States, the array of other, perhaps secondary powers (conceding the continued overall dominant presence of the United States) includes the Soviet Union, West Germany, Japan, Spain, and France.[6] The presence of these several other actors makes the formulation and implementation of U.S. policy in Latin America far more difficult and enormously complicates the job of the U.S. foreign service officer.

It is, of course, the Soviet presence, seen in this broader and more complicated context, that concerns us here. Not only is the Soviet Union a rising influence in Latin America, but also its influence has become more pervasive and complex. Its diplomatic presence has become considerably larger, including relations with and embassies in all but five of the Latin American countries. The size of its diplomatic missions has grown and so has the quality and Spanish-speaking ability of its personnel.[7]

Soviet trade with Latin America, particularly such key countries as Argentina, which supplied wheat to the Soviet Union after the imposition of the U.S. embargo in 1980, has grown enormously in recent years. Such trade has become extensive in a wide variety of products and has been accompanied by an increase in trade missions and other exchanges. Soviet cultural missions in Latin America have similarly been stepped up, and the number of scholarships available to Latin American youths to study in the Soviet Union has been significantly increased, vastly surpassing (by ratios of up to 10 to 1) the U.S. efforts in these areas. The attention devoted to Latin American affairs in official Soviet "think tanks" has also been markedly expanded.[8]

Especially worrisome is the Soviet military buildup, including in the Caribbean Basin. This buildup encompasses the army, navy, and air force, as well as special forces. Details concerning this military buildup are provided in the following chapters. The Soviet Union now has for the first time a deep-water navy capable of projecting Soviet power anywhere in the world. Its air force similarly ranges far and wide. Most recently, the Soviets have begun to build up their marine and amphibious assault forces capable, like those of the United States, of intervening quickly and decisively tipping the balance in a localized conflict virtually anywhere in the world.

Latin America is, of course, far distant from the Soviet Union, and there are immense problems of logistics, resupply, and the like. That is where, among other things, Cuba plays such a vital role. Cuba provides the Soviet Union with a base, port facilities, an "aircraft carrier" for its long-distance planes, a listening post, a launching pad, a refueling depot, and a training facility for guerrillas, terrorists, and political operatives from all over Latin America and Africa. Cuba has, in addition, a Latin American face and voice, which make it easier for other Latin Americans to emphathize with its revolution than with those of the Soviet Union or Eastern Europe. Cuba has its independent interests and capabilities in a number of these foreign policy areas, but it also serves as a proxy, surrogate, and far outpost for all kinds of Soviet machinations. That is why a ring of additional Soviet satellites, encompassing potentially or in the past Nicaragua, El Salvador, Grenada, Suriname, and others, is so worrisome.

It is not just that the Soviet presence has greatly increased in Latin America but that its strategy, tactics, and *understanding* of Latin America have become much more sophisticated as well. The Soviet Union and its operatives are no longer the stumble-bums or comic opera buffoons of movies and television. Rather this is a deadly serious game being played in Latin America by intelligent, trained, capable, often ruthless people, for stakes that continue to get higher.

Finally, the Soviets have learned to use to great advantage the "nationalism" (often automatically translated as anti-Americanism), the "heroism," and the "independence" of the Cubans and now the Sandinistas as a means of increasing their possibilities in Latin America—and meanwhile of twitting, challenging, and causing difficulties for the United States. It has not been hard over the years for the Soviets to find issues to use to take advantage of this latent anti-Americanism; the change now is that they have become more skillful at manipulating Latin American opinion in these directions and that the Latin Americans have become more receptive to those positions. This is a real problem that neither American policy makers nor the informed policy-influencing community is sufficiently or adequately apprised of.

Yet it is also important, even while emphasizing the growth of Soviet activities in Latin America, to recognize the limits on Soviet power and capabilities in Latin America. The Soviet Union is a rising presence in the region, but it remains of distinctly secondary importance. Its influence is by no means equal to that of the United States. Rather, it ranks at a second-level tier along with West Germany and others—except for its military-strategic capabilities that do constitute a threat, current or potential, to the United States. There are severe constraints on what the Soviets can do and accomplish in Latin America—even on what it wants to accomplish. For the fact is that although Latin America is of rising interest to the Soviet Union, the area is not of vital importance to it, as is Eastern Europe, for example, or perhaps even Afghanistan.

Moreover, with the renewed attention of the United States to Latin America in recent years and our military, political, diplomatic, and strategic buildup in the area—coupled with our apparent willingness to use force as in Grenada and Central America to protect our interests—there is evidence that the Soviet Union is reconsidering its Latin American involvements. The Soviets are not about to withdraw from Latin America, but they may well be tempted to concentrate their expansionist ambitions elsewhere. Renewed and wholehearted wooing of India and the stepped-up pressure directed at Pakistan, for example, may well be among the first indications of these shifting priorities.

Hence the purposes of this book: the Soviet Union is emerging as a serious presence in Latin America that must be assessed factually, prudently, and realistically. It will do us little good as a nation for our policy either to overstate or to understate the Soviet role. In the Washington policy community, as well as among the public at large, such exaggerations on both sides of the issue often prevail—and they are counterproductive of good policy. Our purpose here, in contrast, is to provide a reasoned, calm, dispassionate, and, we think, realistic analysis and assessment.

We hope that this study will serve a number of purposes. On the one hand, the Soviet specialists in the United States who are now turning their attention to Latin America need to know far more than they now do about the area. On the other hand, Latin Americanists need to know far more than they now do—or are willing to admit publicly—about the Soviet role in the region. At the same time, foreign policy generalists and the public at large need to know more about both Soviet strategies and Latin America—and the connections between the two. We need, in addition, to be able to distinguish between countries and to analyze the changing and quite different

Soviet strategies from one country to the next. The book seeks to forge links and understandings among these diverse communities and foreign policy issue areas.

The Book: A Look Ahead

Our study begins with an overview by Mark Falcoff, "Communism in Central America and the Caribbean." Dr. Falcoff provides a historical introduction to the region, discusses the Caribbean area in Soviet strategic planning, analyzes the political context of the Caribbean region and the U.S. role, treats the three main Caribbean revolutions (Cuba, Nicaragua, and Grenada), and assesses the options for U.S. policy makers.

In the following essay by the volume's co-author, Howard J. Wiarda, both the opportunities for Soviet policy in the Caribbean and Central America and the constraints on that policy are analyzed. The author begins by examining the quite different perspectives of Sovietologists and Latin Americanists on these issues. He then dissects the new capabilities and tactics employed by the Soviet Union in Latin America. He assesses those factors favoring a larger Soviet role in Latin America as well as those impeding it.

Jiri Valenta and Virginia Valenta next analyze Soviet strategies and policies in the Caribbean Basin. Carefully and in detail, they examine Soviet strategic objectives in the area, trace the rising Soviet presence in all its manifestations, analyze Soviet policies toward a variety of Latin American countries, discuss future Soviet-Cuban strategy in the Caribbean, and conclude with a series of recommendations for new U.S. policy initiatives in the region.

Mark Falcoff then offers a complement to the Valentas' chapter by focusing specifically on Cuba's role. He assesses the Soviet Union's thinking about Latin America before 1959, shows how the Cuban revolution provided a watershed, talks about Cuban-Soviet military links, Cuba's contributions to Soviet expansionism, and Cuba's role in Nicaragua and Grenada. He concludes with a statement on future prospects.

In chapter six Ernest Evans analyzes the development of new strategies among the revolutionary forces in Central America. He studies the earlier generation of revolutionary movements and the revolutionary precepts of Che Guevara and Reges Débray. He contrasts the earlier "foco theory" with the much more nuanced and sophisticated strategy followed today. He also concludes with a section on the implications of these changes for U.S. foreign policy.

Two chapters follow on the Grenadan revolution and the implications of the U.S. intervention there in November 1983. Both chapters are based extensively on the revealing documents captured in Grenada by the U.S. forces. Mark Falcoff offers an "inner history" of the Grenadan revolution and examines the complex interrelations between Grenada, Cuba, and the Soviet Union in the period prior to the U.S. action. Then Howard J. Wiarda provides a preliminary assessment of the implications of the U.S. intervention on revolutionary movements and prospects in Central America.

Mark Falcoff next turns his attention to Nicaragua and offers a lucid assessment of the revolution after its first five years. He describes not only the internal dynamics of the Sandinista regime and its public policies, but also the international context, the ties to the Soviet Union and Eastern Europe, and the manipulation of opinion in the United States. It is not an encouraging picture, either of the revolution or of its foreign machinations.

In his analytical conclusion, Falcoff returns to a number of the themes raised in the introduction, assesses the Soviet role and prospects in Latin America as well as those of its proxies, and offers a commentary and series of suggestions for U.S. foreign policy in the region.

It is an informative discussion of a critically important theme. There is no more crucial issue in American foreign policy than our relations with the Soviet Union, and Latin America has recently become one of the key theaters where both the East-West and the North-South conflicts meet. We seek in this book to bridge some of the gaps that exist in our understanding of these issues and between the policy communities that write, think, and act in these often separate policy arenas.

Notes

1. A good listing and survey is Cole Blasier, *The Giant's Rival: The USSR and Latin America* (Pittsburgh: University of Pittsburgh Press, 1983).

2. Luis Mercier Vega, *Roads to Power in Latin America* (New York: Praeger, 1969), pp. 102–106.

3. Robert S. Leiken, *Soviet Strategy in Latin America* (New York: Praeger, 1982).

4. Blasier, *Giant's Rival;* and Robert Wesson, ed., *Communism in Central America and the Caribbean* (Stanford, Calif.: Hoover Institution Press, 1982).

5. For a full discussion see Howard J. Wiarda, *In Search of Policy: The United States and Latin America* (Washington, D.C.: American Enterprise Institute, 1984).

6. See our study of one such new relationship, Howard J. Wiarda, ed., *The Iberian-Latin American Connection: Implications for U.S. Foreign Policy* (Boulder, Colo.: American Enterprise Institute-Westview Press, 1986).

7. Robert S. Leiken, "Eastern Winds in Latin America," *Foreign Policy*, vol. 42 (Spring 1981), pp. 94–113.

8. Blasier, *Giant's Rival*; also Carmelo Mesa-Lago, *Latin American Studies in Europe* (Pittsburgh: Center for Latin American Studies, University of Pittsburgh, n.d.), pp. 121–30.

2
Communism in Central America and the Caribbean

Mark Falcoff

The Caribbean Basin contains one of the most complex collections of peoples, cultures, and political orders to be found anywhere in the world, particularly within so relatively small a geographical circumscription. It includes large nations not normally thought of as "Caribbean," although their coastlines skirt extensive portions of the water's edge (Mexico, Venezuela, Colombia, and even the United States); smaller Spanish-speaking island states (Cuba, the Dominican Republic, and Puerto Rico); the five Central American republics (Guatemala, Honduras, El Salvador, Nicaragua, and Costa Rica) and Panama; two "Anglo-Saxon" mainland states (Guyana and Suriname); the microstates of the eastern Caribbean (mostly English-speaking but also three that are formally part of Holland and one that is part of France); and Haiti, which shares the island of Hispaniola with the Dominican Republic and which is officially French speaking but possesses deeper cultural ties to Africa than to any other area. The microstates alone comprise thirty-two distinct political entities with a population of 30 million—fifteen independent countries, twelve of which have attained their sovereign personality only since 1960.

Recent discussion of Caribbean issues in the United States and elsewhere has almost uniformly focused on the islands and microstates, excluding the larger mainland countries but often including the Central American republics because of the political and ideological links between Cuba and Nicaragua. These are the boundaries we shall observe in the present discussion.

Even setting aside the United States, Colombia, Venezuela, and Mexico, we are still left with astonishing diversity. The populations of Central America and the islands are either Hispanic, Hispano-Indian, Afro-Hispanic, or African descended, although there are identifiable Indian communities in Guatemala, Nicaragua, and Panama; East Indians in Trinidad and Guyana; and Chinese in Jamaica and elsewhere.

Some prominent political personalities—most notably Prime Minister Edward Seaga of Jamaica—are of Syro-Lebanese extraction. The languages spoken include Spanish, French, English, Dutch, Chinese, and Mayan and other pre-Columbian tongues; East Indian dialects, Chinese, and a mixture of European and African languages generally classified as "Creole."

During the sixteenth and seventeenth centuries the Caribbean region was of vast economic importance to the European powers—an apparently endless source of sugar, tobacco, rum, indigo, cochineal, and hardwoods, produced on plantations by African slaves or Indian laborers. In some cases one or two islands constituted what by modern standards would be an enterprise of multinational dimensions. France, for example, derived more economic benefit from Haiti in the 1750s than Great Britain from the entire thirteen American colonies combined. By the early nineteenth century, however, the depletion of arable land and the emergence of competitive sources of tropical products in Africa and the Far East provoked a gradual but relentless economic decline, from which even now most of the islands show no signs of reversing. Today it could be said that, although scattered individual enterprises have shown some profitability, the value of the region is almost entirely geostrategic. Even Central America, which continued to be a profitable locus of foreign investment for another century and a half, has shrunk in relative economic significance for both the United States and Western Europe. Apart from their tourist attractions, the only thing most of these countries have to offer the Great Powers is their proximity to other, more important communities and resources or, what amounts to the same thing, their place on the international political chessboard. In this consists the contemporary Caribbean drama.[1]

The importance of the Caribbean region has long been recognized by naval strategists and geopoliticians, but for most of the nineteenth and twentieth centuries, it remained either an informal Anglo-American condominium or, since World War I, an area of overwhelming U.S. hegemony. France lost St. Dominique in the 1790s; Spain was finally compelled to withdraw from Cuba and Puerto Rico after an ignominious defeat in 1898; two attempts by Germany to establish a presence in the region during both world wars never rose above espionage. The distance of competing power centers, the overwhelming power of the United States, and tacit recognition of the Monroe Doctrine by all potential interlopers combined to render the Caribbean the one region where U.S. security interests could easily be taken for granted.

Recent challenges to U.S. hegemony in the area have generated a curious and paradoxical response by some who assert that, whatever the importance of the Caribbean in the past, it has all but lost its strategic relevance. Such claims can be accepted only by pushing aside some very large pieces of evidence to the contrary. For one thing, the Panama Canal remains the sole instrument by which the United States can claim a three-ocean capability for what is really a one-and-a-half ocean navy. For another, the canal route is utterly crucial to the economies of key U.S. allies like Australia, New Zealand, and Japan. And for yet another, it is the natural and in some cases the only avenue of transshipment for certain critical raw material imports.

The most important of these is, of course, petroleum. Most of the supertanker traffic from Africa and the Middle East requires lightering facilities in the Bahamas, the Virgin Islands, Trinidad, Curaçao, and Aruba for the transfer of crude oil to standard craft. These carry more than 50 percent of the oil imported into the United States, and refining facilities in the area handle what ultimately becomes 12.5 percent of U.S. domestic consumption. Further, oil from Alaska and Ecuador passes through a trans-Panamanian pipeline, augmenting the tanker routes through the canal itself. When combined with petroleum shipments from Mexico, Guatemala, and Venezuela, the aggregate importance of the Caribbean for American oil imports could easily be likened to the Persian Gulf.

The Caribbean also represents a critical link in the network of American listening posts monitoring ships and subversive activities in the Atlantic Ocean and the approaches to U.S. territorial waters, as well as other communications, tracking, and navigational facilities. Again, for many years the lack of a countervailing power rendered these facilities somewhat honorific—with the very important exception of the years 1941–1945. Since the advent of the Castro regime in Cuba in 1959, however, such assets, where they remain, can no longer be taken for granted. For the Cuban revolution not only established a Soviet client-state within the region, but ultimately led the United States (through the Khrushchev-Kennedy accords of 1962) to accept a permanent if "limited" Soviet military and naval presence there.

Although one school of U.S. foreign policy thinking emphasizes the high monetary costs to the Soviets of this alliance with Castro—as if it were a largely unsought or at any rate unwanted burden—the Soviet strategic literature itself is remarkably free of such ambivalence and repeatedly characterizes the Cuban revolution as one of the most important events in the history of what it likes to call "progressive humanity."[2]

The Caribbean in Soviet Strategic Planning

Much of the current discussion and debate about Soviet intentions in the Caribbean is confused by the frequent failure to draw distinctions between strategy and tactics, between longer-term goals and more immediate objectives. The optimal outcome for Moscow would be the creation, through a Soviet naval and air presence enhanced by upgraded Cuban forces, of an offensive interdiction capability effective enough to block the region's sea lanes, thereby disrupting the "swing strategy" developed by NATO planners in the event of a war in Europe. This strategy posits the movement of three reinforcing U.S. divisions from Hawaii, Washington, and California through the Panama Canal, thence eastward along the southern coast of Cuba. In such an eventuality, modernized Soviet naval and air forces operating from Cuban bases (and whatever other points might subsequently become available elsewhere in the region) could harass such reinforcements. Meanwhile, Soviet surface and submarine fleets could close the four major choke points in the basin. To counter such interdiction, the United States would have to invade Cuba itself, an enterprise that by conservative estimates would require 100,000 troops, roughly the strength of our reinforcements for NATO, and more aircraft carriers than are currently available.

Such scenarios are, of course, excessively dramatic and would be the "worst case" for the United States; in all probability such actions are well beyond Soviet capabilities now. Some medium-term goals lie well within reach, however. These include the transformation of the Caribbean region in such a way that it would stand to the United States roughly as its Western borders stand to the Soviet Union: a region of potential "encirclement" or, at any rate, of such serious security concern as to tie down resources and manpower that would otherwise be free for deployment elsewhere. That such an eventuality could have definite strategic implications is clear: during the critical months of 1982–1983, when the United States and its NATO allies were finalizing the deployment of Pershing missiles in Europe, the Soviet leadership openly threatened to take "retaliatory steps" that would put the other side, including the United States on its own territory, in an "analogous position" and broadly hinted that such steps would include the placement of offensive missiles in Cuba and Nicaragua.

Such a strategy would obviously be greatly assisted by the creation of new client-states in the area, but the Soviets have accepted the fact that it may be necessary to pursue this end in piecemeal fashion. Consequently, they are pursuing several policies at once. These include military, economic, and intelligence support for those genuinely pro-Soviet regimes already in existence (Cuba and Nicaragua and, until 1983, Grenada); intensification of state-to-state relations with nations like Mexico and Panama, which, though themselves not "Socialist" in the Soviet understanding of that word, act as a base for revolutionary activities elsewhere in the basin and with whom the Soviets have certain tactical convergences of policy; and aid and assistance (through the Cubans and other proxies) to armed insurgencies in what are deemed particularly vulnerable targets of opportunity—normally, right-wing dictatorships supportive of (and supported by) the United States but also fragile democracies whose leaders have not yet consolidated a new political order.

All three tactics serve the same longer-term goals: to stir up anti-U.S. feelings throughout the region; legitimize a growing Soviet presence there; and by fomenting political upheaval in the more unstable communities, generate new states of "Socialist orientation," which would provide a broader platform for Soviet activity or, alternatively, would confuse and divide public and congressional opinion in the United States and divert American attention and resources away from areas more central to Soviet concerns. Perhaps the Soviets themselves are not certain which of these last two they would most prefer.[3]

The Political Environment in the Caribbean Basin

Two facts stand out about the societies of the Caribbean Basin: they are small in scale and generally poor in resources. In most cases their economies depend upon the export of one or two items, for which there is limited and often shrinking demand. Moreover, the Caribbean share of the world market for certain traditional products, notably sugar and bauxite, has been falling, and even the region's share of international tourism has declined. Meanwhile, a fourfold increase in the world price of oil, higher interest rates, and the ensuing inflation in the industrial countries have pushed many vital imports— foodstuffs, replacement parts for machinery, and capital goods— almost beyond reach. With small domestic markets, low per capita incomes, and inadequate access to foreign credit, these economies have been, and for some time to come are likely to remain, in very deep trouble.

This deplorable situation, for all its pathetic aspects, is rich in irony. For the islands, probably the most unfortunate event in their histories has been the advent of political independence, freeing the former metropolis (in this case, Great Britain) for responsibility for societies it quite literally created in another time and context. As colonies of declining economic utility they could at least subsist on the imperial dole; as micro nation-states, they are forced to compete for international assistance with an undifferentiated pool of Asian and African states whose claim on the Western conscience (or Western interests) may be considerably greater. Although the ideology of island politics continues to be "anti-imperialism" in some form or another, the real enemy, as V. S. Naipaul has written, "is the past, of slavery and colonial neglect." And he continues: "The small islands of the Caribbean will remain islands, impoverished and unskilled, ringed as now by a *cordon sanitaire,* their people not needed anywhere. They may get less innocent or less corrupt politicians; they will not get less helpless ones."[4]

In Central America the problem is different but no less paradoxical. In the postwar period the five nation-states of the isthmus experienced a truly extraordinary period of impressive and sustained economic growth, an annual average of 5.3 percent for the period 1950–1978. Although the fruits of this development were by no means distributed in a wholly egalitarian fashion, the generalized benefits to the population as a whole were not negligible. Thus, during the period in question, real per capita income doubled, the number of physicians expanded twice as fast as the population, and the number of nurses six times as fast. Between 1960 and 1976 the adult literacy rate rose from 44 to 72 percent, and the number of secondary students as a percentage of their age group more than doubled from 12 to 29 percent. There were dramatic increases in the per capita consumption of calories and in the average lifespan and a notable drop in infant mortality.

These figures mask considerable differences between countries, and they also compress the gap between rural and urban living standards, which in all probability opened still farther as a result of imbalanced (and often unplanned) economic expansion. But even if the process could have continued in a linear fashion, uninterruptedly raising the "floor" to include most of those left out, it would have generated a serious challenge to political stability, since economic growth itself generated new social classes and interest groups—industrial workers, technicians, small businessmen, and even embryonic peasant unions. None of these had any interest in maintaining what in some countries were extremely antique political structures, typically dominated by a handful of families and their allies in the military establishment.

Before this could happen, however, an economic crisis originating in the industrial and oil-producing countries descended upon the Central American nations with tremendous force, reversing the favorable economic trends of three decades. It also created the conditions for a new, structural instability. Whether it also created a "revolutionary situation," as some contended, depended wholly upon definitions, but it did embolden Marxist insurgents and their foreign sponsors to resume efforts that had met with conspicuous failure in the 1960s and early 1970s. In this they were encouraged not only (or even particularly) by the accumulating social crisis, but by the success of a revolution in Nicaragua in 1979, which, against the will of the United States and then finally with its acquiescence, had installed a government controlled by allies of Cuba and the Soviet Union.[5]

Four aspects of the political scene in Central America and the Caribbean are worth careful attention. First, there is a difference between instability and the inevitability of Marxist-Leninist regimes. Some of the economic factors that afflict the more open societies have operated with equal force upon Marxist states already established and played a role in undermining the one that has since expired. Moreover, to the degree to which economic crisis fosters social polarization, it may actually strengthen the forces of the right in some countries rather than prepare the way for a Marxist takeover. Second, the three Marxist states that exist or have existed in the region—Cuba, Nicaragua, and Grenada—came to power as the result of a *political* revolution, not as a response to economic or social deprivation. Indeed, in 1959 by most standards Cuba ranked fourth among Latin American nations in economic development and living standards and, if the urban population of the island alone were taken into account, would doubtless have ranked first.[6] Castro's revolution was entirely aimed at the overthrow of a hated dictator, as was the Sandinista revolution in Nicaragua two decades later; other agendas were revealed only later, and economic development, poverty, and social justice hastily summoned to justify them after the fact. In Grenada, the New Jewel Movement took power through a *coup d'état*, the first in West Indian history, and began the task of building a mass movement and party only after installing itself in power. Third, the economic and social inequalities of the region and its generally low level of development are made more unbearable by the presence of the United States so close at hand, holding up a model that, perforce, can never be fully replicated. This situation generates a complex range of responses and acts as a permanently destabilizing element for all the regimes of the region, including those that claim to have opted out of the race for emulation. Fourth and finally, the diversity that characterizes almost every aspect of the region has been carried over even into the three experiments with Marxism that we shall now explore.

Cuba

The only full-dress Marxist-Leninist regime in the Caribbean is found in Cuba, an island off the coast of Florida that by turns has been Spain's most faithful American colony (1498–1898), the Latin American nation closest to and most admiring of the United States (1898–1959), and now a tropical ally of the Soviet Union (1960–   ), for whom it acts as an international mercenary in exchange for a subsidy variously estimated at between $10 and $12 million a day. In official Cuban mythology, this situation is the result of incomprehension and insensitivity by the United States to the (early) minimal agendas of the revolution, forcing Castro to seek support elsewhere. Although this view has been accepted by much of the international liberal public, particularly in Western Europe, it contradicts another notion also retailed by the regime: namely, that the present state of affairs is the best of all possible outcomes, short of which the country would have had to settle for squalid "bourgeois" reforms that would have left too many evils in place.

What is unique about the Cuban regime is not its anti-Americanism or its loyalty to the Soviet Union—such things can be found elsewhere around the globe—but that Fidel Castro has managed to replicate fully Soviet patterns of political, economic, social, and cultural control in an environment that, in 1959 at least, most observers would have thought highly unlikely. Nonetheless, in many ways today Cuba more closely resembles Bulgaria or East Germany than the Dominican Republic or Venezuela: a one-party state led by a "maximum leader" with life tenure, supported by the full apparatus of a professional "revolutionary" bureaucracy. The regime possesses total control over the media and education, deploys an extensive police and domestic intelligence network, and presides over a huge military establishment, one many times larger than any other found in the region except in the United States. In short, Cuba is, in the most technical sense of the term, a totalitarian state.

Such states obviously possess enormous resources to ensure their preservation, and short of war and foreign invasion none of them has ever succumbed to internal stress or domestic upheaval. In the particular case of Cuba, the regime has also benefited from the outmigration of more than 1 million citizens since 1959, persons who, had they remained, would conceivably have constituted something of a Trojan Horse. Conventional wisdom has it that the regime's achievements in education and health have won it a genuine majority constituency of those who have remained, particularly among Cubans who in 1959 were among the poorest of the poor. Although such things are impossible to measure—and although, as we shall see, there is some evidence to the contrary—even if we accept the claim at its face value, such achievements could be fully appreciated only by those old enough to remember the truly deplorable conditions of the bottom third of Cuban society a quarter-century ago, a generational cohort that over the next twenty-five years will be overtaken numerically by Cubans born since 1960 and that over the quarter-century after that is destined to disappear altogether. The most stabilizing factor for the regime remains the fact that it is the only government many Cubans have ever known. There is no clear alternative to it, either inside or outside the island, and the presence of the Soviet Union as its guarantor lends an air of inevitability and hopelessness to a situation that under other circumstances would provoke widespread and active political disaffection.

Nonetheless, there are serious internal strains within Cuba that the regime cannot ignore and that periodically surface in ways highly damaging to its international image, if not always to its internal hold upon society. The first of these is the patent failure to produce anything resembling sustained economic growth. Indeed, from fourth among Latin American nations in per capita income, Cuba has dropped to twenty-first or twenty-second. In effect, the revolution not only eliminated the upper, upper-middle, and middle classes, but also effected the gradual leveling-down of those classes that remained. There are various ways of measuring this phenomenon, but all of the indicators point unswervingly downward. Official Cuban figures claim that per capita economic growth declined from 8.2 percent in 1978 to 3.1 percent in 1979 and finally to 1.8 percent in 1980, leading Fidel Castro to explain in a speech at the end of 1980 that his people would have to endure shortages of the most basic foodstuffs and clothing for the foreseeable future. In very concrete terms, these rations allow the average Cuban two pounds of red meat per month, one and a half pounds of chicken per month, two ounces of coffee every fifteen days, four meters of cloth per year, two packs of cigarettes per week, and one pair of shoes, one pair of trousers or one dress, and two shirts a year. Significantly, the figures for clothing are 20 percent less than in 1965.[7]

To some degree, the dismal performance of the Cuban economy rests upon one factor utterly beyond Castro's control—the world price of sugar, which has been steadily declining since the end of the Korean War. With a shift in dietary habits in the Western countries and the constant entry of new low-cost producers into the market, this situation is unlikely to reverse itself, and not even Soviet purchases of the Cuban harvest at roughly five times the world price can adequately offset it. In addition, there have been several crop failures, especially in recent years, due to weather or disease.

The larger cause of Cuba's economic failure is, however, political: a highly personalistic form of macroeconomic mismanagement, which first led Castro and his most intimate associates to place excessive emphasis on industrialization, followed by a sudden, erratic shift in priorities, exemplified by the unsuccessful attempt to achieve a 10-million-ton sugar crop in 1970. Similarly, during the 1960s the decision to create a "new Socialist man" encouraged the introduction of economic disincentives to productivity ("moral incentives"), an innovation the regime was finally forced to partially reverse in the next decade when it became apparent that, apart from the fact that it generated no perceptible increase in "revolutionary consciousness," it was having precisely the opposite of the effect intended upon the profitability of state enterprises. Quite apart from these peculiarly local circumstances, Cuba has suffered from the structural inefficiencies, waste, and corruption inherent in Soviet-style central planning: targets are met only by falsifying figures or by reducing the quality of the finished product, and there is a vigorous black market in all items of prime necessity.[8] Finally, the U.S. economic embargo, in place since 1962, has cost Cuba its nearest (and formerly most important) export market, as well as what was once its principal source of imports, adding heavy transportation costs to capital goods and other products that must be brought from Eastern or Western Europe.

Serious improvement in the Cuban economy could come about only as the result of larger changes in the world sugar market, or an equally momentous shift in the way the island's resources are managed at home, or, better still, a combination of the two. The first is frankly difficult to foresee, and the second hardly less so: however unproductive the Cuban system may be, it serves larger political agendas that could not be met without the kind of control that a centrally planned economy provides. The U.S. trade embargo could not be lifted without some important changes in Cuba's international policies, changes that the regime has shown no signs of being willing to make and that in all probability it could not make even if it wished to, given the centrality of the Soviet Union to its economic survival and also its international role, upon which Castro places extraordinary importance.

The second internal stress on Cuban society proceeds from the first: a generalized sense of political alienation and spiritual fatigue by large sectors of Cuban society, who for twenty-five years have had to subsist on a steady diet of promises and exhortations, juxtaposed against recurrent shortages and Draconian rationing. As Carlos Alberto Montaner reports, today in Cuba "the majority of the people no longer believes that the regime's mistakes are partial or that they can be corrected." Rather, they believe "quite simply that the system does not work, and that it is never going to provide them with either happiness or prosperity." This is particularly true for those under twenty-five years of age, for whom the heroic days of the revolution are "foreign and remote."[9]

Through its many outlets for propaganda and "political education," the regime continually reminds Cubans of how much worse things were before the revolution, how bad they are in other Caribbean and Latin American countries, and how dreadful life is in the United States, particularly for Blacks or Hispanics. Nonetheless, this campaign seems not to have fully neutralized the harshness of life in Cuba, since the latest wave of refugees—some 100,000 who fled in 1980—included many Blacks and young people. A report prepared for the Senate Foreign Relations Committee found, moreover, that in contrast to earlier refugee cohorts, which were made up of upper, then upper-middle, then middle-class Cubans, the 1980 group was drawn from "lower, semi-skilled, or unskilled working-class Cubans." Though some were vagrants, bohemians, or criminals, "many [were] respectable family members . . . students, lower-level government employees, truck drivers, restaurant workers, and laborers." The report concluded: "In fact there is some evidence that some of the new arrivals were formerly exemplary militant supporters of the Castro government who have simply lost faith in the power of the government to improve their economic plight."[10]

The third internal stress proceeds from Castro's self-appointed role as a paladin of revolution in the third world, particularly in lands distant from Cuba both geographically and culturally. At issue are the thousands of Cubans operating in military, intelligence, and police advisory capacities in Africa, the Middle East, and the Caribbean. Cuban troops tipped the balance in favor of Soviet allies in Angola in 1976 and in Ethiopia the following year—on that occasion fighting under the command of a Soviet general. Castro himself has admitted that by 1982 more than 120,000 Cuban servicemen had served outside their country, and at present 25,000–30,000 remain in Angola and 10,500 in Ethiopia as props to shaky Marxist dictatorships. Another 2,000 Cubans are now at work in Nicaragua with that country's armed forces and ministry of interior (police). (Such estimates do not include Cuban "internationalists" working in construction, agriculture, or industry, such as the 3,000 currently in Libya.)

The regime does benefit in some ways from this new, worldwide military role, inasmuch as it nourishes Cuban self-esteem and also provides some very modest economic benefits: for example, the Ethiopian government is reportedly paying Castro $6 million a year for the use of his troops. On the other hand, military service in far-off lands also generates considerable disaffection among conscripts and their families, particularly when the former return from distant fields of combat mutilated or dead. There is some evidence—not, however, conclusive—that the latest wave of discontent on the island began with disaffected veterans of Castro's African campaigns. More interesting are the data that point to a significant displacement of economic resources to military purposes, from which one could infer both the deepening shortages of consumer goods and a drop in morale and support for the regime. The figures are clear enough: between 1959 and 1974 imports of foodstuffs dropped from 27 percent of total imports to 19 percent, while those of manufactured goods likewise declined from 31 to 12 percent. (In neither case do the figures reflect a rise in Cuban self-sufficiency in either area.) Meanwhile, the military budget has risen dramatically from 33.8 pesos per capita in 1962 to 85.7 in 1979.[11] If Cuba's only military expenditures were allocated to defense of the island against a hypothetical U.S. invasion, they would have far less potential for domestic controversy. Quite obviously, however, they reflect a combat role in venues far from Cuba's traditional concerns, on missions that could be fully appreciated only by a dwindling minority of genuinely committed Marxist-Leninists.

Options for U.S. Policy Makers. While it must be recognized that no set of U.S. policies will bring down the Castro regime, a proper mix can prevent its further consolidation, deepen its internal contradictions, and leave open the possibility at some future date of its evolution in a more constructive direction, at least with respect to its international conduct. The most important task is to break down the wall of censorship intended to prevent Cubans from knowing what is really going on outside their country and to some extent within it as well. Although at one time the rationale for the Cuban revolution was the regime's stated commitment to both abundance and equality at home, the failure to achieve either has led to a radical shift in emphasis: Cubans are now told that their mission is to contribute in every possible way to an alteration of the international political order and specifically to the position of the United States within it, which is said to threaten the existence not merely of the Castro regime but of the Cuban people itself.

Such perceptions can be maintained, of course, only in an atmosphere of asphyxiating unanimity, which in many ways is self-defeating. Although five major government radio networks blanket the country, there is a "significant demand for non-governmental information . . . due in part to the monotony and perceptively-biased content of [official] programming, which includes verbatim transmission of Castro's four-hour-long speeches."[12] Moreover, given Cuba's geographical situation, this demand can be satisfied relatively easily by clandestine monitoring of foreign broadcasts—not only from Puerto Rico and the Dominican Republic, but from the Spanish-language service of the BBC, the Voice of America (VOA), and commercial radio stations in Florida, many of which broadcast in Spanish.

Despite the small-scale and unfocused nature of U.S. commercial broadcasting. Castro clearly regards it as a serious threat and rightly so, for the advertisements alone suggest a prosperity and well-being among Cubans who have emigrated unthinkable for those who have remained. Not surprisingly, relatively low-kilowatt Spanish-language stations like WQBA in Miami have been repeatedly jammed by high-powered Cuban transmitters, and even before the Reagan administration announced in 1981 intentions to beam new VOA programs to specifically Cuban audiences, new jamming facilities were already under construction on the island.

Such frenzied responses by the Castro regime suggest a vulnerability that the United States would be ill-advised to ignore. In particular, this reaction underlines the potential of Radio Martí, a subdivision of the VOA created precisely to fill the huge information gap in Cuba, resuming a practice that the VOA had dropped for budgetary reasons in 1974 (and discontinued throughout the mid- and late 1970s by the Ford and Carter administrations, who were seeking to normalize relations with Cuba). Although Radio Martí was originally proposed as an independent broadcasting authority, the Reagan administration was forced to scale down its original concept in response to intense lobbying by domestic broadcasters (whom the Cubans had threatened with widespread interference in their programming) and strong opposition from congressional liberals, who feared that the new entity would widen the estrangement between Washington and Havana and postpone still further U.S. acceptance of the Castro regime.[13] Even in its truncated form, however, Radio Martí will provide Cubans with a new source of uncensored international news and news about the United States. Even more important, it will provide information about Cuban activities overseas, particularly the costs of Castro's military adventurism, about which many Cubans—even those relatively well-placed in the bureaucracy—appear to be incompletely informed.

The other way to close the information gap in Cuba would be to increase the number and frequency of visits there by Cuban-Americans who continue to maintain contact with relatives on the island. At present, however, this is merely a hypothetical possibility, since the Castro regime is still reeling from the consequences of the first round of visitations initiated during the Carter administration. The concept was originally accepted by the Cuban dictator to serve two of his most important objectives: to obtain hard currency and to open a political breach within the Cuban-American community. Before either could be accomplished, however, the presence of thousands of prosperous Cuban-Ammericans in their midst immediately awakened within the Cuban people barely suppressed appetites for U.S. consumer goods and, by providing a vivid and direct counter-testimony to official propaganda about conditions in the United States, perceptibly undermined the regime's shaky credibility. Most observers believe, in fact, that the visits of 1977–1979 played a major role in provoking the massive refugee outflow in 1980 and that Castro would therefore be hesitant to resume them. Recognizing their clearly destabilizing (or at a minimum, profoundly neutralizing) potential, however, U.S. policy makers would be well-advised to place these visits high on any list of concessions to be obtained in future "normalization" agreements.

The second primary objective must be to maintain those pressures that raise the economic costs of Castro's policies. Some mention has already been made of these; here we need to focus more clearly on the regime's international economic relations and how they affect domestic performance. Perhaps the most important single fact about the Cuban economic system is that it can function even at its present dismal level only with the aid of massive foreign subsidies and credits. Central to these is, of course, Soviet aid, which amounted to $13 billion in the decade 1972–1982 alone, representing not only purchases of Cuban sugar at inflated prices, but also the sale of crude oil at roughly one-third the price charged by OPEC producers. Without these two elements, Cuba's 1978 global trade deficit, which was reported at $178 million, would have been $2.8 billion.

Although the overall costs of aid to Cuba are small for the Soviets—only 0.4 percent of their gross national product—they are rising, particularly with the OPEC price increases since 1973. Shipments of crude oil to Cuba have forced the Soviets to forgo considerable export earnings; in 1979, for example, these amounted to what otherwise would have been 6 percent of their hard currency income. From this it is possible to deduce that the Soviets would welcome a rapproachement between Havana and Washington, at least to the extent of relieving them of this burden. Evidently they do not desire it enough, however, to seriously pressure Castro to reduce his agressive external profile or scale down his international ambitions.

Cuba's trade with other Communist countries is largely through barter and cannot be accurately measured here; it is unlikely, however, to reflect the kind of subsidies implicit in the Soviet figures. Rather more important is the island's trade with Western countries and Japan, which since 1974 has amounted to $1 billion. These purchases—foodstuffs, some technology, a small amount of high-quality capital, or consumer goods—caused the regime's hard currency debt to balloon to $2.6 billion in 1980, most of which is owed to Western banks. Payments on these obligations fell into serious arrears in 1982 and forced the Cuban government to declare a unilateral moratorium the following year. With access to new Western loans clearly limited, Cuba's hard currency resources will in all probability be limited to earnings on exports to the West, limited income from tourism, and Soviet hard currency aid. All three rest upon imponderables well beyond Cuban influence or control.

Not surprisingly, this situation has reawakened official Cuban interest in resuming economic relations with the United States. Although the trade embargo imposed more than two decades ago has led to substantial retooling of Cuba's industrial plant, even now it possesses considerable relevance for the island's economic welfare. As one economist has written, the embargo condemns the Cuban economy "to stagnation, with some occasional blips of modest improvements tied to sugar price increases."[14] Lifted, at a very minimum it would open potential U.S. markets for some Cuban exports and encourage U.S. banks to relieve their European and Japanese counterparts of part of the burden of supporting Cuba's hard currency economy.

This is precisely what must not be allowed to happen. First, there is no reason to assume automatically that economic relations affect political conduct; in the Cuban case, indeed, the evidence runs precisely opposite. Massive Western lending to Havana during the detente honeymoon of 1975–1979 did not alter the regime's international behavior, which included military intervention in Ethiopia and Angola, and significant assistance to Marxist rebels in El Salvador and Nicaragua. That lending may in fact have subsidized it directly or indirectly. Second, and very much related to this, Western credits extended to Cuba during this period did not encourage investment in socioeconomic development or attempts to raise living standards in Cuba. Havana's claims to the contrary are belied by its own production figures for 1980 and 1981 and the fact that a surprising number of loans were not linked to specific projects but for unspecified "general purposes," which could, and in all probability did, include military expenditures and foreign military and intelligence activities.

Third, there is no reason to make the burden of supporting Cuba easier or cheaper for the Soviet Union, nor should one assume that Castro's foreign policy is for sale to the highest bidder. While the United States may have to accept the Cuban-Soviet alliance as an international fact of life for many years yet to come, it can at least make the economic environment in which that alliance must operate increasingly difficult, not only by retaining the present embargo, but by applying discreet pressures to allied and friendly nations that might otherwise be tempted to breach it. This policy need not visit additional hardships upon the Cuban people, since its sole purpose is to force the regime to shift its priorities to domestic economic growth. In the absence of such disincentives, Castro will continue to regard the world outside Cuba as his primary field of endeavor.

Fourth and finally, because the embargo remains the most important single policy instrument to effect an eventual change of Cuba's international position, it should not be lightly discarded or traded for anything of lesser import.

Another way to keep the Cuban regime permanently off balance is to maintain an open-door policy for Cuban emigration to the United States. As Montaner points out, this option, whether actual or potential, has seriously hindered the regime's final consolidation by enabling many Cubans "to overcome the temptation to accommodate to the system's demands." To many, he writes, "The existence of an accessible exterior world—infinitely richer and freer in material and spiritual terms than their own deprived reality—has been, and continues to be, useful in understanding the wretchedness of Castroism."[15]

The Cuban government itself has blown hot and cold on the subject of emigration for more than twenty years. As noted earlier, the departure of thousands at the beginning of the regime actually helped Castro to tighten his grip on power, not only by removing potential dissidents from the scene, but also by providing him with resources (houses, automobiles, and the like) to confiscate and reallocate. At this point, however, the important thing is not so much whether emigration actually takes place (a decision that lies beyond the control of the United States) so much as that a policy of frank and permanent welcome be unambiguously stated and widely known. At the same time, Washington must be fully prepared to live up to its promises should the opportunity present itself again.

The United States should also make Cuban military adventurism overseas more expensive and difficult by aiding those governments under siege (El Salvador) or movements actively fighting against Cuban expeditionary forces (Angola). The latter is particularly important because a decisive defeat in Africa would deprive the regime of its only legitimate claim to success and raise disturbing questions about its historical inevitability precisely among those cadres, military professionals, generally believed to be most committed to it.

One last option needs to be considered here: that normalization of relations between Cuba and the United States, even without serious preconditions, would drastically undermine Castro's hold on power or, at any rate, force a thoroughgoing liberalization and moderation of the regime. This case has been made most persuasively by Carmelo Mesa-Lago, who argues in effect that so great is the appeal of the American way of life to ordinary Cubans that the regime can survive in its present form only if it walls its people off from such attractions. Conversely, once the floodgates are open, there will be serious pressures, he theorizes, not only from below but even from the middle and higher ranks of the bureaucracy to "de-Stalinize" (my term, not Mesa-Lago's).[16] Interestingly, this view is also shared by many American radicals, who fear that normalization would undermine what, for them, is a vaunted revolutionary purity.

Such hypotheses should be approached with caution. One must assume that these are matters to which Castro and his most immediate associates have given long and serious thought and with which they are prepared to deal when and if the situation arises. "Normalization" of relations could mean nothing more for Cuba than it does for the German Democratic Republic: the opening of an embassy, very limited travel for Americans, even more limited travel for nationals of the Communist state, and, for the latter, a new source of credit and foreign exchange, as well as enhanced opportunities for intelligence operations in the United States. For Castro to open his society beyond this would be so destabilizing as to surpass serious contemplation. In a certain sense such an outcome, however, desirable for the United States, would require that the Cuban regime become something other than what it is.

If one condition of normalization were met—namely, Cuba's withdrawal from the Soviet alliance and its reemergence as a genuinely nonaligned nation—many other desirable things would follow, both for the United States and for the Cuban people. But again, this requires an alteration in the very nature of the regime (or at a minimum, in its self-definition), an event utterly unthinkable as long as Castro is alive. It is somewhat less inconceivable, however, in the event of his death, and the United States should be prepared to offer his successors aid and protection in the event that they demonstrate a serious wish to leave the Soviet bloc. In all probability such a shift would have repercussions in the domestic political system far more significant than in Yugoslavia, a metaphor, which for various reasons, is not, strictly speaking, wholly applicable here. In the meanwhile, more modest efforts should be mounted in the service of shorter-term goals.

Nicaragua

In 1979 an insurrection in Nicaragua, led by the Marxist-Leninist Frente Sandinista de Liberación Nacional (FSLN) but supported by the broadest spectrum of popular opinion, brought down the dictatorship of Anastasio Somoza Debayle. In the process, an entire cycle of Nicaraguan history, characterized since 1934 by the rule of a single family, was brought to an end. In its place, presumably, Nicaraguans would have a range of political choices at least as wide as the coalition that had brought Somoza down. In the best of cases, Nicaragua would become a left-wing social democracy, such as France or Greece; in the worst, a one-party state in which, however, like Mexico, all members of the "revolutionary" family would enjoy a limited but institutionally ensured pluralism. To reassure both domestic and foreign opinion on this score, even before taking power the Sandinista directorate promised the Organization of American States that the new regime would be characterized by free elections, a mixed economy, and a non-aligned foreign policy. Five years later it is apparent that even the worst-case scenario was far too optimistic. Instead of a coalition of diverse interests bound together by a common revolutionary experience, the Nicaraguan government is a left-wing dictatorship whose Marxist-Leninist features have become so prominent as to seriously embarrass its sympathizers abroad and provoke widespread opposition at home.

Even now, however, the true nature of the Nicaraguan regime remains a matter of controversy because, although indisputably authoritarian, it does not fully replicate the system in Cuba. Specifically, Nicaraguans still have considerable freedom to travel abroad, some larger enterprises remain in private hands, and real property both urban and rural has not been fully expropriated by the state. Private schools continue to function, there is one opposition newspaper (*La Prensa*), opposition parties and groups are a visible part of the political scene. This has led many foreigners who have visited the country for short periods of time—typically, from two days to a week—to conclude that the Nicaraguan revolution is completely *sui generis*. Their most frequent claim is that though Marxist-Leninist in its vocabulary, in practice *Sandinismo* is humanitarian and pluralist.

Such differences as do exist between Nicaragua and Cuba are not, however, of a sort to inspire optimism about the future. The failure to consolidate a totalitarian state is due not to an absence of will, but to peculiar political circumstances. Out of the Sandinista revolution has emerged no single charismatic leader: instead, power is shared among nine comandantes who are often at odds over policy and tactics and between whom are considerable personal and political rivalries. This has led, as one scholar has put it, to the "feudalization" of the regime, with functional areas of the revolution parceled out to individual members of the junta: security to Tomás Borge, agrarian reform to Jaime Wheelock, and military affairs to Humberto Ortega. Under these circumstances, ministries function "as if they were almost independent entities." In contrast, during the first two years of the Cuban revolution, Castro had managed to bring virtually everything under his personal control, and not even his brother Raúl or Ernesto Guevara could operate independently.[17] Significantly, the one Sandinista leader capable of playing Castro's role in Nicaragua, Eden Pastora Gómez, has gone over to the opposition and now leads a counterrevolutionary movement. There is also no coherent, disciplined state party such as Castro was able to create by merging his personalistic following with the Cuban Communists. The Sandinista apparatus is still a hodgepodge of organizations (labor, women, students, peasants, and the like) hastily created since 1979, and, what is more to the point, many of these exist more on paper than in reality.

These descriptions hold true only for things as they are now. If one looks at the *direction* in which the regime has been moving, the pockets of freedom that remain appear to be living on borrowed time. The trend toward political dictatorship was evident from the very beginning, when the Sandinistas began to pack the Council of State with "representatives" of bodies that had no previous existence and to crowd out other, more independent or moderate political forces. *La Prensa* has been repeatedly shut down and since March 1982 subject to censorship under "state of emergency" laws. Depending upon the vagaries of official policy, its editors may have to delete entire articles, leaving blank spaces on pages where they would otherwise appear. The two television networks are in the hands of the state, and all radio stations (with the exception of one Catholic station) have lost their independence. Opposition parties operate under conditions of considerable harassment and demoralization. Their meetings are frequently interrupted by government-organized mobs *(turbas)*, they have no open access to the media, and many of their leaders, as well as prominent businessmen capable of financing them, have already left the country.

While the private sector continues to dominate the economy, in and of itself this does not guarantee the survival of political pluralism. As Thomas Anderson observes, two-thirds of the industry and agriculture in China remained in private hands a full seven years after the Communists came to power in 1949. Meanwhile, Sandinista "block committees" (Committees of Sandinista Defense), obviously mimicking those in Cuba, have begun to stretch a gossamer web of domestic surveillance across the country. Advised by a bloated Cuban intelligence and political mission and an East German police adviser, the Sandinistas are busily erecting the repressive apparatus characteristic of a "people's democracy." Once in place, it will be easy enough to close the loopholes and fill the interstices that now make Nicaragua something of a systemic anomaly. In any event, by 1987 there were few loopholes left—the Sandinistas had even closed (at considerable cost in international support) the independent newspaper *La Prensa*.

Although the Sandinista regime has steadily lost popular support since 1979, like any Central American dictatorship it retains the loyalty of a large government bureaucracy, the career military, and their immediate families. In addition, recipients of particular benefits (in this case, pilot health and literacy programs, groups identified for the priority receipt of foodstuffs and other rationed items, and so forth), and younger, ambitious members of the middle class who hope and expect to derive future career benefits from the status quo also support the regime. In the case of the Sandinistas, two additional groups have been, at least until recently, particularly supportive of the regime. One is composed of young people between the ages of fifteen and twenty-five, who under other circumstances would have nothing to do between leaving school and finding their first serious employment. To these, the regime has given an identity by putting them into uniforms and placing them on militia duty, a particularly exhilarating adventure for young women who before 1979 would have been forbidden by their parents to remain away from home over night, much less for days at a time. The other is a stratum of *lumpen* elements in Managua and some of the larger cities who survive by selling their support in one form or another to whatever government happens to be in power. Not surprisingly, many of these, formerly fervent supporters of Somoza, have become active members of block committees and of the *turbas*.

Unlike the Cuban regime, the Sandinista dictatorship cannot as yet depend primarily upon force and fear, inertia, and the lack of an alternative. It must elicit some measure of genuine popular support. At the beginning this was done by symbolic acts (confiscating the Somoza family holdings, dissolving the National Guard), positive benefits (literacy programs and the distribution of food and other forms of international assistance), and propaganda aimed at creating a sense of national pride in the revolution and its accomplishments, particularly the expulsion of a dictator represented as an extension of the will of the United States. These acts supposedly showed that tiny Nicaragua could somehow "defeat" the most powerful nation on earth. Implicit in all of this was the assumption that a new political order would also mean a vastly improved standard of living for the Nicaraguan people.

Far from fulfilling this fundamental promise, the Government of National Reconstruction (as the Sandinistas call their regime) has launched the country into a process of what can only be called de-development. Mismanagement, the flight of skilled managers and workers, misallocation of resources, and corruption, combined, have pushed most economic indicators steadily downward. At this writing, virtually all lines of activity were performing well below their prerevolutionary level. With 1978 as a base year, for example, in 1982 agriculture (the country's fundamental source of foreign exchange) had declined 17 percent, industry 18 percent, and commerce 27 percent—a combined drop in gross domestic product of 14 percent. By 1984 things had gotten worse: inflation had risen to over 50 percent a year, and the country was running a balance of payments deficit of about $500 million a year, with a foreign debt that had more than doubled since the fall of Somoza, amounting to $3.6 billion. The only sector in that four-year period that showed significant growth was the government, which has tripled in size since the Sandinistas took power.

Reduced production and declining world prices for tropical agricultural products (combined with several natural disasters) caused Nicaragua's export earnings to fall to $400 million in 1982, down from $500 million in 1981. Although a cutback in imports has helped to reduce the trade deficit somewhat, this has been more than offset by increasing payments for foreign debt service. Although the country's obligations to foreign banks inherited from the Somoza regime were originally rescheduled under very generous conditions, increasing financial problems caused it to fail to meet installment deadlines in 1983; although the 1980 "rollover" fell due once again in 1985, the government was incapable of meeting its obligations. In June of that year Nicaraguan finance officials reached an agreement with 130 foreign banks (more than half of them in the United States) to pay an initial sum of $3 million as a gesture of good faith and a future $17 million in 1986, rolling over the rest of the $381 million in principal and interest (including arrears) into the coming year. The growing impossibility of meeting these obligations is evident from the fact that by July 1985 the total foreign debt stood at $4.5 billion, and its service, $870 million per annum, was roughly twice the country's anticipated export earnings.[18]

A combination of low productivity, mismanagement, and lack of ready foreign exchange has resulted in a steady drop in living standards for the ordinary Nicaraguan. Private consumption dropped in real terms by 12 percent from 1982 to 1983 (the latest figures available), and official sources concede 20 percent unemployment. Salary levels have been frozen since 1981, and the annual rate of inflation has run in excess of 25 percent (Nicaraguan government figures). Government subsidies for basic foodstuffs have stemmed declining purchasing power somewhat, but at the same time there have been increasing shortages of staple items like rice, beans, and cooking oil.[19]

The Nicaraguan economic picture would be gloomier still were it not for massive international assistance, which has been steadily pouring into Nicaragua since 1979. This includes $3.3 billion in new foreign loans and $250 million in outright donations, combined with concessional aid and the sale of oil by Mexico and Venezuela under preferential terms (similar to those offered other Central American countries under the San José accords). Several aspects of this external assistance are worth noting, however. First, in spite of a foreign policy that almost from the very beginning was blatantly pro-Soviet, most of the aid through 1982 came from Western sources (including approximately $110 million in outright grants from the United States during the last year of the Carter administration) and an average of $12 million per month during roughly the same period (July 1979–November 1981) from the World Bank and the Inter-American Development Bank. Second, although most of the Western European governments are reported to be disillusioned with the evolving nature of the Sandinista regime—some strongly so—until very recently there has been no significant reduction in aid.

Third, there has been a significant increase in Soviet bloc aid. While in 1981 some 15 percent of the country's foreign assistance came from that source, the figure jumped to 47 percent in 1982 and to nearly 60 percent in 1983. Originally Moscow provided mainly commercial credits and military equipment; by 1984, however, it was compelled to ship machinery, spare parts, fertilizers, and other items formerly acquired from Western sources. But the Soviet contribution was greatest (by dollar value) in petroleum imports; whereas the U.S.S.R. supplied some 45 percent of these in 1984, because Nicaragua had fallen hopelessly behind in its payments to Mexico and Venezuela, by mid-1985, the figure had jumped to 85–90 percent.[20] Fourth, no new sources of economic assistance (or significant increases from Western sources) are on the horizon unless and until the regime alters its fundamental character.

Meanwhile, a storm of domestic political discontent has been brewing, which probably not even a modest improvement in economic trends could fully turn back. The arrogant ruling style and evident corruption of the Sandinista comandantes has led many Nicaraguans to refer to them as "the nine Somozas," and the peremptory confiscation of ration cards for nonattendance at Sandinista public meetings has provoked widespread resentment.[21] The introduction of conscription in January 1984, ostensibly to raise forces to fight counterrevolutionaries supported by the United States, has introduced a new element of alienation among young people and particularly among their parents, who fear that their sons will be sent to the front without adequate training or who regard the Sandinista government as basically indefensible. Under the new law, the first such in Nicaraguan history, all men between the ages of seventeen and forty-five must register, although only those between the ages of seventeen and twenty-two are now being called. Refusal to serve is punishable with two to five years in prison, and a draft card is now required for job and school applications and for legal contracts. Demonstrations against conscription have become commonplace in many Nicaraguan cities and towns, and there has been widespread evasion on the part of many young men, particularly those whose families have been able to send them abroad.[22]

The gathering political opposition to the Sandinista regime has formed around four entities—the Roman Catholic church, the independent labor movement, the Democratic Coordinator (an umbrella organization of political parties), and a small but mounting counterrevolutionary insurrection. Perhaps the most important in many ways is the church, since religion ranks highest on the list of values indicated by Nicaraguans in the last public opinion poll (January 1981) permitted by the Sandinistas. Moreover, unlike some other countries in the region, in Nicaragua the church has not been particularly associated with the privileged classes, and its spiritual leader, Monsignor Miguel Obando y Bravo, was a conspicuous leader in the fight to bring down the Somoza dictatorship. Having failed to co-opt Archbishop Obando y Bravo and his bishops, the Sandinistas sought to divide the Nicaraguan church by creating a schismatic "people's church." In this they have been supported to some degree by the Jesuits (who have not controlled a Latin American country since the seventeenth century and view the possibilities in Nicaragua with unbecoming relish), by some foreign missionary clergy (particularly from the United States), and by several leading Sandinista personalities who are ordained clergy and who serve—in disobedience to papal orders—as ministers or other government functionaries. The sharpening confrontation between the Sandinista government and its supporters in the clergy on one hand and the Vatican on the other hand was made embarrassingly manifest during the visit of Pope John Paul II to Nicaragua in March 1983, when halfway through the pontiff's homily, Sandinista technicians apparently connected microphones to the main public address system, thus allowing progovernment mobs to drown him out with cries of "popular power."[23]

The divisions the Sandinistas have provoked within the church have turned out to be extremely lopsided, with the majority of the clergy and the overwhelming majority of the laity remaining faithful to their bishops and to the pope. More than that, in an environment of increasing political repression and harassment of dissidents, the church has become a quasi-opposition party, much as its counterpart in Poland. That is, while it cannot hope to overthrow the government or even replace it, it can challenge it in very important ways. Concretely, the Nicaraguan bishops have strongly articulated the opposition to conscription in a pastoral letter, in which they proclaimed that "no one can be forced to bear arms in defense of an ideology." Subsequent attacks by the government on Archbishop Obando y Bravo as "an agent of the CIA" have proven counterproductive; his popularity has never been higher.[24]

Sandinista attempts to take over the independent labor movement have been equally unsuccessful. Before 1979 there were two federations in Nicaragua: one, the Confederación de Unificación Sindical (CUS), which like the AFL-CIO was affiliated with the International Confederation of Free Trade Unions (ICFTU), and the other, the Confederación de Trabajadores Nicaragüenses (CTN), which is part of the Christian Democratic trade union international, the World Confederation of Labor headquartered in Brussels. Within hours of assuming power, the Sandinistas created their own Central Sandinista de Trabajadores and announced their intention to "unify" the labor movement under its banner. In October 1980 this new creation affiliated with the World Federation of Trade Unions (WFTU), based in Prague.

When the established unions failed to affiliate with the CST, the government began to abuse physically, jail, and deport their leaders; to organize disruptive factions; to falsify union elections; and then to ban strikes, collective contracts, demonstrations, and meetings under a "state of emergency" decree promulgated in March 1982. Although the official unions were exempted from these provisions, the Sandinistas have alienated even the workers in these, and there have been an increasing number of wildcat strikes. Labor unrest has aggravated an already difficult economic situation but, what is probably of greater political importance, has created the embarrassing spectacle of a grass-roots, working-class rebellion against a Marxist government—again, as in the case of the church, reminiscent of Poland.[25]

The Democratic Coordinator, an umbrella organization of three centrist political parties, two independent labor federations, and several professional groups, was established in early 1984 to contest the elections the Sandinistas held to meet an obligation to the Organization of American States incurred when they took power in 1979. In choosing as its presidential candidate Arturo Cruz Porras, the Coordinator has offered the Nicaraguans a non-Sandinista alternative that is not, strictly speaking, "counterrevolutionary"; Cruz was an important leader in the struggle against the Somoza dictatorship, served the new regime as Central Bank president and ambassador to the United States, and is a Social Democrat with close ties to the Socialist International. Consequently, the Sandinistas have been hard pressed to find ways to limit his influence and to restrict the electoral prospects of the Coordinator as a whole.

Although after many delays the Sandinistas finally announced in the fall of 1983 an election for November 4, 1984, they have since then alternated between attempting to exclude the Coordinator from participation altogether and to restrict Cruz's movements and opportunities to address crowds. Thus, for example, under the State of Emergency decree, he was forbidden to hold open-air meetings, which in a country like Nicaragua, with few really large indoor facilities, in effect restricts his audience at any one time to several hundred people. Officially sponsored violence was also used to discourage attendance at rallies and to intimidate Cruz physically with an evident view to forcing his withdrawal from the race.[26]

By mid-October 1984, the Coordinator was demanding postponement of the elections on the grounds that its candidates had been denied a fair opportunity to present their case to the public. Complicated negotiations failed to resolve the issue, and not even a personal appeal from the president of the Socialist International, Willy Brandt, who had traveled to Nicaragua expressly for that purpose, could move the Sandinistas. Among other things, official intransigence in Managua was attributed to the notion that the comandantes believed that by "legitimizing" their regime before the elections in the United States two days later, they would stay the hand of a victorious Reagan administration, allegedly planning a military invasion of the country.[27]

The course of opposition in Nicaragua cannot be fully understood without some reference to the insurgents who have taken to arms against the regime. In reality, there are three such groups: the Nicaraguan Democratic Force (FDN), Democratic Revolutionary Action (ARDE), and the Nicaraguan Armed Revolutionary Force (FARN). Although outsiders have a tendency to lump all these formations under the omnibus term *contras* (a shortened form of the Spanish word for counterrevolutionary), there are many differences between them; in fact, as Richard Millett has written, the *contras* "are a disparate amalgamation of forces unified only by their opposition to Nicaragua's current rulers."[28]

The largest of the groups, the FDN, has put between 5,000 and 10,000 men in the field, operating from bases in Honduras and supported more or less openly by the U.S. government through the Central Intelligence Agency. Although the Sandinistas claim that the *contras* are *somocistas* intent upon restoring a military dictatorship, it is only the FDN that provides evidence for that accusation, and very imperfectly so. While the majority of its military staff, many of its field officers, and an undetermined number of its NCOs were formerly on the rolls of Somoza's National Guard, the FDN's most important military personality, Brig. General Enrique Bermúdez, was distrusted by the late dictator because of his popularity with his troops and also because of what was perceived as insufficient devotion to the interests of the Somoza family. Much of his military career was spent in virtual diplomatic exile in the United States and Japan; consequently, his record is free of the atrocities committed by Somoza and his guard generals during their final years in power. Again, while it is true that the political directorate of the FDN is based in Miami and made up of conservative Nicaraguan politicians and businessmen, many of these figures, including Calero himself, were staunch opponents of Somoza, particularly during his last years in power, and the rank and file of FDN's tiny army, as Millett notes, is made up of "peasants, small landowners, or shopkeepers who are unhappy with the Sandinistas for religious or ideological reasons."[29] Many are Miskito Indians, a distinctive ethnic group living on Nicaragua's Atlantic Coast, long neglected by the central governments in Managua (including that of Somoza) and almost everyone else save a handful of former missionaries, until the Sandinistas, in a totalitarian urge to bring all elements of Nicaraguan society under their control, forcibly attempted to relocate them. In the process, they uprooted ancient communities from their ancestral lands, destroyed their homes, and transformed many of them into bitter refugees.[30] In the process, they also freed many of their young men for service in the ranks of the FDN.

The ARDE, a smaller group estimated at between 2,500 and 4,000 men, of which fewer than 2,000 are regular combatants, is led by Eden Pastora Gómez, a former hero of the revolution against Somoza who has since broken with his former Sandinista comrades over the issue of Marxism-Leninism. Based somewhat insecurely in Costa Rica (where its presence has provoked a major domestic political controversy), the ARDE enjoys no apparent support from the United States and derives only small amounts of financial assistance from democratic parties in Colombia and Venezuela and reportedly from Israel and some parties and groups in South America and southern Europe, as well. Most of the ARDE's fighting force is made up not of former guardsmen but of former Sandinistas, and its political leader, Alfonso Robelo, was a longtime opponent of Somoza. The tiny FARN, led by Fernando Chamorro, is unabashedly conservative, but neither its leaders nor its followers have any connections with the former regime.[31]

None of these groups have as yet established any major territorial footholds within Nicaragua itself, but they represent a serious challenge to the regime nonetheless. For by merely existing and surviving in much the same form as the Sandinistas themselves did for so many years, they make it impossible for the regime to claim that its revolution has passed the point of no return.

The present situation in Nicaragua could be described as a classic stalemate. On one hand, a government intent upon imposing a Marxist dictatorship upon a largely unwilling population can influence the conduct of ordinary citizens through preferential access to rationed goods and services, through propaganda, or, if need be, through intimidation and violence. As yet, however, this government lacks the means to extinguish independent thought and action completely. On the other hand, opposition is at once widespread, increasingly embittered, and willing at this point to contemplate the overthrow of the regime for which, however, it now lacks the politico-military means. The government can break the stalemate in its favor only if it can put its projected totalitarian political institutions into place at a rate faster than Nicaragua's present economic and political deterioration; a truly free Nicaragua, with pluralistic political institutions but under Sandinista leadership, is no longer a serious possibility, if indeed it ever was. For its part, the opposition can survive only by recourse to civil war; failing this, even massive popular disaffection will be insufficient to prevent the consolidation of a new dictatorship.

Both government and opposition attempted to negotiate a compromise in September and October 1984 when talks were held between the FSLN and the Coordinadora. Their breakdown, however, came as no surprise: no doubt the Sandinistas wanted to hold an election of some sort, but given the imperatives of their ideology (and the likely outcome), they could not afford to observe normal democratic procedures. For one thing, they might have lost; for another, even a "victory" on a scale of 51-55 percent would not constitute a mandate sufficient to reconstruct society along Leninist lines. And of course, the very notion of free elections obligates the winner to recognize the right of an opposition to continue to participate freely in the political process. This is a concession most Sandinista leaders believed they could not afford to make, and for all one can know, they might have been right.

The result was an election that combined aspects of Eastern European and *somocista* political practice: with a result just sufficiently ambiguous to satisfy die-hard apologists of the regime at home and abroad, but also capable of solidifying the hegemonic position of the ruling party. Although the Sandinistas supposedly received 67 percent of the popular vote and nearly two-thirds of the seats in the National Assembly, two of the parties that agreed to participate at all were split-off factions of Nicaragua's historic parties (Conservatives and Social Christians), Sandinista in all but name; three were self-described Marxist-Leninist formations. The only true opposition party to participate then was the Independent Liberal Party (and it, too, had a pro-FSLN faction); it received nine out of the ninety-six seats in parliament.[32]

Options for U.S. Policy Makers. Although few issues since the Vietnam War have provoked so much heated debate, particularly in Congress and the prestige press, as U.S. policy toward the Sandinistas, its most important aspect seems thus far to have been largely overlooked: namely, that both "soft" and "hard" policies have already been tried and found wanting, if "success" is defined either as a self-willed transformation of the regime or as its overthrow and replacement by something else. This does not mean that all possible methods of persuasion have been tried, but it does suggest that since the two policies so far tested lie somewhere close to polar extremes, it is highly unlikely that anything in between would yield more satisfactory results.

Between mid-1979 and late 1980, the Carter administration made a concerted effort to moderate the course of the Nicaraguan revolution by accepting the Sandinistas at face value, flooding the country with economic aid (slightly more than $100 million worth, including 100,000 tons of surplus foods), and asking as few questions as possible about Nicaragua's new foreign policy, which was unabashedly pro-Soviet and intimately linked to that of Castro's Cuba. This approach was not inspired so much by sympathy for the new government (in fact, the Carter administration had labored almost to the final hour to find a non-Sandinista alternative to Somoza), but rather by the assumption that in gracefully accepting its diplomatic defeat, the United States could recoup its losses in the future. Underlying such calculations was a deep-seated belief on the part of many administration officials that Castro's embrace of the Soviets in 1959–1960 had been provoked by Washington's refusal to accept his revolution at a time when its goals were at their most minimal; although there was no empirical proof that this had been the case, and much evidence to the contrary, Washington proceeded as if the matter were beyond discussion. In time, it was expected that the Sandinistas' Marxist ideology would lose its political content, that the post-Somoza coalition would solidify into a true national consensus, and that relations with the United States would eventually assume the quality of business as usual, much as occurred, after many contretemps, between the United States and revolutionary Mexico in the late 1920s.

Almost immediately it became apparent that this scenario was unreasonably, even insanely, optimistic. In spite of (or possibly, because of) Washington's generosity, patience, even self-effacement, the Sandinistas were becoming more, not less, tolerant of other political forces in Nicaragua. They were also becoming more, not less, active in efforts to destabilize their neighbors. By late 1980, disturbed by the expulsion of moderates from the Council of State and the overwhelming evidence of Nicaraguan arms shipments to El Salvador, the Carter administration temporarily suspended economic assistance. This is where things stood when Ronald Reagan took office in January 1981.

The new administration extended Carter's sanctions and added several more: Nicaragua was deprived of its portion of the U.S. domestic sugar market through cancellation of its import quota; U.S. representatives at the World Bank and Inter-American Development Bank were ordered to vote against Nicaraguan projects; and the Central Intelligence Agency was ordered to assist those anti-Sandinista forces eventually known as the FDN. Although the stated purpose of these actions was to force the Sandinistas to live up to their 1979 promises to the Organization of American States and, secondarily (by supporting the *contras*) to intercept Nicaraguan arms shipments to El Salvador effectively, Democratic members of the House and Senate argued that their true purpose was to overthrow the Nicaraguan government, which outcome they apparently found more deplorable than its consolidation. By October 1984 the Congress had suspended funding for *contra* operations for a five-month period, during which the Sandinistas would presumably have the opportunity to reestablish their *bona fides* by holding an honest election.

What half-measures between appeasement on one hand and confrontation on the other have been proposed? First is a more thoroughgoing U.S. economic embargo. In spite of repeated accusations of an economic "blockade" (which applies wholly to the sugar quota), most commerce between the United States and Nicaragua remains uninterrupted. The entire Nicaraguan banana crop is sold in California, and coffee, meat, and shellfish from that country are regularly unloaded at U.S. ports. Further, the government-owned airline, Aeronica, still makes regular flights between Managua and Miami. These activities constitute a vital source of foreign exchange, the lack of which, according to one report, is the government's most serious economic problem, since it is heavily dependent upon imports of manufactured goods and must service a foreign debt now estimated at $3.5 billion. So far the United States has been reluctant to impose a full trade embargo for fear of violating American obligations under the General Agreement on Tariffs and Trade and other international accords.

Second, the United States could pressure other Western countries to reduce their aid to the regime. In effect, this is already happening, probably more in reaction to the growing climate of political repression in Nicaragua than to any efforts from Washington. At this writing West Germany has suspended such aid, and the Netherlands is in the process of doing so; in Western Europe, only Spain and Sweden continue to fund significant aid programs there.

Third, the United States could attempt to isolate Nicaragua diplomatically and militarily. This is presumably what Democratic presidential candidate Walter Mondale had in mind when he suggested a possible U.S. "quarantine" of Nicaragua in an important newspaper interview shortly before the 1984 U.S. elections. Exactly how such a policy would be implemented in practice is difficult to say; two efforts that might be described as falling within that general concept, mining the Nicaraguan harbors and increasing arms shipments to El Salvador, have been consistently opposed by a substantial minority of Mondale's own party, and mining the harbors was specifically rejected by the candidate himself in his second debate with President Reagan on October 21, 1984.

At this point the real division of opinion within the United States is whether it can accomplish its goals in Nicaragua by falling back from "hard" policies toward more indirect and less violent "soft" alternatives (such as those outlined above), or whether it should persist in its present course and perhaps move even further along the "hard" end of the continuum: increased aid to the *contras*, selective bombing of airfields, or an outright invasion. Part of the reason for the present policy stalemate in Washington is that there is no agreement between the two major parties over what our goals should be, other than in some vague way to alter the conduct of the Nicaraguan government. The root of that division is a fundamental confusion over the very nature of the regime in Managua. For if one acknowledges the fundamentally Marxist-Leninist character of Sandinista rule, then it is fairly obvious that in and of themselves no half-measures—blockades, embargoes, or "quarantines"—will be persuasive with people for whom retention of power is the supreme and perhaps, by this point, the only good. *In combination with* other forceful measures, however, such as continued assistance to the anti-Sandinista insurgents, they could effectively undermine Sandinista attempts to consolidate power.

Even if such actions brought about only a "historic compromise" in which the FSLN retained the commanding heights of political and economic authority, but permitted (as in Mexico) a multiplicity of pluralistic institutions and wide areas of individual freedom, the United States could regard this outcome as a technical victory, since for all practical purposes it would constitute an abandonment by the Sandinistas of Leninist principles and practices; in effect, the "regime" would be overthrown, though not in so many words. Admittedly, this has never happened before, and it is not likely to happen now: but it is at least a possibility that will persist as long—but only as long—as the Sandinistas have not fully consolidated the regime they are now striving to build. Once that occurs, the United States will be forced to choose between writing Nicaragua off to the Soviet-Cuban alliance (with all that implies for our regional security interests), or mounting a full-scale military invasion.

Grenada

In March 1979, a group of revolutionaries from the New Jewel Movement under Maurice Bishop seized power in the tiny island of

Grenada, one of the smallest of the former British principalities in the eastern Caribbean. The result was a regime that defined itself as Marxist-Leninist in ideological orientation, that consciously allied itself with Cuba and the Soviet Union, and that set out to transform its society along Eastern European lines. By the summer of 1983, the New Jewel leadership was quarreling among itself, both over the direction the revolution was taking and over Maurice Bishop's competence to lead it. After several lengthy meetings of the Central Committee, on October 15, Bishop was expelled from his own party, disarmed, and placed under house arrest; Bernard Coard, a long-time rival, assumed power. Popular riots on October 19 in favor of Bishop, however, succeeded in securing his temporary release. Reapprehended several hours later, he and several associates were executed on orders of the new leadership. Before Coard could consolidate his rule, however, and before a potential civil war could erupt, troops of the U.S. Army and Marines and soldiers of the Organization of Eastern Caribbean States invaded the island and reestablished order.

The fact that Grenada's Marxist regime has expired allows us to know far more about it than would otherwise be the case, particularly since the captured archives of party and state have now been made available to scholars.[33] These documents plot with remarkable specificity the difficulties of transforming an Afro-Caribbean island of slightly fewer than 100,000 people into a thoroughly regimented society with a centrally planned economy. They also strongly suggest that Cuban attempts to export revolution to Caribbean societies of vastly different cultural and linguistic traditions may be doomed from the very start.

The greatest assets the New Jewel Movement obtained by joining the Cuban-Soviet alliance were arms; scholarships for students and for party, military, and government functionaries in the Soviet Union, Cuba, and Eastern bloc countries; access to the world of front groups and international organizations; and assistance in organizing a secret police and a domestic surveillance network. In spite of repeated requests, however, the Bishop regime did not receive significant economic aid from the Soviet bloc; rather, most funds (including several million dollars to complete a highly controversial airport far larger than needed for tourism) were obtained from the European Economic Community, Iran, Iraq, and quite possibly Libya.

Economic assistance, even from Western sources, never approached the levels necessary to make a serious impact on living standards, and mismanagement and incompetence squandered what modest sums were obtained. Further, a diplomatic chill with the

United States over Grenada's evident alignment with the Soviets complicated its relations with private U.S. banks and the multilateral lending institutions, although it is still unclear whether Bishop's failure to obtain relief from that quarter was due to opposition from Washington or to poor project planning.

The most serious obstacle to the consolidation of a Marxist-Leninist regime in Grenada was, however, the very nature of the society itself: "firmly petty bourgeois," in the words of one party commission, "by law rebellious to any form of strict discipline and organization." Moreover, in Grenada as in most small island societies, there was a well-established tradition of seeking work abroad—in Canada, Great Britain, or the United States. This led to "an unsatisfactory level of patriotism among the masses—a visa mentality." Because the country's minuscule economy was heavily dependent upon remittances from Grenadians abroad (with whom the regime studiously labored to maintain good relations), it was frankly reluctant to abridge freedom of travel. The same party commission also doubted that it would be possible to forbid wholly the distribution of "imperialist" books, magazines, and films and lamented the strong popular resistance to conscription, which deprived families of an able-bodied wage earner without corresponding remuneration.[34]

To be sure, other Marxist regimes have overcome societal resistance to regimentation, but none of these have previously been shaped by British cultural and political traditions. In Grenada this meant that repression would automatically be less acceptable and also that institutions would already be in place to resist it. The most important of these were the Grenadian churches, which avoided direct confrontation with the government while nonetheless managing to act as a focal point of opposition. Almost from the beginning of the New Jewel regime, the Anglican bishop was calling for early elections and the release of political prisoners; he also strongly criticized the government for its seizure of the island's two independent newspapers. His Roman Catholic counterpart sponsored the publication of pamphlets the regime regarded as anti-Marxist and used his control of the Catholic Youth Organization to resist recruitment of young people to its New Jewel analogue. Both Catholic and Anglican churches possessed independent school systems to which the regime had no alternative to offer. The regime was unable to split the church as in Nicaragua, because there was no sector particularly attracted to "liberation theology." This was so because unlike many Spanish-speaking countries of the Caribbean, in Grenada neither the Anglican nor the Roman Catholic hierarchy was particularly associated with large landowners or the wealthier classes, of whom there were precious few in any case. Moreover, the presence of numerous missionaries from "nontraditional" Protestant denominations (Seventh Day Adventist, Mormon, Jehovah's Witness) acted as an additional brake on any "progressive" trends within the religious communities.[35]

The regime also faced resistance from the most nontraditional (but also most characteristically Afro-Caribbean) religion of all—the Rastafarians, a sect that believes that the late emperor of Ethiopia is God and whose braided hair, disheveled appearance, and irregular lifestyle ran strongly counter to the notion of a new "Socialist man." The Central Committee of the New Jewel Movement discussed the Rastafarian threat at its meeting on June 24, 1981, where it appeared, apparently in opposition to conscription, that a group was planning to attack an army encampment; they were also reported to be planning to "go on the offensive in the northern part of the country" and were "weak[ening] . . . [the regime's] support base." A proposal to have the police selectively pick up several hundred Rastafarians and forcibly cut their hair was strongly opposed by Bishop and the Cuban ambassador (who normally attended these meetings *ex officio*), both of whom warned of likely unfavorable international and regional repercussions. Significantly, on that occasion Bernard Coard tartly reminded the meeting that "the Party for the last two and a half years . . . [has] been reluctant to take firm decisions on key issues."[36]

The regime's relationship to the labor movement was only slightly less problematical. As Bishop explained it in a speech to a closed session of the Central Committee on September 13, 1982, Grenada suffered from "underdeveloped class formations," which meant that the working class alone was too small upon which to base a movement toward socialism. Hence, he favored a "class alliance" with other elements—the petit and grand bourgeoisie—an alliance in which, however, "we [the party] have a hegemonic control on power." This left open the question of how the interests of the trade unions would be balanced against other groups, a conflict never fully resolved. Bishop continually had to renegotiate his alliance with a labor movement where "economism and consumerism" were reportedly rampant and where failure to deliver the goods could have negative political consequences.[37]

The New Jewel Movement had an even more tenuous grasp on the peasantry. Although there were a few large landowners in Grenada, most country folk were smallholders, making it difficult to use land reform as a political instrument. In effect, a rough democracy of poverty tended to blunt class conflict. As in much of the English Caribbean, the most explosive social class was not a landless peasantry, but the unemployed youth (many of recent rural origin), who clustered in the streets and squares of the towns—bored, listless, with serious mob potential. This was the segment of society that was most affected by Maurice Bishop's charisma and the group that in the end almost saved his life.

Between 1979 and 1983, then, the New Jewel Movement attempted to build a Marxist-Leninist state within Grenada, only to succeed in erecting a radical populist dictatorship allied politically and militarily to the Eastern bloc. By mid-1983 it was apparent that neither its connections abroad nor its resources at home were sufficient to meet even minimally the popular expectations that Bishop himself had raised. Thus he went to the United States to appeal for a detente in political relations, an arrangement that presumably would provide new sources of economic assistance. Before the sincerity of his intentions could be measured, he was overthrown and murdered by a faction of his own party loyal to Bernard Coard. In some interpretations, Coard was provoked to action by Bishop's trip to Washington, a sign of serious ideological backsliding. But precisely what form the Grenadian state would have assumed within the context of a full rapprochement with the United States can never be known.

Implications for U.S. Policy Makers. In spite of frequent allegations by apologists of U.S. attempts to "destabilize" the Bishop regime, both before and after its demise, the immediate cause of its downfall was an internal quarrel that arose at least in part from its inability to attract significant international economic assistance. Having promised far more than the elected governments in other parts of the eastern Caribbean, the Bishop regime also delivered less, possibly because the only thing it had to offer the world besides nutmeg and beaches— its international allegiance—was negotiable only in weapons and political advice from the Soviet bloc. What "conscience money" could be obtained from the West was too modest to make a difference.

To be sure, U.S. policy was not irrelevant to these events. Had the United States wished to, it could have offered the island vast amounts of aid to create a "showcase" of Marxist populism in the region. At a minimum, it could have supported Bishop's requests at the World Bank and the Inter-American Development Bank more vigorously. The United States obviously had no incentive to do so, however, and in any case it is virtually certain that, at least until 1983, such conciliatory efforts would have been sharply turned aside for ideological reasons.

This was true as much for the Carter as the Reagan administration. Admittedly, the Reagan administration was more visibly hostile to Grenada than its predecessor, to the point that the president deliberately raised the temperature of bilateral relations through a broadcast address on March 10, 1983, in which he called attention to the ominous security implications of the airport project. By that time, however, the Bishop regime had also moved very far out front in its support of Soviet objectives worldwide, so that it is impossible to know to what degree Washington acted on its own impulses or to what degree it merely reacted to deliberate Grenadian provocations.

The violent downfall of Maurice Bishop was no triumph for U.S. policy, since it temporarily brought to power a regime even more pro-Soviet than Bishop's; the threat of civil war and the prospect of an indiscriminate slaughter of civilians, though, afforded ample pretext for a multinational military expedition, the result of which was the downfall of Coard's dictatorship and the expulsion from Grenada of several thousand Cuban advisers and construction workers, not to mention the dismantlement of an entire intelligence apparatus in the service of the Soviet bloc. In addition to retrieving Grenada for the West, the intervention served notice on "progressive" political forces in other islands in the eastern Caribbean that the international behavior of their governments was a matter of deep U.S. concern. In that sense, events in Grenada may have converged to neutralize pro-Soviet forces in the region for a decade or more. Nevertheless, it is difficult to extract from these events any other lesson that could be readily applied in the future.

Notes

1. Abraham Lowenthal, "The Pencil of God," *Wilson Quarterly* (Spring 1982).

2. R. Bruce McColm, "Central America and the Caribbean: The Larger Scenario," *Strategic Review* (Summer 1983).

3. Jiri Valenta and Virginia Valenta, "Soviet Strategy and Policies in the Caribbean Basin," in Howard J. Wiarda, ed., *Rift and Revolution: The Central American Imbroglio* (Washington, D.C.: American Enterprise Institute, 1984); see also Morris Rothenberg, "The Soviets and Central America," in Robert S. Leiken, ed., *Central America: Anatomy of Conflict* (New York: Pergamon Press for the Carnegie Endowment for International Peace, 1984).

4. V.S. Naipaul, *The Overcrowded Barracoon* (London: Andre Deutsch, 1972), p. 250.

5. Robert Pastor and Richard Feinberg, "Far From Hopeless: An Economy Program for Postwar Central America," in Leiken, *Central America*.

6. Theodore Draper, *Castroism: Theory and Practice* (New York: Praeger, 1964), esp. pp. 97–103.

7. Laurence H. Theriot, "Revolutionary Balance Sheet," in U.S. Congress, Joint Economic Committee, *Cuba Faces the Economic Realities of the 1980s* (Washington, D.C.: GPO, 1982).

8. René Dumont, *Is Cuba Socialist?* (New York: Viking Press, 1974).
9. Carlos Alberto Montaner, "Toward a Consistent U.S. Cuban Policy," in Irving Louis Horowitz, ed., *Cuban Communism*, 5th ed. (New Brunswick, N.J.: Transaction Books, 1983), p. 522.
10. Barry Sklar, "Cuban Exodus, 1980: The Context," in U.S. Senate, Committee on Foreign Relations, *The Political Economy of the Western Hemisphere: Selected Issues for U.S. Policy* (Washington, D.C.: GPO, 1981), pp. 100–16.
11. Ernesto F. Betancourt and Wilson P. Dizard III, *Fidel Castro and the Bankers: The Mortgaging of a Revolution* (Washington, D.C.: Cuban American National Foundation, 1982).
12. *U.S. Radio Broadcasting to Cuba: Policy Implications* (Washington, D.C.: Cuban American National Foundation, 1982).
13. U.S. Senate, Committee on Foreign Relations, *Hearings on Radio Broadcasting to Cuba* (Washington, D.C.: GPO, 1982).
14. Theriot, "Revolutionary Balance Sheet."
15. Montaner, "Toward a Consistent U.S. Cuban Policy," p. 528.
16. Carmelo Mesa-Lago, *Cuba in the 1970s: Pragmatism and Institutionalization* (Albuquerque, N.M.: University of New Mexico Press, 1974).
17. Thomas P. Anderson, "The Two Revolutions: Nicaragua and Cuba," Paper prepared for the Office of Long Range Assessments and Research, U.S. Department of State (Washington, D.C., 1982).
18. *Keesing's Contemporary Archives*, November 1985, p. 33968A.
19. U.S. Department of Commerce, International Trade Administration, *Foreign Economic Trends and Their Implications for the United States: Nicaragua*, January 1984; see also Stephen Kinzer, "With Economic Woes Deepening, Managua Sees Years of Shortages," *New York Times*, October 22, 1984.
20. Congressional Research Service, Library of Congress, *International Assistance to the Sandinista Government* (Issue Briefs 1B 82115 and 84-505F); Stephen Kinzer, "Soviet Help to Sandinistas: Blank Check," *New York Times*, March 28, 1984; and *Keesing's Contemporary Archives*, November 1985, p. 33968A.
21. Ronald Radosh, "The Drift toward Repression," in Mark Falcoff and Robert Royal, eds., *Crisis and Opportunity: U.S. Policy in Central America and the Caribbean* (Washington, D.C.: Ethics and Public Policy Center, 1984).
22. Juan O. Tamayo, "Sandinista Draft Triggers Resistance," *Washington Post*, August 4, 1984; Stephen Kinzer, "Military Draft in Nicaragua Is Meeting Wide Resistance," *New York Times*, June 26, 1984.
23. Alan Riding, "Sandinistas Are Indignant at Pope, Dissidents Delighted at His Policies," *New York Times*, March 6, 1983.
24. "The Subversion of the Church in Nicaragua: An Interview with Miguel Bolanos Hunter," Institute on Religion and Democracy, *Briefing Paper* no. 1, 1983; "Embattled Archbishop," *New York Times*, March 5, 1983.
25. William C. Doherty, "Nicaragua—A Revolution Betrayed" (American Federation of Labor–Congress of Industrial Organizations, 1984, mimeographed); Sam Leiken, "Labor under Seige," *The New Republic*, October 8, 1984.
26. Arturo J. Cruz, "Democracy Rears Its Ugly Head in Nicaragua," *Wall Street Journal*, August 10, 1984.

27. Stephen Kinzer, "Brandt Visits Managua but Fails to Settle Nicaragua Vote Dispute," *New York Times*, October 15, 1984.

28. Richard Millett, "Praetorians or Patriots? The Central American Military," in Leiken, *Central America*, pp. 69–91.

29. Ibid., p. 84.

30. *Report on the Situation of Human Rights in Nicaragua* (Washington, D.C.: Organization of American States, 1983).

31. Millett, "Praetorians or Patriots?" p. 83.

32. Robert S. Leiken, "The Sandinistas' Tangled Elections," in Mark Falcoff and Robert Royal, eds., *The Continuing Crisis: U.S. Policy in Central America and the Caribbean* (Washington, D.C.: Ethics and Public Policy Center, 1987), pp. 377–99.

33. This analysis draws upon portions of those documents released to the public by the U.S. Department of Defense and U.S. Department of State, *Grenada Documents: An Overview and Selection* (Washington, D.C., 1984); a slightly more convenient edition is available in Paul Seabury and Walter A. McDougall, eds., *The Grenada Papers* (San Francisco, Calif.: Institute for Contemporary Studies, 1984).

34. Ibid., Document 102602. Progress Report of Commission Number Five (no date).

35. Ibid., Document JJ1. Top Secret, "Analysis (of) the Church in Grenada" (March 15, 1983); Document KK1, "Analysis of the Church in Grenada" (July 12, 1983); Document II1, "Report of the Delegation Sent to Grenada by the Americas Department (of the Cuban Communist party) with the Aim of the Gathering of Sources for the Characterization of the Religious Situation in the Country and the Contracts for Further Cooperation between the PCC and the NJM Regarding the Question" (October 14, 1982).

36. Ibid., Document 105449. "Minutes of the Political Bureau Meeting, June 21, 1981."

37. Ibid., Document 001560. "Line of March for the Party"; Document 104060, "Minutes of the Central Committee Meeting, June 26, 1982"; Document 105416A/103415, "Central Committee Report on First Plenary Session," July 13–19, 1983.

3
Soviet Policy in the Caribbean and Central America: Opportunities and Constraints

Howard J. Wiarda

Sovietologists and Latin Americanists: A Meeting of the Minds?

The heightened crisis in Central America and the Caribbean and the stronger and more assertive role of the Soviet Union in that part of the world have given rise to a new phenomenon in what we might call the sociology and politics of knowledge, specifically that branch of knowledge relating to foreign policy analysis. What is new involves the infusion into Latin American area studies of a vast array of Soviet specialists, global foreign policy analysts, Kremlinologists, and experts in Eastern Europe and in Soviet foreign policy. For the first time (even including the 1962 Cuban missile crisis, which, though deadly serious, was only a brief interlude in a long history of indifference), Sovietologists and U.S. foreign policy generalists are paying serious attention to Latin America. In the process, they have increasingly come into conflict with long-time regional experts on Central America, the Caribbean, and the Latin American area as a whole. The result has frequently been not so much a meeting of the minds or a mutual enrichment that comes from regard for each other's expertise, but rather discord and disagreement. The battle is fought out in the op-ed pages, in the journals and magazines, and in the wealth of new books on the area. It has the potential to develop into a major scholarly battle, with important implications for policy as well.[1]

Latin America specialists, for the most part, tend to like the area they study. They enjoy traveling there. Most of them feel at home in Latin America. Many went there first as youthful and idealistic Peace Corps volunteers, or as young scholars caught up in the romance of the 1960s development literature, which sought not only to analyze development but also to *bring* it, in an ethical and moral sense, to those in what were then known as the "emerging" or "developing" nations. Latin America specialists sympathize with their area's aims and aspirations. They develop empathy and understanding—indeed those are usually inculcated in their graduate training. They have come to learn, and appreciate, Latin America's language or languages, its literature, its culture, and even the distinctiveness of its modes of sociopolitical development. They value the area and see its worth. As area specialists, they have been steeped in Latin America's history. Moreover, they are inclined to look with favor on the region's efforts to break out of its vicious circles of dependency and underdevelopment.[2]

Latin Americanists, however, frequently exaggerate their area's significance both as a major region worthy of study and as an area of presumed importance to the United States. They value Latin America as a *civilization,* and they are still somewhat defensive about that older notion, prevalent during the 1950s but still residually present in the thinking of some academics and policy makers today, that Latin America constitutes a second-rate area for second-rate minds. Latin Americanists generally employ a culture area approach to their region, and the conceptual frameworks they use have traditionally held little room for exogenous actors. That perspective is now changing under the impact of dependency theory. Hence when Latin Americanists do analyze external forces, they usually blame the United States for the area's troubles and its position of dependency. Furthermore, many Latin Americanists suspect, with considerable reason historically and perhaps with some validity currently, that the new wave of attention to the area is a prelude to new covert, CIA-inspired initiatives directed against "their" countries, especially when that attention comes from Soviet specialists within the U.S. government. Nor do Latin Americanists always appreciate the attempts by the newcomers to analyze or write about the area, let alone issue policy prescriptions for it, without steeping themselves in the language or culture or spending much time there.

That is precisely the position in which the new wave of Sovietologists and foreign policy generalists who have in fact recently turned their attention to Latin America now find themselves. Few know the languages of the area. Few have ever been there—or if they have, for only a brief visit—long enough in most cases to confirm prejudices already strongly held. Few care about the area, and they would probably not want to live there. To them, Latin America is a relatively minor and probably temporary sideshow, a current stage where the U.S.-Soviet rivalry is acted out. The present locus of the battle, they believe, should not be permitted to distract from the global character of the struggle, which is certain next week or next year to pass on to another theater, which will then similarly receive temporary attention. Sovietologists, hence, have little interest in Latin American culture or civilization per se. For them, Central America and the Caribbean constitute only another *object* of Soviet foreign policy, rather like Vietnam or Afghanistan, but not itself a region of intrinsic importance. Having little empathy with the area, many such analysts tend to denigrate its importance, except as it affects the U.S.-Soviet rivalry. They view the professional Latin Americanist rather like the proverbial anthropologist who has "gone native" and become so closely identified with his area of study that his objectivity has been lost. They may even suspect that Latin Americanists have stronger loyalties to their area of specialization or to other agendas than to the United States and its foreign policy objectives. They feel further that Latin Americanists are blind to the realities of Soviet, Cuban, and now Nicaraguan machinations in the area, tending to ignore or belittle the rising Soviet presence and both its capacity and its willingness to meddle in this formerly "American lake."

These differences between Sovietologists and Latin Americanists as outlined here are reflected in the debate over East-West and North-South approaches to foreign policy. The Sovietologists, naturally, see the world mainly in an East-West perspective; they are generally older and have tended to dominate the main U.S. foreign policy agencies since World War II. The Latin Americanists, North-South oriented, are generally younger; they have also tended over the years to be critical of U.S. foreign policy. In fact, as William Luers emphasizes in a set of comments based on attendance at the professional association meetings of both these groups, the two bodies sound as if they "come from different planets and their visions of foreign policy and American society are at opposite poles of the American scene."[3]

U.S. Latin Americanists, again following Luers, are often influenced by Latin American dependency analysis, are supportive of Latin American criticism of the United States, are influenced by critical perspectives of the Latin American Left, and are sympathetic to Latin American efforts to break the ties of dependency to the United States. Influenced by the North-South perspective as well, their preoccupations are usually development-related problems, human rights and social justice issues, the furtherance of democracy, and economic asymmetries between the developed and the developing worlds—and not issues of U.S. national security or national interests at stake in Latin America. These groups, in academia, journalism, churches, and government, tend to be idealistic about Latin American motivations and the capacity and desire of the United States to realign its foreign policy in accord with these objectives. At the same time, they are often strongly critical of existing U.S. policies toward the third world and specifically the Latin American part of it, almost regardless of whether those policies emanate from a Carter or a Reagan administration.[4]

Sovietologists, in contrast, tend to be highly critical of their area of specialization, critical regarding both Soviet goals and the Communist ideology, and innately suspicious of revolutions and revolutionary movements. In Luers's words, they are not given to idealism, they are hard-nosed about the limits of U.S. policy, and they are convinced no issue is so important as the U.S.-Soviet relationship. Whereas the Latin Americanist is suspicious of U.S. power and seeks to build restraints into U.S. actions abroad, the Sovietologists try to increase U.S. power and the capacity to use it abroad. Soviet specialists usually give low priority to North-South issues and are often either patronizing toward those who do or, worse, "instant experts" when they do engage the issues. To a Latin Americanist, his region should be of major interest to the United States for humanitarian and political reasons that are only confused by the introduction of "extraneous" East-West issues. The Soviet specialists and foreign policy generalists, in contrast, see Latin America as a minor and relatively insignificant region in which the U.S.-Soviet rivalry is now being carried out.

The potential obviously exists for the absence of any meeting of the minds on these issues. The two groups, coming from different backgrounds as well as different intellectual and socialization experiences, are largely talking past each other. Indeed there is a strong possibility for hostility and downright conflict between these clashing groups and points of view. Albeit for different reasons, both Latin Americanists and Sovietologists may reinforce each other's low tolerance for serious discussion of Central America or the rising Soviet presence there.

It might be hoped that some better and mutually beneficial exchange could be established between these two groups. Without being unduly optimistic, it might be suggested that the Sovietologists and East-West specialists could appropriately stop denigrating the importance and *worth* of the area, begin reading about and paying it serious attention, and actually learn something about Latin America. At the same time, Latin America specialists need to recognize that there *is* a new Soviet (and Cuban) presence, capability, and interest in the Central American–Caribbean area (without elevating that fact into a single, all-encompassing explanation of the region's troubles) with important implications for the future of the region and U.S. foreign policy there. Latin Americanists could also be reminded, in their encounter with the generalists, that in the broader global context, theirs is an area of distinctly secondary importance for the point of view of U.S. policy.

Both groups, it seems to me, can stand to learn from each other. That, in any case, is the thrust and intention of this paper.

The U.S.S.R. and Latin America: New Capabilities and Tactics

This chapter does not presume to offer a complete analysis of Soviet foreign policy, strategy, and tactics in Latin America, or in Central America more specifically.[5] A consensus is emerging among serious scholars regarding the new Soviet presence and capabilities in the area and the changed strategy of the Soviet Union, however, and that consensus is reflected here. Furthermore, a brief overview is necessary as a prelude to the discussion that follows on both the possibilities for the Soviet Union in the region *and* the constraints limiting Soviet activities there.

Capabilities. The Soviet capacity to function effectively in Latin America is far greater now than it was thirty years ago.[6] Then, the notion of Stalinist legions, military or political, playing a serious role in Latin America was dismissed as ludicrous, as it deserved to be. Today, the situation is not so simple: the Soviet Union is a rising presence in the region, a fact that needs to be recognized and treated realistically. We need not fall prey to scare tactics or shibboleths or be tempted to blame all the region's troubles on Soviet or Cuban machinations. But we should not fall into the opposite trap either: a failure to recognize this rising presence or, worse, an attempt to deny entirely the importance of Soviet activities. One should neither minimize the Soviet role nor confer upon it an importance it does not have, but rather one should assess it carefully and dispassionately. Several aspects of the new presence and capabilities of the Soviet Union in Latin America should be noted, here presented in summary outline form and detailed in the bibliographic references accompanying this chapter.

First, diplomatic and normal state-to-state relations. Prior to World War II the Soviet Union had established temporary relations with only two Latin American countries (Mexico and Uruguay), and only three (Argentina, Mexico, and Uruguay) sustained relations with Moscow throughout the postwar period. By 1980, however, the Soviet Union had established diplomatic relations with all the major Latin American countries and most of the smaller ones (except the Dominican Republic and Guatemala). These ties have given the Soviet Union a diplomatic and political presence throughout the hemisphere that it lacked before. Such a presence is useful to the Soviets for gathering information, establishing regular channels of communications, and influencing developments. It provides a stronger basis for Soviet participation in United Nations, nonaligned, and third world events. Such normal state-to-state relations give further legitimacy to the Soviet Union as a great power and weaken the stigma of evil incarnate long attached to it. Indeed, one could argue that in contrast to the strategy of fomenting revolution with which Soviet machinations are most closely associated in the popular mind, it is the building of "normal" state-to-state relations—and the legitimacy that goes with them—that is currently the primary focus of Soviet policy.[7]

Second, the Soviet military presence. Over the past two decades the Soviet military has become an increasingly global military. The Soviet Union cannot match the U.S. military presence in the Western Hemisphere, its role is still limited, and one could say that, so far as Latin America is concerned, the Soviet Union is not yet a superpower there. It has, however, considerably increased its naval and air presence and capability, especially in the Caribbean and the South Atlantic. Moreover, some of its forces have acquired, or are about to acquire, an amphibious landing capability. The day may not be very far off when a crisis somewhere in the Caribbean will find both the U.S. and the Soviet fleets setting sail simultaneously and arriving at the same time, *both* with helicopters in the air, landing craft dispatched, and marine forces ready to take control—or to face down each other.[8]

Third, Cuba. Over the years the island of Cuba has been turned into a major military, air, naval, and intelligence base, offering numerous advantages to the Soviet Union. Cuba is a refueling station, an arms depot, a center for training, a propaganda center, and a launch pad for naval operations and reconnaissance flights. Cuba acts to a degree as an independent nation and to a degree as a proxy,[9] to further Soviet (as well as Cuba's own) military-strategic and political objectives in such far-flung regions of conflict as southern Africa, the Horn of Africa, the Arabian Peninsula, and Central America and the Caribbean. The situation is enormously advantageous to the Soviet Union in that it can rely on a proxy without itself seeming to be directly involved.[10] Marxist (and increasingly Marxist-Leninist) Nicaragua may augment these possibilities, as Grenada for a time seemed to promise. In addition, the Soviet paramilitary presence (spy and communications ships, agents, "fishing boats," channels for arms and training, and the like) has been considerably increased.

Fourth, expanded Soviet trade relations with the area. The Soviet Union is not prepared to bankroll very many needy third world countries, and the volume of trade is still sufficiently low that, except in one or two countries, it is inadequate to buy much political influence. Although the level of commerce between the Soviet Union and the major Latin American countries does not nearly equal that of the United States in Latin America, it has reached the level of trade with other industrial countries (for example, Japan or West Germany). The increase and above all the *regularization* of trade permitted the Soviet Union to achieve levels of cooperation with several Latin American governments—Argentina or Peru—that while themselves not Socialist could nevertheless accept Soviet technical assistance and commercial offers in a spirit of amicability. Expanding commercial relations enable the Soviet Union to maintain regular contact with a country like Bolivia, despite its frequent changes of regime. Argentina remains the Soviet Union's largest trading partner in Latin America, but in Central America and the Caribbean its economic connections have also been expanding.[11]

Fifth, improved Soviet diplomatic and political representation. Far more than before, quite a number of Soviet and Eastern European personnel know Spanish and have lived in the area. Moreover, the quality and sophistication of Soviet scholarship and analysis of Latin America have improved markedly in the past two decades.[12] And unlike American diplomatic personnel, who are generally moved from region to region every three years and their expertise lost, Soviet personnel are more often kept in their area of specialization.

Sixth, expanded Soviet cultural exchanges. The matter of cultural exchanges should be of particular interest to the U.S. Information Agency. Soviet and Marxist-Leninist literature is omnipresent; the number of scholarships being offered to young Latin Americans far outdistances our own. Strenuous efforts are being made to influence Latin American opinion molders: young journalists, party leaders, student leaders, labor and peasant leaders, and scientists. Whole plane loads of such future opinion leaders are flown from such countries as Bolivia, Nicaragua, Cuba, Colombia, and Peru for extended visits to the Soviet Union and Eastern Europe. By this time there is in Latin America a whole new generation of young people who, sometimes because of Soviet indoctrination and in other instances quite independent of it, have swung radically to the left and for whom Marxism (if not Marxism-Leninism) constitutes *the* cognitive map by which they interpret the world.[13]

Seventh, an increased Soviet commitment to involvement in Central American and Latin American affairs. Previously the Soviets looked on the Caribbean Basin—indeed on all of Latin America, with the exception of Cuba—as rather hopeless from their point of view, part of the American sphere of influence, sociologically backward, disorganized, and chaotic, not worth their involvement. Now the Soviets see both opportunities to be pursued and advantages to be gained from embarrassing the United States in its own back yard, tying up U.S. military and political resources that might otherwise be used elsewhere, allowing and even encouraging another divisive issue to fester in the domestic U.S. body politic, and furthering the Soviets' own foreign policy goals—all this at no or minimum costs to the Soviet Union. The Soviets obviously recognize their limitations in operating in the Western Hemisphere, but they have seen that even a modest investment on their part can reap considerable political and strategic gains—hence their willingness to make a greater commitment. Their willingness to increase such commitments is also fueled, in Latin America and the Soviet Union, by the widespread perception that the United States, historically the dominant power in the hemisphere, is a confused, divided, and declining power. As the presence of the United States in Latin America diminished in the past decade, that of the Soviet Union correspondingly increased.[14] It will be interesting to see if the U.S. intervention in Grenada, the strong U.S. presence in Central America, and the overall U.S. military buildup fundamentally alter these Soviet views of the area.

The Soviet Union, there can be no doubt, has significantly augmented its presence in Latin America in the past two decades—diplomatically, politically, commercially, militarily, and culturally. But to talk of a rising Soviet presence is insufficient by itself. What is also required is information on Soviet tactics, capabilities, purposes, and level of sophistication in pursuing its foreign policy goals, as well as Latin America's response or receptiveness to these. Let us turn to these matters next.

Strategies and Tactics. While the Soviet Union's presence has been expanding in Latin America, its strategies and tactics have been shifting as well. Overall, the Soviet approach has become much more sophisticated than in the past.[15]

First, a better-defined, more aggressive policy. In the past twenty years Soviet policy toward Latin America has become much more focused and activist. That is the central thesis of the important paper written at Princeton University by William Luers,[16] former U.S. ambassador to Venezuela, counselor to the Kissinger Commission, and former ambassador to Czechoslovakia. The more aggressive Soviet posture, Luers argues, which for the first time is openly directed toward the violent overthrow of the governments of El Salvador and Guatemala, is the product of changed Soviet perceptions of conditions in the region, of U.S. capacities and policies, and of a bolder military approach vis-à-vis the United States outside the NATO area. A major influence on this changed Soviet posture is Cuba, which, Luers argues, has finally convinced Moscow after twenty years of debate that the promotion of violent revolution in Central America can be a productive and relatively low-risk policy. Luers suggests that the evolution of a greater Soviet role in the area was due as much to changed conditions there as to its own ambitions and machinations: the declining U.S. presence since the early 1970s, the growing assertiveness and independence of the Latin American nations, the triumph of the Nicaraguan revolution, the successes registered for a time by guerrilla groups in El Salvador and Guatemala, and the growing trend in the region toward third worldism and nonalignment. There is, overall, an increased Soviet commitment to affect the course of events in the Caribbean Basin.

Second, an emphasis on long-term rather than short-term gains.[17] Che Guevara's abortive and unsuccessful guerrilla campaign in Bolivia in the 1960s helped force this reassessment. Obviously the Soviets are not opposed to short-term gains either, as in Nicaragua, Grenada for a time, Suriname, and perhaps El Salvador. But the main thrust is now long term. The Soviets recognize that the level of industrialization and the class situation in Latin America are not sufficiently strong to produce successful workers' revolutions very soon. They do, however, see strong possibilities for building a solid base for securing future gains. The strategy relies on caution, prudence, and gradualism rather than on accomplishing quick or easy victories. It seeks to build up sympathy for the Soviet Union, to increase trade and cultural exchanges, to play upon rising Latin American nationalism, and to be sympathetic toward nonaligned and third world orientations. Naturally the Soviets would not be displeased if another country, rather like Cuba or Nicaragua, simply fell into their hands, but the main thrust of Soviet policy has shifted away from quick guerrilla victories and toward securing long-term advantages.

Third, anti-Americanism. The Soviets have learned to play cleverly on the growing anti-Americanism throughout the region and to take advantage of it. To various target groups—students, peasants, and workers especially—the Soviet Union has sought to present itself as a viable alternative to U.S. dominance. It offers itself as a counterpoint to the United States, ideologically, politically, and economically. As the U.S. presence there has declined, the Soviet Union has positioned itself to help fill the vacuum. As the U.S. erects greater tariff barriers to the import of Latin American products, the Soviet Union and Eastern Europe stand ready to increase their trade. If the United States follows a reactionary policy of aiding chiefly Latin America's most repressive and backward-looking forces and regimes, the Soviets are prepared to assist the progressive elements. As the debt issue heats up and the United States and U.S. banks, fairly or not, are seen as responsible for the depressed conditions, rising food prices, and downward-turning economies, the Soviets again stand ready to take advantage of the strong anti-Americanism thus engendered.

Fourth, fine-tuned policy. Soviet policy has become far more flexible and nuanced.[18] The Soviets have learned that they need not go so far as to support guerrilla action everywhere. Rather, they pursue multiple strategies at the same time, ranging from normal state-to-state relations in some countries to destabilization and subversion in others. The Soviets distinguish rather closely between different types of regimes in Latin American and adjust their strategies accordingly. Although they will oppose the more reactionary and repressive regimes in Latin America and may seek to overthrow them, they may simultaneously work out amicable and mutually beneficial relations with military regimes like those formerly ruling in Argentina and Brazil. Where democratic and populist governments are in power (Costa Rica and the Dominican Republic, for example, or Torrijos's Panama a few years back), they recognize that advantages can still be gained from playing on both nationalism and anti-Americanism. They may, at one and the same time, support democratic governments at one level (Peru, Costa Rica, and Colombia), while at the same time fomenting terrorism and antigovernment guerrilla groups directed against them.

Fifth, changed guerrilla tactics. From an emphasis on the "foco theory" and on promoting more Cuba-like revolutions two decades ago, the Soviet Union has now evolved a strategy emphasizing broader anti-imperialist positions and building on more broadly based opposition coalitions.[19] The Nicaraguan revolution, which brought together peasants, workers, students, intellectuals, some clerics, young professionals, a sizable part of the middle class, and even some businessmen, helped precipitate this change; similar tactics are being employed in El Salvador and Guatemala.

Sixth, forced unity. In key revolutionary contexts like Nicaragua in the mid-1970s and later in El Salvador and Guatemala, the Soviets have been instrumental in forcing several antiregime groups to come together for the common struggle. This tactic has afforded a unity and coherence to the revolutionary struggle not present before. In meetings in Havana and Moscow, unity and a common strategy have been forced on these groups as a condition of further military assistance. In this way the often competing factions and leaders have been obliged to work together despite long years of rivalry and feuding. The results, as in Nicaragua, are plainly visible.

Seventh, increased international support. The Soviets have skillfully built international support, including support not just from the Communist countries but also from the nonaligned movement, the third world, the Southern Hemisphere, and other Socialist and social-democratic movements such as the Socialist International. This effort involves, in addition, infiltrating such groups and building a base of support among their sympathizers, agents, and, more important, well-intentioned but often naive persons, themselves not Communists, in the United States, in particular some church, student, and human rights groups. The strategy makes extensive use of propaganda to discredit U.S. policy, to legitimate their own thrusts into the area, and to prejudice third parties against the United States. The Soviet propaganda and disinformation networks became effective just at the time exposure and denunciation of them became unfashionable and they were labeled "McCarthyism."[20]

Eighth, more thorough Communist indoctrination. As the Soviets have grown more sophisticated in their analyses of Latin America, they have taken a stronger and more direct hand in devising strategy for the region. The Soviets and their Eastern European allies have themselves been providing training and indoctrination, ideologically orienting the Central American and Caribbean revolutionary groups, providing day-to-day instructions and guidance, and enforcing tighter canons of ideological orthodoxy. The warehouse of papers captured by the United States in the Grenada invasion provides ample evidence of the heavy, deep, everyday involvement of the Soviet Union in all aspects of the revolutionary process.[21]

Ninth, a realistic approach. The Soviets do not believe that all Central America and the Caribbean, let alone South America, will fall into their hands tomorrow. They do see situations there to take advantage of, however, to embarrass the United States and frustrate its intentions, to immobilize U.S. resources and raise the level of U.S. commitments that might otherwise be spent in other areas, to secure some advantages for themselves, and to deny possibilities to the United States, if not yet to seize them for the Soviet Union—and all this without expending many resources of their own. The Soviets see they can make gains in Latin America at very low costs to themselves, without risking confrontation with the United States, as would be the case in Europe, the Middle East, or the Pacific Basin, for example. They are exploiting the current situation and securing gains on the cheap, allowing local possibilities to develop. Our recent preoccupation in the United States with the Soviet-Cuban role in Central America, moreover, has distracted our attention from Soviet gains farther south. Actually, both areas have been the scene of impressive Soviet advances in the past decade, and both command our serious attention.

The Soviet Union and Latin American Realities

Although the Soviet Union is undoubtedly a considerably stronger presence in Latin America now than it was two decades ago and although its policy is now more nuanced and sophisticated, the Soviets nevertheless have immense problems to surmount in advancing their interests farther. While the Soviets enjoy some advantages, they also operate under severe constraints. Indeed, as we examine the problems the Soviets must overcome, we see how similar these problems are in many respects to those faced by the United States in pursuing its policies there. As we weigh those features favorable to an expanding Soviet presence against those impeding it, the point becomes clearer.

Aspects Favoring an Expanded Soviet Influence. Many aspects of society, culture, economics, and class relations in Central America and the Caribbean—and in Latin America more generally—favor an expanded Soviet influence there.

First, nationalism. Nationalism and anti-Americanism are strong and probably growing. The Soviets and Cubans have, as indicated, been clever in exploiting these factors to their own advantage.

Second, economic conditions. The prevailing economic and social conditions are such that Soviet arguments, propaganda, and blandishments often find a receptive audience. The poverty is endemic and widespread, with the wide gaps between the classes probably widening. The middle class is small, allowing few avenues for ambitious and energetic young people to rise in the social scale. Rigidities in the social structure are difficult to overcome, and the sense of "relative deprivation"[22] is also growing. The national economic "pie" in most of the countries is shrinking, resulting in rising unemployment and underemployment. Depression and discontent are increasing.

Third, revolutionary potential. Because the Latin American countries occupy intermediary positions in the rank orderings of developed and developing countries, their revolutionary potential is thereby further increased. That is, they are neither so traditional and backward that they are politically inert, nor so developed and advanced as to have developed some immunity to revolutionary appeals. Rather they occupy that in-between and hence potentially revolutionary category analyzed by Crane Brinton and other students of modern-day revolutions,[23] where development is occurring but not fast enough to satisfy the new expectations that have been raised, or else the development that has occurred has been perverted in corrupt and unacceptable directions as under Batista and the later Somoza.

Fourth, profound social changes. Latin America is in a state of flux. We mean this not in some superficial sense that the area is always unstable and prone to coups and violence, but in a deeper sense that profound sociological and structural transformations are under way. The old order in Latin America is breaking down, and a new one rising to replace it. But the institutions of this new order are weak, and its precise configuration is still unknown. In the meantime the endemic instability will offer numerous opportunities for the Soviet Union to achieve advantage. The traditional countryside is awakening and mobilizing, as deep class changes alter the political culture in fundamental ways. The severe economic depression has also weakened the historical model and structure on which the area's political systems have functioned,[24] creating not just temporary instability but a long-term degenerative crisis in which Latin America's entire political system and historical accommodation to change are being undermined. These conditions indeed provide ample opportunities for the Soviets to fish in troubled waters.

Fifth, conformity to Marxist model. Latin America does—let us face it—conform to many aspects of the Marxist model. It is undergoing a long-term transition from a form of feudalism to a kind of capitalism. It does have intransigent oligarchies and, in some places, rapacious multinationals. What passes for capitalism in the area does exhibit numerous internal contradictions. The workers are poor and exploited. The bourgeoisie are often greedy and grasping. At these most general levels, the Marxist explanation and categories do have relevance and applicability. As one becomes more specific and treats of specifics and individual cases, however, these general explanations often prove less than satisfactory. It is not difficult to see, however, why the Marxist paradigm would have a certain validity and maybe even an attractiveness to some groups in Latin America.[25]

Sixth, disaffection within specific societal groups. A class of disaffected young people, students, intellectuals, and professionals, for whom the systems of Central America and of the region more generally have not yet found an appropriate place, provides a primary source of the leadership cadres of the area's guerrilla groups.[26] And if the disaffected, educated, middle-class young people form the leadership of these movements, it is the poor—both urban and rural—who constitute the rank and file.

The widespread discontent, the depressed living standards, and the absence of hope throughout the area, due to prevailing social, political, and economic conditions, have made these poorer elements, again especially the young people, a prime recruiting ground for the guerrillas.

Seventh, an affinity with monolithic systems of thought. Another characteristic of the area that may also work to the Soviets' advantage is a certain cultural affinity with monistic and wholistic solutions. In a famous passage historian Richard Morse cautioned against overoptimism for the cause of liberal-pluralist democracy in Latin America and suggested that it was a shorter and easier step from monolithic and theocratic Thomism and corporatism, which is the historical Latin American system, to monolithic and "theocratic" Marxism-Leninism than it is from Thomism to liberalism.[27] Further, it is a relatively short step from the form of state capitalism characteristic of the area (90 percent of GNP is generated through the public sector of Bolivia, 60 percent in Brazil, and similarly high figures in the other countries) to a system of state socialism. All that is required is a shift in political leadership at the apex of these historically pyramidal systems, as in Peru in 1968 or Portugal in 1974, and a form of socialism can quickly be implanted, not from below but from above.

Eighth, U.S. ineptitude. Let us recognize that the United States may, at times and inadvertently, play into the Soviets' hands. The issue has several dimensions and cannot be fully discussed in this space. Nevertheless, in some instances the United States, in its haste to push modernization throughout the area, may have helped undermine some Latin American traditional institutions that might otherwise have helped ease these nations through a difficult transition. The social programs we have pushed, in addition, while often enlightened, have sometimes had the effect of increasing the pace of destabilization in the area rather than providing for a smooth and stable transition. In fact, to the degree that U.S. policy toward the area is ill-informed, unenlightened, based on misperceptions, and downright incompetent, the United States may have contributed to the possiblities for Soviet expansionism in the region.

Aspects Impeding an Expanded Soviet Presence. While many conditions in Central America and the Caribbean help make that area seem ripe for expanded Soviet influence, numerous cultural, sociological, and political factors impede that influence. Any balanced assessment of Soviet possibilities in the area must therefore take into account both the advantages that the Soviets enjoy and the constraints that hinder their activities.[28]

First, cultural differences. The Soviets do not always like Latin America or get along very well there. They often have the same language and cultural prejudices as we—arguably even greater ones. Since they are also Western, European, and Weberian, more or less, in their expectations of rational and routinized bureaucratic behavior, as we are, the more informal, charismatic style of decision making of a Fidel Castro tends to annoy and frustrate them. For this reason the Soviets have come out strongly against the "cult of personality."[29] They are impatient with the delays and inefficiencies in the area that sometimes seem to impede a more "rational," from their point of view, system of organization. The Soviets do not generally understand let alone empathize with Latin American ways of doing things any more than Anglo-Saxons do; in fact, in this regard they are often considerably behind the United States. They live in their own compounds, seldom socialize with local Latin Americans, seldom speak the language, make fun of Latin American inefficiencies behind their backs, tell demeaning ethnic and racial jokes, and the like. In some regimes the Soviets may be admired for their power, their technology, their rubles, and their developmental accomplishments, but they are seldom loved.

Second, little good will toward Soviets. Another constraint on Soviet expansion in the region is the absence of a large base of good will toward the Soviet Union. Public opinion polls are not favorable toward the Soviet Union or its policies. The Latin Americans neither like nor admire the Soviet political or economic model, because it is too rigid, monolithic, structured, bureaucratic, totalitarian, godless, and anti-Christian for their taste. In addition, the Soviet invasion of Afghanistan and subsequent brutality, the suppression of Poland's Solidarity movement, the subservience and subordination of the European satellites, the shooting down of the Korean Airlines passenger plane, and the revelations of Soviet machinations in Grenada have all had a major impact on popular attitudes in Latin America. Many Latin Americans, again especially the younger generations, find Marxism intellectually appealing and may wish to alter their ties of dependency with the United States, but Marxism-Leninism as an ideology and system holds little attraction for them. Very few Latin Americans wish to replace the United States with the U.S.S.R.

Third, democratic sympathies. Another inhibiting factor, the reverse side of the previous point, derives from the strong feelings that favor democracy, liberalism, and representative government throughout Latin America. Liberalism, though, has seldom represented a sentiment of the majority in the hemisphere, and many Latin Americans doubt their capacity for democratic rule. Too, representative democracy like the United States is probably more attractive to the older generation of Latin Americans than the younger. Still, despite these limits, democracy does have strong support, which may now be on the increase. Certainly it is the case that the overwhelming majority of Latin Americans strongly prefer representative democracy to Marxism-Leninism.[30]

Fourth, the weakness of the traditional Communist parties in Latin America. The old-line Communist parties tend to be tired, run-down, overly bureaucratic, and overly Stalinist, often consisting of a few professors and their students at the national university—"pocket parties" with little popular following. Their communiqués often sound fierce, and their strength seems impressive if judged by party posters plastering a capital city. But squads of poster painters can almost literally cover a city overnight at low costs, and the number of posters is not an accurate guide to party strength. When they have chosen to participate in national elections or been permitted to do so, Communist parties in the region have usually done very poorly. The traditional Communist parties do not offer a base for the launching of Soviet expansionary policies.[31]

Fifth, weak trade unions and peasant organizations. Moreover, the region lacks the organizational base, in the form of strong trade unions and peasant organizations, for the launching of a large-scale rebellion. Trade union weakness is especially characteristic of the Central American and Caribbean countries, where seldom is more than 10 to 12 percent of the work force organized. And the unions that do exist increasingly tend to be bread-and-butter oriented, not necessarily inclined toward provoking full-scale social revolution.

The peasant leagues are also weak, internally divided, and ineffectual in national politics. In some countries they may be strong enough to seize some landholdings for themselves, but they are not sufficiently well organized to topple a government. Such large-scale mobilization and organization ordinarily require years and even decades, and in most of Latin America that form of mass organizational infrastructure simply does not exist.[32]

Sixth, geographical limitations. The sheer distances involved and the logistics make it difficult for the Soviet Union to carry through an effective and, most important, sustained effort in the Caribbean. For the Soviets, the Caribbean is halfway around the world; the problem for them is in some ways comparable to our own difficulties in maintaining a long-term military presence in the Indian Ocean or the Persian Gulf. Time, problems of resupply, and the absence of many good and well-developed bases all work against the Soviets in the Caribbean. Many of these limitations are changing, as we saw earlier, as the Soviet presence increases and the ports and facilities in Cuba are built up. So far, however, the Soviets have recognized that they cannot match U.S. power and influence in this part of the world. Their strategy is realistically adjusted to these facts: the Soviets have moved to consolidate their economic, political, technological, and commercial links in the area, but so far they have prudently avoided any direct strategic or military confrontation with the United States in the Western Hemisphere.[33]

Seventh, financial strains. So far the Soviets have shown great reluctance to commit very much more financial support to the region. Cuba receives upward of $5 million *per day* from the Soviets—more than the U.S. commitment to the entire region—and the Soviet Union is obviously willing to accept any plums (Cuba, Nicaragua, Grenada for a time, and Suriname perhaps) that fall into its lap. Until now, though, the economic commitment to regimes and movements other than Cuba's has been quite modest, and there are strong indications the Soviets have already told the Nicaraguans that they are unwilling to put anything close to the amount they provide to Cuba into the defense of the Nicaraguan revolution. Of course, we should be a little skeptical of such statements since the Soviets obviously think their

Cuban investment worthwhile and they may reach the same conclusion about Nicaragua. Until now, however, the Soviets have provided quite limited financial support to the region.

Eighth, no revolutionary groundswell. The objective conditions, may not favor immediate revolutionary upheaval throughout the area. The evidence from Latin Americanists indicates that neither the peasantry nor the workers, and not even the students, are in all countries, or necessarily, particularly revolutionary. Many are conservative; others are oriented toward bread-and-butter issues more than toward revolutionary action.[34] It may be that the mass base does not now exist for the successful launching of very many Soviet- or Chinese-like revolutions.

Ninth, a healthy respect for U.S. power and local advantage in the Caribbean. This factor is obviously related to the earlier geographic and logistical limitations. Beyond question, in this region the United States is still the dominant outside presence. It would be foolhardy for the Soviets to engage the United States seriously in an area where the United States has all the advantages. In areas closer to the Soviet base (Afghanistan, Southeast Asia, the Middle East perhaps, the Eastern Mediterranean, and perhaps the Baltic) the Soviets might be willing to undertake a major commitment, but not in Central America. Not only is the United States the dominant power in the Caribbean, but there has recently been, with the Grenada action and the military buildup in Central America, a reassertion of U.S. power and influence there. Hence it is only prudent for the Soviet Union to devise a policy of gradual and evolutionary gains, without provoking a direct confrontation with the United States in its own back yard.

Tenth, ideological preconceptions. A close examination of Soviet writings on Latin America reveals that the Soviets have a variety of "blinders" and ideological perceptions about the area that frequently block realistic analysis. In this, although the specific ideological blinders are obviously quite different, they are somewhat like us. Soviet understandings of Latin America are frequently based on quite rigid notions about social classes and the class configuration of the area, about the interrelations of these forces, about class conflict, and about Latin American development, which are not entirely accurate.[35] The Marxian categories are sometimes useful starting points in understanding *some aspects* of Latin American society and development, but by themselves they are not sufficient or adequately refined for a full understanding. It has been said that the United States does not understand Latin America very well and seldom comprehends the full ramifications of its policy measures there, failures that help account for our various missteps and the unanticipated consequences of many U.S. initiatives.[36] But if anything the Soviet Union has a worse problem in this regard because its ideological straitjacket is even more narrow and confining than our own. Furthermore, the notion now becoming widespread in U.S. scholarly and action-oriented policy groups and almost universally accepted in Latin America that the Latin Americans know their own societies better than any outsiders and are best equipped to deal with their own problems in their own ways is still anathema to the Soviet Union, which presumes to know better. This, too, retards the Soviets' effectiveness in the area.[37]

Eleventh, incompatible political models. The dynamics and prevailing models of Latin American politics may not be especially susceptible to Marxist-Leninist appeals or interpretations. Politics in the area is still often based on family, clan, and/or patronage rather than on class. The traditional accommodative and cooptive model of politics is still strong in most countries. Liberalism and a form of organic corporatism are probably more popular as ideologies and national organizing principles than is a rigid Marxism-Leninism. The traditional wielders of power are still strong, and the dominant historical institutions—church, army, *hacienda,* local community, extended family, and patrimonialism—still have immense influence. All this is now changing in the course of contemporary events in Latin America, but so far in most countries of the area these institutions and practices remain dominant while Marxism-Leninism still represents a minority strain.[38]

Twelfth, domestic considerations in the Soviet Union itself. The Soviet economy has not performed well. It faces pressure to streamline, modernize, and decentralize the economy as well as to provide a higher standard of living and more consumer goods to the long-suffering population. The Soviets have made the decision, in a context of finite resources, that they cannot afford to bail out every third world charity case that comes along, regardless of the self-proclaimed purity of its Marxism. The Soviets subsidize Cuba massively, but Nicaragua has received very limited economic assistance (arms transfers are another matter, however). These domestic economic constraints serve as an enormous deterrent to further Soviet expansion in Latin America. From the Soviet point of view, however, some hard choices have had to be made, and the conclusion is clear: the Soviet Union should not expend a great amount of its scarce resources in an area of the world where its interests are very limited and where the United States has overwhelming local advantage.

Conclusions and Implications

The Soviet Union, operating both on its own and through Cuba, is a rising presence in Central America, the Caribbean, and Latin America more generally. Its capabilities are far greater than they were ten, twenty, or thirty years ago. Although a growing "presence" and certain expanding capabilities are insufficient by themselves to predict and understand Soviet behavior in the area, we have also seen that Soviet strategies and tactics have become more complex and sophisticated than before. A review of Soviet strategic thinking on Latin America similarly reveals a set of policies aimed at registering long-term gains in the area, embarrassing the United States in its own back yard, and all this at extremely low costs and without provoking a major confrontation with the United States in a disadvantageous location.

The Soviet Union has become a formidable but by no means yet equal rival to the United States in Latin America. Yet, conditions in Latin America also make that area susceptible to greater Soviet influence and possible expansion. Hence, the time when the Soviet threat and potential could be dismissed as nonexistent and ludicrous is over. The evidence for this expanded Soviet presence, capacity, will, and ambition is now quite overwhelming. It is time for realistic students of Latin America to recognize this new force in the Western Hemisphere and to come to grips with it realistically.

Some would even argue they can sense, even *feel*, the United States palpably giving way to the Soviet Union throughout the region. This was particularly true in the 1970s during a period of "benign neglect," when the United States was a largely uninterested and declining presence throughout the area and when Soviet prestige and power were rising rapidly. But the United States is nevertheless unlikely soon to be supplanted by the Soviet Union as the dominant power in the Western Hemisphere. Despite their increased presence and capability, the Soviets also face strong impediments, at least in the near and medium terms, to playing a much stronger role throughout the area: their contacts and prospects are still quite limited, they do not as yet constitute a serious military threat, there are finite limits on their resources and capacities, and they have other priorities. Hence for the most part in Latin America the Soviets to date have been quite prudent and cautious. Nor, with the major military, political, and diplomatic buildup in the last few years, is the United States quite the impotent giant it earlier appeared to be in that region.

Cole Blasier sums up the situation well when he suggests that although the Soviet Union does not now have great influence in the area, it does have the possibilities of acquiring it.[39] Moreover, these constraints have been recognized in the Soviet Union itself where the following conclusions have been reached: (1) the United States has been a declining presence in Latin America; (2) anti-Americanism and nationalism are rising; (3) social and class tensions are rising; (4) the Soviet Union can take advantage of these situations; (5) its position and influence can be enhanced without risking a head-on clash with the United States; and (6) these gains can be registered without heavy financial or military commitment, problematic from their point of view in any case.[40] More recently, however, in the aftermath of Grenada, the immense U.S. strategic and military commitment throughout the Caribbean Basin, and the atrophy of the guerrilla forces in countries such as Guatemala and El Salvador, the Soviets have again reassessed their Latin American possibilities. Whether that reassessment will lead to a decision to reduce its efforts in Latin America or is just part of the normal ebb and flow of Soviet policy awaiting perhaps a more opportune moment, cannot at this time be ascertained.

The real problem for U.S. policy is not the possibility of Soviet military forces suddenly descending on Latin America, nor is it really the appeals of Communism and the Soviet model, which remain quite limited. Rather, it is the capacity of the Soviets to assist and to be seen as sympathetic to Latin America's most fundamental aspirations, and attach themselves to the calls of nationalism and revolutionary socialism independent of the United States that *are* widespread throughout the area and that *do* often appeal to local hopes and desires. The Soviets seek to use the nationalist revolutions stirring throughout the area to cause problems for the United States and to secure advantages for themselves. The Soviets realistically recognize their own limits in operating in the area, but they also see the possibilities there and have adjusted their tactics accordingly. Although the new Soviet policy goal in this area has military and strategic components and implications, it is essentially a political strategy and it requires essentially a political response. Whether the United States has the will, capacity, and political sophistication to counter this challenge effectively is a question we must grapple with, and that will be at the center of the debate in this country in the next few years and maybe even decades. That is essentially what the Kissinger Commission recommendations and the accompanying legislation provided: a preeminently political response to a political challenge.[41]

Beyond these important considerations, another one commands our attention. That involves the issue with which we began: the new relations between professional Latin Americanists and their counterparts in Soviet studies. Both these groups need to learn from each other. Latin Americanists need to acknowledge the real role the Soviet Union is playing in Latin America and not be too frightened to consider and seriously research the topic rather than acting on 1950s myths and shibboleths. In fact, Latin America is no longer isolated from the world, including the Soviet Union; rather, the new role the Soviets are playing in Latin America is part of the same trend toward multipolarity and the breakdown of the older power blocs that gives the Latin American nations themselves the chance to pursue greater international independence. Latin Americanists could also learn some greater modesty regarding the importance of their area in the broader world arena. By the reckoning of most foreign policy experts, Latin America, even with the attention now focused on Central America, ranks lower on the list of U.S. foreign policy priorities than the Soviet Union, Western Europe and NATO, Japan, China and the Pacific Basin, the Middle East, Eastern Europe, South Asia, and maybe even southern Africa. For Latin Americanists, talking with a U.S. foreign policy generalist should be a somewhat humbling experience.

Soviet specialists, however, also need to learn something about Latin America. They need to get from Latin Americanists an understanding of the role of the military, Church, elites, middle class, peasants, students, and bureaucracy in Latin America, as well as the dynamics and processes of the region's politics. Sovietologists and American foreign policy generalists often exhibit an appalling lack of knowledge of the basics of Latin America, the behavior of major groups, and their interactions, or even an interest in the subject. If the knowledge of the Soviet and foreign policy experts is not increased, especially now that serious attention is being devoted to Latin America really for the first time, U.S. foreign policy is likely to continue to be shaped by the same mistaken stereotypes, ethnocentrism, problematic assumptions, and lack of understanding that it has often been in the past. One hopes that a mutual learning process will evolve from the new interaction between these two groups of scholars.

Notes

1. For some parallel comments developed independently see William Luers, "The Soviets and Latin America: Three Decades of Tangled U.S. Policies" (Paper prepared for the Woodrow Wilson School of Public and International Affairs, Princeton University, 1983).

2. These comments are based on some twenty-five years of studying Latin America, working with and among Latin Americanists, and participant observation in the culture and mores of the profession. But see also the journals of the profession, such as the *Latin American Research Review, Journal of Inter-*

American Studies, and *Hispanic American Historical Review,* as well as the various publications and newsletters of the Latin American Studies Association.

3. Luers, "Soviets and Latin America," esp. pp. 5-7.

4. For some comments on why Latin Americanists are prone to be critical of all U.S. foreign policy agendas, whether emanating from Democratic or Republican administrations, see Howard J. Wiarda, "The United States and Latin America: Change and Continuity," in Alan Adelman and Reid Reading, eds., *Confrontation in the Caribbean Basin: International Perspectives on Security, Sovereignty and Survival* (Pittsburgh: Center for Latin American Studies, University of Pittsburgh, 1984) pp. 221-25; also Wiarda, *In Search of Policy: The United States and Latin America* (Washington, D.C.: American Enterprise Institute, 1984).

5. The main literature is listed in the bibliography appended to this chapter.

6. An excellent and detailed recent overview is Jiri Valenta and Virginia Valenta, "Soviet Strategies and Policies in the Caribbean Basin," in Howard J. Wiarda, ed., *Rift and Revolution: The Central American Imbroglio* (Washington, D.C.: American Enterprise Institute, 1984), pp. 197-252. (Chap. 4 in this book.)

7. See Cole Blasier, *The Giant's Rival: The U.S.S.R. and Latin America* (Pittsburgh: University of Pittsburgh Press, 1983), chap. 2; also Augusto Veras, "Ideology and Politics in Latin American-U.S.S.R. Relations," *Problems of Communism* (January-February 1984), pp. 35-47.

8. Blasier, *Giant's Rival;* Robert Leiken, *Soviet Strategy in Latin America* (New York: Praeger, 1982); and Jiri Valenta, "The U.S.S.R., Cuba, and the Crisis in Central America," *Orbis,* vol. 25 (Fall 1981), pp. 715-46.

9. A good discussion of this complex issue is Jorge Domínguez, "Cuba's Relations with the Caribbean and Central American Countries," in Adelman and Reading, eds., *Confrontation in the Caribbean Basin,* pp. 165-201; see also Domínguez, ed., *Cuba: Internal and International Affairs* (Beverly Hills, Calif.: Sage Publications, 1982).

10. M. R. R. Frechette, "Cuba-Soviet Impact on the Western Hemisphere," *Department of State Bulletin,* vol. 80 (July 1980), pp. 77-80; and Morris Rothenberg, "Latin America in Soviet Eyes," *Problems of Communism* (September-October 1983), pp. 1-18.

11. Blasier, *Giant's Rival,* chap. 3; and Veras, "Ideology and Politics in Latin American-U.S.S.R. Relations."

12. Blasier, *Giant's Rival,* appendix; Jerry Hough, "The Evolving Soviet Debate on Latin America," *Latin American Research Review,* vol. 16, no. 1 (1981), pp. 124-43; and Leon Gouré and Morris Rothenberg, *Soviet Penetration of Latin America* (Miami: Center for Advanced International Studies, University of Miami, 1975).

13. This swing to the left of an entire younger generation in Latin America has been solidly documented in numerous studies; for an essay that puts these changes in a larger context, see Howard J. Wiarda, "Changing Realities and U.S. Policy in the Caribbean Basin: An Overview," in *Western Interests and U.S. Policy Options in the Caribbean Basin: Report of the Atlantic Council's Working*

Group on the Caribbean Basin (Boston: Oelgeschlager, Gunn and Hain Publishers, 1984), pp. 55–97.

14. Morris Rothenberg, "The Soviets and Central America," in Robert Leiken, ed., *Central America: Anatomy of Conflict* (New York: Pergamon Press, 1984), pp. 131–52; also Blasier, *Giant's Rival.*

15. See especially Jiri Valenta and Virginia Valenta, "Soviet Strategies and Policies"; also Raymond Duncan, *Soviet Policy in the Third World* (New York: Pergamon Press, 1980); R. H. Donaldson, "The Soviet Union in the Third World," *Current History,* vol. 81 (October 1982), pp. 313–17; Roger Kanet, ed., *The Soviet Union and the Developing Countries* (Baltimore: Johns Hopkins University Press, 1974).

16. Luers, "The Soviets and Latin America," chap. 2.

17. Ernest Evans, "Revolutionary Movements in Central America: The Development of a New Strategy," in Wiarda, ed., *Rift and Revolution.* (Chap. 6 in this book.)

18. See Valenta and Valenta, "Soviet Strategies and Policies," for both an overview of strategy and a country-by-country analysis.

19. The best analysis is Evans, "Revolutionary Movements."

20. See the essays by Mark Falcoff, "The El Salvador White Paper and Its Critics," *AEI Foreign Policy and Defense Review,* vol. 4 (1982), pp. 18–24; and "The Apple of Discord: Central America in U.S. Domestic Politics," in Wiarda, ed., *Rift and Revolution,* pp. 360–81.

21. Jiri and Virginia Valenta, "Soviet Strategy in the Caribbean Basin: The Grenada Case Study" (Paper prepared for delivery at the Kennan Institute of Advanced Russian Studies, Woodrow Wilson Center, Washington, D.C., March 2, 1984); also Jiri Valenta and Herbert J. Ellison, eds., *Grenada and Soviet/Cuban Policy* (Boulder, Colo.: Westview Press, 1986).

22. On this see Ted Robert Gurr, *Why Men Rebel* (Princeton, N.J.: Princeton University Press, 1970).

23. Crane Brinton, *Anatomy of Revolution* (New York: Random House, 1965); also Gurr, *Why Men Rebel.*

24. See the editor's introduction in *Rift and Revolution.*

25. For a review of various approaches, see Howard J. Wiarda, "The Political Systems of Latin America: Development Models and a Taxonomy of Regimes," in Jack W. Hopkins, ed., *Latin America: Perspectives on a Region* (New York: Holmes and Meier, 1986).

26. Seymour M. Lipset, *Rebellion in the University* (Chicago: University of Chicago Press, 1976); Richard Gott, *Guerrilla Movements in Latin America* (New York: Doubleday and Co., Inc., 1971); Daniel Goldrich, *Sons of the Establishment: Elite Youth in Panama and Costa Rica,* Studies in Political Change Series (Chicago: Rand McNally and Co., 1972).

27. Richard Morse, "The Heritage of Latin America," in Louis Hartz, ed., *The Founding of New Societies* (New York: Harcourt, Brace, Jovanovich, 1964); also Glen Dealy, *The Public Man: An Interpretation of Latin American and Other Catholic Countries* (Amherst, Mass.: University of Massachusetts Press, 1977).

28. For some overviews of these socio-cultural and political considerations, see Howard J. Wiarda, *Politics and Social Change in Latin America: The Distinct Tradition* 2nd rev. ed. (Amherst, Mass.: University of Massachusetts Press,

1982); *Corporatism and National Development in Latin America* (Boulder, Colo.: Westview Press, 1981); *In Search of Policy: The United States and Latin America;* and, with Harvey F. Kline, *Latin American Politics and Development* (Boston, Mass.: Houghton-Mifflin, 1979; 2nd rev. ed., Boulder, Colo.: Westview Press, 1985).

29. G. Volsky, "Soviet-Cuban Connection," *Current History,* vol. 80 (October 1981), pp. 325–28.

30. For considerable discussion, see Howard J. Wiarda, ed., *The Continuing Struggle for Democracy in Latin America* (Boulder, Colo.: Westview Press, 1980).

31. Claudio Veliz, ed., *The Politics of Conformity in Latin America* (London: Oxford University Press, 1967); Luis Mercier Vega, *Roads to Power in Latin America* (New York: Praeger, 1969).

32. Robert J. Alexander, *Organized Labor in Latin America* (New York: Harper and Row, 1965).

33. Augusto Veras, "Soviet-Latin American Relations under United States Regional Hegemony," Latin American Program, Woodrow Wilson Center, Washington, D.C. (1984).

34. Henry A. Landsberger, ed., *Latin American Peasant Movements* (Ithaca, N.Y.: Cornell University Press, 1969); Landsberger, "The Labor Elite: Is It Revolutionary?" in Seymour M. Lipset and Aldo Solari, eds., *Elites in Latin America* (New York: Oxford University Press, 1967).

35. A good statement is Wayne S. Smith, "Soviet Policy and Ideological Formulations for Latin America," *Orbis,* vol. 15 (Winter 1972), pp. 1122–46; Morris Rothenberg, "Since Reagan: The Soviets and Latin America," *Washington Quarterly,* vol. 5 (Spring 1982), pp. 175–79.

36. See such journals as *World Marxist Review, Latinskaia Amerika,* and *New Times.*

37. For a full discussion of the U.S. ideological blinders, see Howard J. Wiarda, "At the Root of the Problem: Conceptual Failures in U.S.–Central American Relations," in Leiken, ed., *Central America,* pp. 259–78.

38. For a full discussion, see Howard J. Wiarda, *Politics and Social Change in Latin America, Latin American Politics and Development,* and *Corporatism and National Development in Latin America.*

39. Blasier, *Giant's Rival,* p. 151.

40. The consensus on these points among scholars is strong: see Blasier, *Giant's Rival,* p. 150; Richard Feinberg, "Central America: The View from Moscow," *Washington Quarterly,* vol. 5, no. 2 (Spring 1982), pp. 171–75; Rothenberg, "The Soviets and Central America"; James Theberge, *The Soviet Presence in Latin America* (New York: Crane, Russak, 1974), p. 91.

41. See especially the collection of lead consultant papers prepared for the Commission and published in the *AEI Foreign Policy and Defense Review,* vol. 5, no. 1 (1984).

Bibliography

Barceló, C. Romero. "Russian Threat to the Americas." *Vital Speeches* 47 (May 15, 1981): 452–58.

Bialer, S., and A. Stepan. "Cuba, the U.S. and the Central American Mess." *New York Review of Books* 29 (May 27, 1982): 17–18.

Blasier, Cole. *The Giant's Rival: The U.S.S.R. and Latin America.* Pittsburgh, Pa.: University of Pittsburgh Press, 1983.

Chappel, W. V. "Caribbean Sea: Another Russian Puddle?" *Vital Speeches* 46 (September 1, 1980): 689–91.

Crozier, B. "Targets of Opportunity." *National Review* 31 (November 23, 1979):1481.

"Cuba's Role in the World." *International Affairs* (Feb. 1980): 141–42.

Debray, Régis. *Revolution in the Revolution?* New York: Penguin, 1965.

Domínguez, Jorge. "Cuba's Relations with the Caribbean and Central American Countries." In *Confrontation in the Caribbean Basin: International Perspectives on Security, Sovereignty and Survival,* edited by A. Adelman and R. Reading. Pittsburgh, Pa.: University of Pittsburgh Press, forthcoming.

Donaldson, R. H. "The Soviet Union in the Third World." *Current History* 81 (October 1982):313–17.

Duncan, W. Raymond, ed., *Soviet Policy in the Third World.* New York: Pergamon Press, 1980.

"El Salvador: Soviet-American Contention." *Beijing Review* 24 (March 9, 1981):10–11.

Evans, Ernest. "Revolutionary Movements in Central America: The Development of a New Strategy." In *Rift and Revolution: The Central American Imbroglio,* edited by Howard J. Wiarda. Washington, D.C.: American Enterprise Institute, 1984:167–93.

Feinberg, Richard. "Central America: The View from Moscow." *Washington Quarterly* 5, no. 2 (Spring 1982):171–75.

Flint, J. "More Cubas in the Making." *Forbes* 125 (March 31, 1980):6, 41–46.

Frechette, M. R. R. "Cuba-Soviet Impact on the Western Hemisphere." *Department of State Bulletin* 80 (July 1980): 77–80.

Garfinkle, A. M. "Salvadorans, Sandinistas, and Superpowers." *Orbis* 25 (Spring 1981):3–12.

Gouré, Leon, and Morris Rothenberg. *Soviet Penetration of Latin America.* Miami: Center for Advanced International Studies, University of Miami, 1975.

"Growing Communist Threat in Central America." *Business Week.* April 14, 1980:50.

Hough, Jerry. "The Evolving Soviet Debate on Latin America." *Latin American Research Review* 16, no. 1 (1981):124–43.

"Is Central America Going Communist?" *U.S. News and World Report* 91 (December 21, 1981):20–24.

Jackson, D. Bruce. *Castro, the Kremlin and Communism in Latin America.* Baltimore: Johns Hopkins University Press, 1969.

Kanet, Roger, ed., *The Soviet Union and the Developing Countries.* Baltimore: Johns Hopkins University Press, 1974.

Klochkovsky, C. "The Struggle for Economic Emancipation in Latin America." *International Affairs* (April 1979):39–47.

Legvold, Robert. "The Super Rivals: Conflict in the Third World." *Foreign Affairs* 57 (Spring 1979):755–78.

Leiken, Robert S. "Eastern Winds in Latin America." *Foreign Policy* 42 (Spring 1981):94–113.

———. *Soviet Strategy in Latin America.* New York: Praeger, 1982.

Luers, W. H. "Department Discusses Allegation of Communist Influence in Certain Western Hemispheric Countries." *Department of State Bulletin* 75 (July 12, 1976):49–58.

———. "The Soviets and Latin America: Three Decades of Tangled U.S. Policies." Paper prepared for Woodrow Wilson Center for International Affairs, Princeton University, 1983.

Migdail, C. J. "Marxist Cloud over Central America." *U.S. News and World Report* 88 (March 10, 1980):37–38.

———. "Nicaragua: Cuba All Over Again?" *U.S. News and World Report* 85 (September 11, 1978): 37.

New York Times. March 8 and 17, 1981; December 6, 1981; and March 5, 12, and 16, 1982.

Peter, R. "Moscow Reaches for America's Slim Waist." *National Review* 31 (July 20, 1979):920–21.

Rabkin, R. P. "U.S.-Soviet Rivalry in Central America and the Caribbean." *Journal of International Affairs* 34 (Fall–Winter 1981):329–51.

Ratliff, William E. *Castroism and Communism in Latin America.* Washington, D.C.: AEI and the Hoover Institution, 1973.

Rothenberg, Morris. "Latin America in Soviet Eyes." *Problems of Communism* (September–October, 1983):1–18.

———. "Since Reagan: The Soviets and Latin America." *Washington Quarterly* 5, no. 2 (Spring 1982):175–79.

———. "The Soviets and Central America." In *Central America: Anatomy of Conflict,* edited by Robert Leiken. New York: Pergamon Press, 1984.

Rubenstein, Alvin Z., ed. *Soviet and Chinese Influence in the Third World.* New York: Praeger Publishers, 1975.

Russia in the Caribbean. Washington, D.C.: Center for Strategic and International Studies, 1973.

Singer, Max. "The Record in Latin America." *Commentary* 74, no. 6 (December 1982):43–49.

Smith, A. "How the Russians Look at Managua." *Esquire* 100 (November 1983):15–16.

Smith, Wayne S. "Soviet Policy and Ideological Formulations for Latin America." *Orbis* 15 (Winter 1972):1122–46.

Theberge, James D. *The Soviet Presence in Latin America*. New York: Crane, Russak & Co., 1974.

U.S. Central Intelligence Agency. National Foreign Assessment Center. *Communist Aid Activities in Non-Communist Less Developed Countries*. Washington, D.C. 1978.

U.S. Congress. House. Committee on International Relations. *The Soviet Union and the Third World: A Watershed in Great Power Policy?* May 8, 1977.

U.S. Congress. House. Subcommittee on Inter-American Affairs. *Impact of Cuban-Soviet Ties in the Western Hemisphere: Hearings*. 96th Cong. 2d sess., March 26–27, April 16–17, May 14, 1980.

U.S. Department of State. *Communist Interference in El Salvador*. Special Report no. 80, February 23, 1980.

U.S. Department of State. Bureau of Public Affairs. *Cuba's Renewed Support for Violence in Latin America*. December 14, 1981.

U.S. Department of State. Bureau of Public Affairs. *Strategic Situation in Central America and the Caribbean*. Current Policy No. 352. December 14, 1981.

Valenta, Jiri. "The U.S.S.R., Cuba and the Crisis in Central America." *Orbis* 25 (Fall 1981):715–46.

———, and Virginia Valenta. "Soviet Strategies and Policies in the Caribbean Basin" in Howard J. Wiarda (ed.), *Rift and Revolution: The Central American Imbroglio* (Washington, D.C.: The American Enterprise Institute for Public Policy Research, 1984):197–252.

———, and Virginia Valenta. "Soviet Strategy in the Caribbean Basin: The Grenada Case Study" (Paper prepared for the Kennan Institute of Advanced Russian Studies, Woodrow Wilson International Center for Scholars, Washington, D.C., March 2, 1984).

Valkenier, Elizabeth Kridl. "The U.S.S.R., the Third World, and the Global Economy." *Problems of Communism* 34 (July–August 1979):17–33.

Veras, Augusto. "Ideology and Politics in Latin American–U.S.S.R. Relations." *Problems of Communism* 39 (January–February 1984):35–47.

———. "Soviet–Latin American Relations under United States Regional Hegemony." Latin American Program, Woodrow Wilson International Center for Scholars, Washington, D.C., 1984.

Volsky, G. "Soviet-Cuban Connection." *Current History* 80 (October 1981):325–28.

Wesson, Robert, ed. *Communism in Central America and the Caribbean*. Palo Alto, Calif.: Hoover Institution Press, 1982.

4
Soviet Strategies and Policies in the Caribbean Basin

Jiri Valenta and Virginia Valenta

Since 1979 there has been constant upheaval in some countries of the Caribbean Basin—a geostrategic concept encompassing both the Caribbean island nations and such littoral nations as Mexico, Venezuela, and Colombia. This has occurred primarily in the countries of Central America, as opposed to the majority of the relatively small, English-speaking Caribbean islands, which appear considerably more stable. A revolutionary transformation has been under way in Nicaragua since 1979 and was in Grenada until 1983. In several other countries—El Salvador, Guatemala, and Colombia—guerrilla groups have posed a serious challenge to existing regimes.

An understanding of this activity has frequently been obscured by the perception that conflicts in the area are strictly national. As a result, greater regional and international trends have been either confused with national issues or ignored. The sources of instability in the countries of Central America are not always contained within national boundaries. Consequently, ensuing conflicts tend to assume a wider, regional dimension. A strong Soviet and Cuban presence in the region has given local and regional problems an added international significance; for Cuba, backed by the Soviet Union, has played a pivotal role in their maintenance by assisting the revolutionary guerrilla movements.

Internal conditions in the Central American states helped to generate the current problems. In most of these countries new middle classes remain weak and underdeveloped; they are consequently polarized between very small but highly privileged upper classes and the masses of the very poor. Until very recently an oppressive, autocratic system of governing has been the norm in these countries. Lately the decay of these and other outmoded political, economic, and social structures has made Central America the most disturbed and potentially destabilized area of the Caribbean Basin, if not the entire Western Hemisphere. Several decades of U.S. hegemony and shortsighted policies, ranging from intervention to benign neglect, have contributed to the nationalist reaction in the region.

Contrary to the belief of many analysts, Soviet and Cuban policies in the region are having a serious impact. According to one school of thought, the area is unimportant to the Soviet Union; the Soviets' "initial bravado [after the Nicaraguan revolution] gave way to indecisiveness."[1] Here we do not suggest that revolutionary turmoil in the region is due solely to Soviet and Cuban influence. Yet it is certain that if the Soviet Union and Cuba withdrew their support, their disengagement would render more effective the individual or cooperative efforts to alleviate the crisis by concerned local actors such as the United States, Mexico, Venezuela, Costa Rica, Colombia, and Panama.

The second widely accepted premise to which we take exception is that Cuba and more recently Nicaragua are the main external sources of turbulence in other countries of the region. This view, often found in government and scholarly analyses concentrating on Cuban (and lately Nicaraguan) activities in the Caribbean Basin, tends to isolate the phenomenon from the all-encompassing Soviet-Cuban relationship and fails to perceive these activities within the general framework of Soviet strategy.[2] According to this theory, the Caribbean Basin is of only peripheral interest to the Soviets. As one policy-level State Department official bluntly put it, "I don't think the Soviets give a damn about Nicaragua. There's nothing to demonstrate their willingness to put a lot of resources in there."[3]

The leaders of some Caribbean nations are more realistic in their appraisal of Soviet intentions and regional interrelations. In the words of former Mexican President López Portillo, the Caribbean Basin has been converted into a "frontier" between the United States and the Soviet Union: "The U.S. problem is not with Nicaragua or with Cuba. . . . The U.S. problem is with the Soviet Union."[4] Although perhaps he overstated it, López Portillo does identify our central task and concern, which is to correlate Cuban and recent Nicaraguan activities with Soviet strategy in the region—including the Soviet support for Cuba that makes possible Cuba's revolutionary actuation.

This essay tries to capture the actual Soviet reading of the situation, not the Western mirror-imaging of Soviet views and behavior. First, we briefly trace the history of Soviet policies in the region, showing how they have undergone three major changes and may be in the process of changing again. Second, we name the primary factors that have influenced these policy shifts—the presence of opportunity, the degree of Soviet and Cuban concurrence regarding joint strategy, internal Soviet and East European politics, and Soviet perceptions of the global correlation of forces with the United States. Third, we state the long-term, more or less permanent Soviet strategic objectives in the region—which are primarily ideological, political, and military—and the extent to which Cuba is responsible for their implementation. We show how the policies of the Soviets are tailored to their perceptions of a particular regime's ideological orientation, be it "revolutionary," "progressive," "bourgeois-liberal," or "reactionary." In conclusion we discuss the prospects for Soviet-Cuban policies in the late 1980s and make suggestions for a U.S. counterstrategy.

Unlike Cuba, the Soviet Union has no longstanding cultural, political, or commercial ties with the countries of the Caribbean and Latin America. That it began to develop such ties only as recently as the 1960s was initially due to the area's geographic remoteness and therefore marginal importance to the Soviet Union but also to traditional U.S. hegemony in the region.

With time the element of geographic remoteness became an asset for the Soviet Union. Like the United States in Eastern Europe, the Soviet Union does not have a strong imperial record in Central and South America. Comintern and Soviet officials have traditionally proceeded with caution in these areas, where they were doubtful about the prospects for Communism. Like Marx and Engels, they have viewed the region within a colonial framework under firm U.S. command, while displaying a certain Eurocentric disdain for Latin American leaders and their peoples.[5] Until the Cuban revolution the Communist party of the Soviet Union (CPSU) had only sporadic contacts with the Latin American Communist parties and solely through individual party and Comintern officials.

Shifts in Soviet Policies, 1960–1986

The turning point in Soviet relations with the Caribbean Basin nations was the Cuban revolution of 1959–1960. When the U.S.-Cuban differences became unbridgeable and the United States withdrew from Cuba, the Soviets tried to fill the political, economic, and, ultimately, security vacuums thereby created. Since that time three major shifts have occurred in the Soviets' Caribbean Basin policies. These were influenced by a number of interacting factors, the most crucial being (1) Soviet-perceived opportunities in countries of the region, (2) the status of the Soviet-Cuban alliance in general and particularly vis-à-vis the Caribbean, (3) the dynamics of Soviet internal politics and East European politics, and (4) changing Soviet perceptions of the "correlation of forces" with the United States.

Perceived opportunities. Soviet activities in the Caribbean Basin tend to reflect optimism or pessimism, depending on and corresponding to observable trends in the region—that is, the presence or absence of local revolutionary activities, deteriorating socioeconomic conditions, and anti–United States nationalism. Soviet optimism triggered by these perceived opportunities reached the first of two distinct highs after the revolution in Cuba in 1959–1962. The Cuban success led to a certain euphoria on the part of the Soviets, who became hopeful about the revolutionary potential of other countries in the region.

The Cuban missile crisis in 1962, however, soon reminded the Soviets of the limits of their power in the area and had a sobering effect on their perceptions. The failure (in the 1960s) of Cuban-backed guerrilla revolutionaries in Guatemala, Nicaragua, Colombia, and Venezuela, as well as in Bolivia and Peru, further convinced the Soviets of Latin America's and the Caribbean's unreadiness for revolution. Moreover, in the late 1960s and early 1970s the Soviets were preoccupied with developments in other regions: the Vietnam War in Southeast Asia, the deepening Sino-Soviet dispute, and conflict in the Middle East. The overthrow of Salvador Allende in Chile in 1973 quelled any renewed enthusiasm. In the middle and late 1970s the Soviets were less encumbered, but no immediate revolutionary opportunities were available in Latin America. The contrary was true in Africa, where the Soviets intervened with Cuba in Angola in 1975–1976 and in Ethiopia in 1977–1978.

Soviet perceptions regarding the climate for revolution in the Caribbean Basin changed again dramatically between 1979 and 1981. The Nicaraguan revolution, the coup in Grenada, the growth of the insurgency movement in El Salvador, and the considerable worsening of socioeconomic conditions in Central America particularly brought about this third policy shift, characterized by active support of the more militant aspects of anti-imperialism. Cuba played a pivotal role. The shift in Soviet policies of the early 1980s occurred when the Soviets had become preoccupied with the war in neighboring Afghanistan and the crisis in Poland. Thus it appears to have been motivated not only by the existence of opportunities in the Caribbean but also by a desire to preoccupy the United States in its "strategic rear" and thus direct attention away from the equally troubled Soviet periphery. This second wave of Soviet optimism was dampened by intervention by the United States and the Organization of Eastern Caribbean States (OECS) in Grenada in October 1983 and some decline in revolutionary ferment in El Salvador in 1984–1986.

The Soviet-Cuban Alliance. The dynamics of Soviet-Cuban relations is another important variable for change in Soviet policy. Beginning with Cuban dissatisfaction over Soviet behavior during the missile crisis, the Soviets and Cubans had profound disagreements about which strategy to pursue in Latin America. Castro, who was in favor of a "genuinely revolutionary road," criticized the Soviet Union for dealing with capitalist governments in Latin America. In adhering to Ernesto ("Che") Guevara's concept of guerrilla-peasantry insurgency, Castro's strategy in the Caribbean Basin and elsewhere in South America in the 1960s contradicted and even challenged the Soviet doctrine allowing for diversified roads toward socialism. The Soviets in the late 1960s were unwilling and unable to sponsor Castro's call to create "two or three" or even "four or five more Vietnams" for the United States in Latin America. As a result of these doctrinal and tactical differences, Soviet-Cuban relations in the late 1960s were unsatisfactory and at times strained almost to the breaking point.

After the death of Che Guevara in 1967, when most of the guerrilla movements in Latin America were wiped out, the Cubans soon recognized the need to overcome existing differences and coordinate their policies with Moscow. By making mutual concessions, the Soviets and Cubans were able to arrive at a compromise strategy in the 1970s. It is misleading to suggest, as was common practice in the 1970s, that the Soviet Union had given up the notion of supporting revolutionary movements in the region. Their posture was pragmatic, not acquiescent. Neither the Soviets nor the Cubans had entirely renounced the validity of armed revolution against unfriendly, anti-Communist political forces and governments. Thus the Soviets approved support for guerrilla activities in some Latin American countries having pro-American and anti-Communist regimes. Meanwhile the Cubans agreed to pursue diplomatic, commercial, and cultural channels with other friendlier, "progressive" regimes (those having independent foreign policies often opposed to U.S. policies). The growing dependency and Sovietization of Cuba were conducive to a merger of the strategic outlook of the two countries in the 1970s and to their basic agreement on the dialectics of "anti-imperialist" strategy in the third world in general and in Africa and the Caribbean in particular. In spite of occasional tactical differences and arguments over economic issues, the Soviet-Cuban de facto alliance had become stronger than ever by the mid-1980s.

Soviet and East European Politics. Changes in Soviet strategy and tactics have also been affected by the dynamics of Soviet and East European internal affairs. It is fairly accurate to say that the Soviets have been more constrained in their behavior abroad when they were experiencing severe internal problems such as succession and power struggles in the Kremlin or crises in Eastern Europe. This was true in

1953–1957 after Joseph Stalin's death and again in 1964–1968 after Nikita Khrushchev had been forced from power. Conversely, conditions became more propitious for Soviet global activity when there were no serious domestic or East European problems and when there was strong leadership in the Kremlin. Both conditions prevailed (only to an extent, since Soviet globalism was then premature) after Khrushchev had crushed the Hungarian revolution in 1956 and defeated his rivals in the Politburo in 1957. Later Moscow was able to pursue a more successful policy of selective globalism because of Leonid Brezhnev's consolidation of power in the wake of the Soviet invasion of Czechoslovakia in 1968 and the dismissal of various rivals in the early 1970s. Undoubtedly, Brezhnev's succession in 1982–1985 by Yuri Andropov, Konstantin Chernenko, and Mikhail Gorbachev imposed some constraints on Soviet global activism, and this affected the Caribbean Basin.

The Correlation of Forces between the Superpowers. Finally, but not least important, Soviet policies in the Caribbean Basin are influenced by the state of Soviet-American global relations and by Soviet perceptions of the evolving worldwide balance of power. Judging from the historical record, it appears that the worse Soviet-American relations are, the more the Soviets tend toward an activist posture in the basin. This was true during the Soviet-American confrontation over Berlin in 1958–1961, when the Soviets vigorously sought to exploit opportunities in Cuba and (with the Cubans) elsewhere in the region, and again in 1980–1981, when Soviet-American relations deteriorated after the Afghanistan invasion and the Soviet intimidation of Poland. To qualify this assessment, the Soviets have pursued assertive policies in other third world nations during times when Soviet-American relations were more cordial. Détente in the 1970s did not prevent their bold military aid to Arab clients in the Middle East war of 1973 or the joint Soviet-Cuban military interventions in Africa in 1975–1978.

Within the framework of Soviet-American relations, what appears to matter most is the Soviet perception of the correlation of forces, or balance of power, between the Soviet Union and the United States. During Stalin's time the Caribbean Basin's geographic remoteness, along with limited Soviet sea- and air-lift capabilities, qualified the region as only marginally important. Gradually the Soviet Union evolved from a basically regional and premature global power in the 1960s under Khrushchev to a fully developed, globally oriented superpower under Brezhnev. The attainment by the Soviet Union of strategic parity with the United States in the early 1970s and its immeasurably improved conventional capabilities helped to make possible the Soviet-Cuban ventures in Angola and Ethiopia as well as support for Nicaragua and other clients. In the second part of the 1970s the Soviets repeatedly demonstrated a more assertive strategy in third world countries by means of direct or indirect military intervention and increasing military aid. Cuba's emergence as a pivotal player in Africa and the Caribbean in the 1970s unfolded within the context of this perceived global shift, marked by growing Soviet military power.

Since the mid-1970s the most significant perceptual change concerning the balance of forces has been the image of declining U.S. ability to counter Soviet activity in the third world in general and in Africa and the Caribbean Basin in particular. In previous decades U.S. policy makers were believed to have not only the power to obstruct Soviet plans but also the will. This image had been shaken only briefly during the short period marking the transition from Dwight Eisenhower's to John Kennedy's administration and during the unsuccessful Bay of Pigs invasion shortly thereafter. Khrushchev's appraisal of Kennedy as weak and inexperienced[6] led the Soviets to conclude prematurely that the Kennedy administration was unable to curtail revolution in the Caribbean. The humiliating defeat suffered by the Soviet Union a year later dampened for a long time to come Soviet enthusiasm for an easy revolutionary transformation of the Caribbean Basin. Soviet perceptions regarding U.S. strength and conviction were reconfirmed by the U.S. intervention in the Dominican Republic in 1965, when the motto "Never a Second Cuba" became the imperative for U.S. policy in Latin America throughout the early 1970s. This changed in the mid-1970s. Since then the Soviets have noted a weakness on the part of U.S. policy makers, which they attribute to (1) the defeat in Vietnam and the subsequent fear on the part of the American public and Congress of slipping into a new quagmire, (2) the damaging political and economic effects of the 1973 oil embargo, and (3) the weakening of the U.S. presidency because of the Watergate scandal. Soviet writings point to these phenomena as having slackened the U.S. will and propensity to resist "anti-imperialist" trends in the third world. Thus U.S. support for proxies (in Guatemala in 1954) as well as the direct use of military force (in the Dominican Republic in 1965) was viewed as improbable or at least much more difficult to stage during the decade before the 1983 Grenada operation.

Soviet Strategic Objectives

By the 1970s the Soviet Union and Cuba had arrived at a joint strategic vision with regard to the third world and specifically the Caribbean Basin, and they have orchestrated their actions accordingly. After almost a decade of discord comprehensive strategic cooperation now exists, aimed at achieving specific ideological, political, security, and economic objectives.[7]

Ideology. It is misleading to assume that the Soviets support revolutionary movements in the Caribbean Basin solely as part of a grand design to create Leninist regimes. Still, ideology cannot be discounted among their motives. The Cuban trajectory of the 1970s, resulting finally in conformism to true Leninist development and Soviet recognition of Cuba as a member of the community of Communist countries, is one the Soviets would like to see emulated by other radical regimes in the region. Because of numerous bad experiences in the 1960s and 1970s, however—when many such radical regimes in various parts of the third world, including Latin America, were overthrown and others substantially reduced the Soviets' presence and influence—the Soviets feel compelled to exercise caution when making commitments to would-be Leninist regimes.

With the probable exception of Cuba, the Soviets in the early 1980s hardly view the new radical regimes in developing countries as truly Leninist, in the Soviet understanding of the term. For the moment it is enough that Central Committee officials responsible for dealing with Caribbean Basin revolutionary forces see fit to refer to them as progressive, anti-imperialist, and, at most (in the case of Nicaragua and, before October 1983, Grenada), as on "the path toward socialist orientation" (without yet being truly "Leninist"). This cautious terminology reflects the Soviets' guarded expectations, conditioned by Cuba's long and arduous evolution toward real Leninist development, and the desire that there be no confusion about which is the model regime embodying the most advanced and mature form of Communism—that is, the Soviet regime. At the same time the Soviets appreciated and applauded the Leninist orientation of the new vanguard, socialist-oriented regimes in Nicaragua and Grenada (see the Grenada documents) since their tendencies enabled them to justify better—to their domestic constituencies and allied Communist countries—the aid extended to these regimes.

Disillusioned over the prospects for revolution in Latin America after the fall of Allende in Chile in 1973, the Soviets were unable to anticipate the revolution in Nicaragua, the coup in Grenada, or the momentum of the revolutionary struggle in El Salvador. But they did recognize later that these events were pregnant with the potential for promoting Soviet ideological interests, both abroad and at home. The Soviets see the revolutionary process in the Caribbean Basin and elsewhere in the third world within the context of the worldwide struggle between capitalism and Communism. Because these conflicts are "tipping" the global balance of power "in favor of the socialist camp," argues Victor Afanasiev, who is editor in chief of *Pravda* and a member of the Central Committee of the CPSU, the Soviet Union "will spare no support or sympathy for countries seeking [revolutionary] transformation."[8]

Politics. The Soviets' most important political objective in the basin is to ferment and further the forces and regimes they consider antiimperialist. Because the Soviets view the region as the strategic rear or internal security zone of the United States, their policy has been cautious, until recently respecting in action if not in word the Monroe Doctrine. This attitude changed in 1960 when Khrushchev stated that the Monroe Doctrine had "outlived its times" and that U.S. acceptance of the Cuban revolution was proof that it had died a "natural death."[9] Still, because of a number of constraints, Soviet strategy in the Caribbean during the past two decades has continued to be refined and subtle, allowing for revolutionary transformation by violent or peaceful means (the parliamentary road to socialism—a prolonged political process during which anti-American forces build national coalitions to challenge U.S. hegemony). The choice of means is dictated by internal, national conditions, which vary from country to country, and by external variables, the most important being the state of Soviet-American relations.

The criteria for deciding which tactics to employ in each country were clearly delineated in Soviet behavior throughout the 1970s. During this decade peaceful, diplomatic channels were pursued avidly vis-à-vis the late Omar Torrijos's military yet "progressive" Panamanian regime and the likewise "progressive" regime of Michael Manley in Jamaica (until Manley's electoral defeat in 1980). The Soviets also courted the nationalist and externally progressive regime of Mexico and in lesser degrees the liberal-democratic regimes of Costa Rica, Colombia, and Venezuela. It is important to note that until Anastasio Somoza's overthrow in Nicaragua became imminent, the Soviets dissuaded at least some of the local Communist parties and other more radical leftist groups from trying to overthrow the regimes mentioned above, encouraging them rather to expand their influence gradually and work toward building anti-imperialist coalitions and the wide popular support necesssary to sustain eventual revolutionary changes. The Soviet strategy in Central American countries having pro-American, anti-Communist regimes—that is, Nicaragua before the fall of Somoza in 1979, El Salvador, and Guatemala—was to give steady encouragement to the revolutionary struggle, though not necessarily by fostering terrorism or warfare.

Soviet strategy changed in the late 1970s when, in the Soviet view, the correlation of forces began to shift worldwide because of the U.S. setbacks in Vietnam, Angola, Ethiopia, and Afghanistan. The growing wave of radical anti–United States sentiment in Central America was seen as another manifestation of this change. Furthermore, the 1973 ouster of Allende in Chile seems to have caused the Soviets to doubt the feasibility of following the purely parliamentary path toward socialism in Latin America. "In contrast with the usual 'parliamentary' path," wrote Yu. N. Korolev, the Chilean revolution "through peaceful means" was "nothing more than a form of class *coercion* by a majority of the revolutionary people." (This path is not the "only one possible."[10]) Because of these perceptions and propitious global and regional conditions, the Soviets in the late 1970s once again began, though guardedly, to promote the more militant aspects of the struggle by revolutionary forces. The successful revolutions in Nicaragua and Grenada increased Soviet confidence in the militant path. As in the past, the Soviets pushed two tactical lines: Leninist forces, and especially the Communist party, should (1) gradually build coalitions among all revolutionary forces while (2) always positioning themselves in the vanguard of the struggle.

In the early 1980s the Soviets appear to have further conceptualized and perfected their anti-imperialist strategy in the Caribbean Basin. Careful research of Soviet sources suggests that in the Soviet view four kinds of regimes exist in the Caribbean: (1) revolutionary, pro-Soviet, Leninist regimes, or regimes evolving along a Leninist course—actually Soviet clients; (2) capitalist, yet "progressive," "anti-imperialist" regimes that are basically friendly toward the Soviet Union and willing to stand up to U.S. "imperialism"; (3) capitalist, liberal, "bourgeois" regimes of a democratic character that depend, some more and others less, on the United States; and (4) reactionary, right-wing, military regimes, generally not liked but, until the mid-1980s, selectively supported by the United States.

Revolutionary regimes. The first class of regimes, consisting of Soviet clients such as Cuba, Nicaragua, and, before October 1983, Grenada, either are developing along Leninist lines or, in the case of Cuba, have already achieved a full-fledged Leninist identity. The Soviets support these regimes with ample political, economic, and military aid and advisory assistance. Their political and economic support and arms transfers to Nicaragua and revolutionary Grenada are patterned after their relationship with Cuba and, as such, manifest Soviet faith in the eventual Leninist transformation of these countries.

Progressive regimes. These are the capitalist countries of the Caribbean Basin, such as Mexico and Panama (under Torrijos), that, for a variety of reasons, have conducted policies independent of and sometimes contrary to those of the United States and whose policies the Soviets therefore describe as anti-imperialist. Because of their size, large populations, plentiful resources, or strategic location, they are seen as important nations worthy of being courted. In these countries, for the moment, the Soviet Union and Cuba do not support armed insurgency but rely exclusively on political, cultural, and, to a lesser degree, economic instruments to gain influence. (Through Mexico and Panama, however, the Soviets and Cubans coordinate the political activities of Communist parties and radical groups from other Caribbean Basin nations through large embassy staffs.)

Liberal, bourgeois regimes. In dealing with the democratic regimes of larger countries having plentiful natural resources and foreign policies independent of those of the United States, revolutionary means, including armed insurgency, are not entirely excluded by the Soviets, Cubans, and Nicaraguans. For the moment, however, legal means of gaining influence are preferred. Yet in countries such as Costa Rica and Colombia—which are viewed by Moscow as less significant because of their lesser size, population, resources, and, most important, perceived dependence on the United States—the Soviets see little jeopardy to their interests stemming from their acquiescence in Cuban efforts to aid the local revolutionaries. This reflects an important readjustment in Soviet thinking from the late 1960s and 1970s, when the Soviets seemed to prey only on "right-wing" regimes. Now, apparently, selected "liberal" regimes can also be targets of revolutionary tactics. The fact that Cuba, not the Soviet Union, *appears* to be the main coordinator of insurgency activities in these countries has enabled the Soviets to continue, though in a more limited fashion, diplomatic and economic intercourse with Costa Rica and Colombia.

Reactionary regimes. Policy toward what the Soviets call reactionary regimes—those that are traditionally anti-Communist—is to promote violent revolutionary tactics, which, since the late 1970s, include acts of terrorism. Thus, at least until 1985, the regimes in El Salvador and Guatemala, seen as hostile toward the Soviet Union and Cuba, should if possible be overthrown. Some of these regimes were until recently the worst offenders against human rights in all of Latin America, making it attractive for the Soviets to support the guerrilla movements there. Backed by the Soviets, the Cubans have played a pivotal role in uniting splinter movements and providing at least minimal arms and training to these insurgents. The continuation, scope, and intensity of this policy depend on available opportunities and the perceived costs and risks of such a strategy both within the various countries and for the overall state of Soviet-American relations. Although Cuba can be an autonomous actor in the coordination and support of armed insurgency, this activity would not be possible without continuous Soviet economic and military aid to Cuba and to new clients in Nicaragua and (until 1983) Grenada, as well as Soviet coordination through local Communist parties. (In August 1981, for example, such coordination was said to take place in Panama City when a visiting senior CPSU official discussed regional strategies with Cuban officials and the leaders of local Communist parties.)[11]

One motive for the change in Soviet strategy between 1979 and the early 1980s to support armed as opposed to peaceful struggle in democratic countries of the Caribbean Basin was to preoccupy the United States in its strategic rear and divert U.S. attention from the Soviet periphery, where Poland and Afghanistan, the Soviet Union's western and southern guard, were embroiled in unresolved conflict. Soviet officials view the already deeply troubled Caribbean Basin as pregnant with a potentially unending series of conflicts. Georgi Arbatov, member of the Central Committee and director of the USA and Canada Institute, suggested this to visiting American scholars, saying that the Caribbean region confronts the United States with a series of "delayed-fuse land mines," which the United States will be no more able to defuse than those in Iran. According to him, the Soviet Union has "great sympathy for the struggle" in that region.[12] Arbatov's deputy director, V. Zhurkin, declared further that the Soviet Union would "not accept the Monroe Doctrine" in the region. Yet another adviser to high Soviet officials warned that Soviet policies in the Caribbean Basin will ultimately "reflect the overall state of U.S.-Soviet relations."[13]

Security. Another important component of Soviet strategic vision regarding Central America and the Caribbean concerns security. Here the primary Soviet objective is gradually and cautiously to secure access to and maintain naval facilities so as to improve the projection of Soviet power while undermining that of the United States. The basin constitutes a key passage zone for oil and other vital raw materials from Guatemala, Venezuela, and the Caribbean islands to the United States and for all seagoing vessels using the Panama Canal. About 1.1 billion tons of cargo pass through the Caribbean annually, of which almost half originates in ports of the Gulf coast of the United States. The region would assume crucial strategic importance if the United States were to be engaged in a conventional war. A substantial Soviet military presence in the basin at such a time would endanger logistical support for U.S. allies in Europe and the delivery of oil and other strategic materials to the United States. During wartime Cuba, though highly vulnerable, might serve as a forward base for submarines and aircraft carriers. Accordingly Soviet Air Force Lieutenant Viktor Belenko, who defected to the West in 1976, revealed that the Soviets referred to the island as "our aircraft carrier" in the Caribbean.[14]

So far, however, the Soviet military presence in the region is limited by a lack of facilities and the logistical support necessary for the permanent deployment of a fleet. Moreover, Soviet warships scheduled for deployment in the Caribbean must pass first through NATO checkpoints. The only significant Soviet military presence is in Cuba. It includes modern docks and repair facilities; airport facilities for reconnaissance craft; and satellite stations and intelligence facilities for monitoring U.S. satellite and microwave conversations, U.S. ship and air movements, and advanced NATO weapons testing in the Atlantic. Since 1975 Soviet Tu-95 "Bear-D" long-range reconnaissance planes have been periodically deployed from Jose Martí Airport in Havana on missions monitoring U.S. naval activities in the Atlantic. (In September 1972 for the first time, Tu-95s were observed being deployed from Cuba for the purpose of reconnoitering U.S. naval units off the east coast of the United States.)[15] These aircraft often cross the Atlantic and refuel at Soviet facilities in Luanda, Angola. The Africa-based Bear-D was also used to conduct reconnaissance of the British task force deployment toward the South Atlantic in the 1982 Falkland Islands war.

Overall, the Soviets do not now have sufficient strength in the region to be able to disrupt important sea lanes to the United States, as feared by some analysts. Moreover, they would probably attempt such action only in case of all-out war, and then probably closer to Europe or in the Persian Gulf. Although they proceed with caution, the Soviets would undoubtedly like to see their naval presence in the Caribbean upgraded and expanded. This has been indicated by Soviet plans to make permanent use of the facilities at Cienfuegos, partly shelved in 1970 because of vociferous U.S. protests. Unfettered, the Soviet Union is likely to establish additional facilities. This trend is suggested by recent Soviet tactics in Grenada until October 1983 and in Nicaragua, a country the Soviets view as the most anti-imperialist in the region, which they expect will become a future client.

Given the Soviets' awareness of the basin's paramount importance to the United States, Soviet naval activities in the area, including regular visits by warships, until now have seemed rather scaled down in comparison with U.S. naval visits to areas in Western Europe close to the Soviet Union. Such visits are initially designed to establish the legitimacy of a Soviet naval presence. Soviet naval task groups have made a few dozen such visits to the Caribbean Sea in the past twenty years, all of which (except that of August 1979) made calls at Cuban ports. The Soviets deploy not only warships but also intelligence, merchant, oceanographic, space-supporting, salvage and rescue, and fishing vessels. Many of these also have intelligence missions. (Soviet intelligence collectors, under the pretext of fishing, patrol off the U.S. east coast almost continuously—in the vicinity of Norfolk, King's Bay, Charleston, and Narragansett Bay—as well as in the Caribbean Basin.)

Economics. Economic objectives play a relatively minor role in the Soviets' Caribbean strategy. Sixty percent of total Soviet exports to South America in the early 1980s were to the South American countries of Brazil and Argentina. In Central America, however, Soviet trade remains low both absolutely and relatively. Soviet trade, investment, and credits in early 1982 were limited to Cuba, Mexico, Costa Rica, and the new clients Nicaragua and Grenada. Since they generally must pay for imports in hard currency, the Soviets probably do not view the Caribbean as a priority interest for foreign trade alone. Their patient nurturing of the Caribbean market, however, may be expected to pay off in the future, barring unforeseen changes in the international economic order.

The presence of vital natural resources, however—particularly in Mexico, Venezuela, and elsewhere—has spurred increasing interest in the basin. Accordingly, the Soviets are working with the Mexicans on long-term cooperation in oil matters and may be interested in similar cooperation with other oil producers in the region. Thus Mexico has agreed to furnish Cuba with crude oil and later to assist with oil exploration. Meanwhile Venezuela has become one of Cuba's oil suppliers. Until now Soviet and Eastern bloc trade and economic aid to client regimes such as Cuba and Nicaragua have been ancillary to Soviet strategy in the area.

Soviet Policies toward Revolutionary Regimes: Cuba, Nicaragua, and Grenada

Cuba. The Soviets' gradual involvement in Cuba over the past twenty-three years, in spite of ups and downs, suggests that the long-term Soviet strategic objective there is to ensure the survivability and development of the Cuban revolutionary regime along Leninist lines. Cautious commercial and diplomatic ties preceded military aid and security involvement. Thus, although Castro came to power on January 1, 1959, the Soviets did not begin to provide economic aid to Cuba until early 1960. Soviet loans and other economic aid, such as donations, technical assistance, and trade agreements, including provisions for the Soviet purchase of Cuban sugar, were not forthcoming until a full year later. Diplomatic relations were reestablished even later, in May 1961.[16] At that time the Soviet Union and other East European countries signed a number of diplomatic, commercial, scientific, and technical treaties with Cuba. By 1961 transactions with the countries of the Council for Mutual Economic Assistance (COMECON) accounted for 75 percent of Cuba's total trade.

Economic relations. After the period of ups and downs characterizing their relations between 1962 and 1969, the Soviet Union and Cuba reached an understanding on the coordination of foreign policy strategy, which was in part related to the Soviets' continuing economic, political, and security support of the island. Cuba's economic dependency on the Soviet Union grew substantially during the late 1960s and 1970s and was one of the factors influencing Castro's decision to compromise on foreign policy matters. In the 1980s the Soviet Union sustains the Cuban economy with an estimated $8 million per day (thought by some to be a low estimate). Annually this amounts to about $3 billion, or approximately 25 percent of Cuba's gross domestic product.

Because of the active Cuban role in the Soviets' anti-imperialist strategy in Africa and in the Caribbean from the mid-1970s through the 1980s, Cuba gained the status of a privileged ally, becoming what Soviet officials call "the first socialist country in the Western Hemisphere." As such, Cuba was able to insist on further adjustments in Soviet-Cuban economic relations, mainly commodity subsidies and credits to bolster the Cuban sugar and nickel industries. For the planning period 1981–1985, for example, COMECON gave the faltering Cuban sugar industry a major injection of economic aid equivalent to U.S.$643 million. Another U.S.$451.2 million should be made available between 1985 and 1990. The Soviets also subsidize petroleum prices, enabling the Cubans to purchase oil at roughly one-third of the world market price. According to Konstantin Katushev, former Soviet ambassador to Cuba, the extent, depth, and high level of Soviet-Cuban cooperation in the 1980s were demonstrated by the joint Soviet-Cuban space flight, the inclusion of Cubans in the Soviets' scientific expedition to Antarctica, and (Soviet) joint construction of the first nuclear power plant in Cuba.[17] Privileged Soviet economic treatment allows the Cubans to sustain political and military operations compatible with Soviet foreign policy objectives in Africa and the Caribbean Basin.

Security relations. Soviet economic and political ties with Cuba were followed by military aid and Soviet involvement in Cuban security affairs. These occurred after the signing of a secret agreement in the fall of 1960. Subsequently, in early 1961, the Cuban armed forces openly displayed Soviet and Czechoslovak weapons. Since the summer of 1962 the Soviets have maintained a military presence in Cuba—an advisory group of a few dozen military intelligence specialists and a few thousand ground forces (ascertained in 1979 to be a brigade of 2,600). Also in 1962 the Soviets deployed the missiles that led to the October crisis with the United States. Soviet seaborne arms transfers to Cuba reached their peak that year. They declined and reached the lowest point in 1968, when overall Soviet-Cuban relations were at a correspondingly low level. Arms transfers increased slightly in 1969 and then remained constant until 1974. New increases in the mid-1970s coincided with the Soviet-Cuban interventions in Angola and Ethiopia.

In 1981–1982 the Soviet arms transfers to Cuba reached the highest level since the missile crisis. As in 1962, this increase was intended as a manifestation of Soviet commitment and determination to give military support to a client during a period when, in the Soviet view, the U.S. threat to Cuba was greater than at any time since 1962. This assessment was prompted by statements of Reagan administration officials who threatened to "go to the source" of the Caribbean Basin problem. In response Castro decided to enlarge Cuba's territorial militia from 500,000 to 1 million men and to acquire a corresponding increase in arms. Another likely reason for the sharp increase in Soviet seaborne military deliveries to Cuba in 1981–1982 was the need to build up Cuban stockpiles for supplying Nicaragua, Grenada, and other revolutionary forces in the basin.

In Latin America the armed forces of Cuba (population, 10 million) are second in size only to those of Brazil (population, 120 million). They number 225,000 regulars, of whom 200,000 are army, 15,000 are air force (not including the formidable airborne contingent and assault brigade of 3,000 special troops), and 10,000 are navy. (The last number includes a small yet elite marine corps.)

Soviet modernization of Cuba's armed forces with sophisticated weapons has made them, in both size and equipment, the most formidable force in the Caribbean Basin, with the exception of the U.S. military. By the early 1980s Soviet assistance had equipped the Cuban armed forces with a significant, if indeed limited, interventionist capability throughout the region. But, as the Grenada crisis demonstrated, the Cubans still do not have sufficient air- and sea-lift or amphibious assault capabilities to conduct military interventions in the Caribbean opposed by U.S. forces. The Cuban inventory at this time contains, among other items, 200 MiG fighters, two squadrons of MiG-23 "Flogger" type jet fighters, several An-26 short-range transport planes, and seven Il-62 long-range transport aircraft. The army's inventory includes sophisticated weapons such as Soviet T-62 tanks and Mi-24 HIND-D assault helicopters.

The Soviets have also helped Cuba to build small yet modern and efficient naval and merchant fleets. In the past few years they have furnished Cuba with nine guided-missile attack boats of Osa and Komar class and Turya-class hydrofoil patrol boats, as well as an antisubmarine frigate, mine sweepers, several landing craft, and two Foxtrot-class torpedo-attack, diesel-powered submarines. In 1981 the Soviets delivered what became the largest vessel in the Cuban navy, a 2,300-ton Koni-class frigate. Although this ship is considerably smaller than the new U.S. frigates, it is viewed as a major improvement over the Cubans' existing naval inventory. The Soviets have also helped to enlarge Cuban ports and update the Cuban merchant marine with passenger ships, oil tankers, and container ships.

Obviously, the essentially defensive Cuban navy cannot challenge U.S. naval power in the Carribean Basin. Yet, in the case of a U.S. confrontation with the Soviet Union in another region (the Persian Gulf or Europe), the Cubans could put constraints on U.S. mobility and capacity to respond, causing significant delays in U.S. deployment. A more immediate concern is that Soviet-backed Cuban forces, if unchallenged, will continue to provide military aid to revolutionary forces in other countries of the Caribbean region.

Cuba's strategic role. Cuba is not totally subservient to the Soviet Union in the Caribbean, and at times in the past it has appeared to be even more assertive and activist than its mentor. Castro undoubtedly exercises some autonomy in formulating policy toward other countries in the region and even influences Soviet policy making. Elsewhere one of the authors has discussed these mutual constraints and leverages in detail. It is not possible here to dwell at length on the complex personality of Castro, who appears to be more Machiavellian than Leninist and more Bonapartist than Communist in his ambitions and perceptions of the payoffs of maintaining close Soviet ties. Despite Castro's biases and interesting personality, however, overall Cuban economic and military dependency on the Soviet Union makes it unthinkable for the Cubans to initiate any major overt or covert support operation for guerrilla forces in the Caribbean Basin without Soviet approval and assistance. Such operations, furthermore, would be impossible without Soviet strategic cover and commitment to protect Cuba in the event of an attack on the island. Obviously a strategic understanding exists between Cuba and the Soviet Union regarding coordination and implementation of their strategy in Africa and the Caribbean Basin. The Soviet Union, however, plays the dominant role.

Cuba's great vulnerability to Soviet economic coercion was used to Soviet advantage in the late 1960s. At that time the Soviets slowed down the supply of oil and arms when Castro failed to appreciate the subtleties of Soviet anti-imperialist strategy. The Soviets are likely to use this leverage again should the need arise. Castro himself made it clear to American officials during secret negotiations that despite his wish for better relations with the United States, he "cannot abandon his friends, the Soviets, who have supported his revolution unequivocally."[18] Day-to-day Cuban policies in the Caribbean region are probably not subordinated to a grand Soviet strategy, but there is, as Cuban leader Carlos Rafael Rodríguez admitted, "a high level of agreement" on foreign affairs as Cuba and the Soviet Union share "the same compass" —that of "Marxism-Leninism." This will probably continue. Fidel Castro's brother and deputy Raúl, who will very likely succeed Fidel, has said that Soviet-Cuban relations, which in the early 1980s were at "the highest level ever recorded in the past two decades," are the "cornerstone" of Cuban foreign policy.[19]

Nicaragua. Since 1980 the Sandinista regime has had close and growing ties with the Soviet Union and its allies. As early as January 1980 former Soviet Central Committee secretary and Politburo member Boris Ponomarev equated the Nicaraguan revolution with the struggles of "socialist-oriented vanguards" in Afghanistan, Ethiopia, Angola, and elsewhere.[20] Soviet commentary has also grouped the Sandinista regime, along with the New Jewel Movement (NJM), under the rubric "popular democratic," a term that was used to describe the transitional stage of post–World War II regimes in Eastern Europe on their way to becoming full-fledged Leninist systems. When these and other ideological labels are applied, they usually indicate increased Soviet political and moral support for given movements. Expanded ties between the Soviet bloc and Nicaragua are evident in the areas of interparty affairs, military-security assistance, and economic relations.

Party-to-party relations. In the Sandinista Front for National Liberation (FSLN), Moscow was dealing with a relatively small yet elitist party that had the distinction of having come to power through a popular revolution. Although the Soviets recognized the Sandinista regime diplomatically precisely one day after it took power, on July 19, 1979, party-to-party relations were probably formalized during the visit of an FSLN delegation to Moscow in March 1980. Interior Minister Tomás Borge and Defense Minister Humberto Ortega were members of this delegation. Any agreement signed then would have been similar to the agreement signed between the CPSU and Grenada's NJM in July 1982, establishing a broad framework for party-to-party cooperation—including consultations on international matters, all-round development of state-to-state relations, and extensive cooperation between mass organizations in the two countries.[21] The political closeness of the two parties is suggested by the strong pro-Soviet bias in subsequent Nicaraguan foreign policy.

It is evident that the FSLN conceives of itself as a revolutionary bridge between the CPSU and the Communist party of Cuba (PCC) on the one hand and leftist forces in the Caribbean Basin (particularly Central America) on the other. The FSLN coordinates regional support for revolutionary movements in El Salvador (the Farabundo Martí National Liberation Front—FMLN) and Guatemala (the Guerrilla Army of the Poor—EGP) and for the Costa Rican revolutionary underground. Members of other Latin American revolutionary movements, such as the M-19 guerrillas of Colombia and the Montoneros of Argentina, also cooperate with the FSLN in Nicaragua, as do the Palestine Liberation Organization and Libya, both of which are represented in Managua.

Military assistance. During the Sandinista insurrection, Cuba supplied weapons and advisory assistance to the FSLN and helped it obtain weapons on international markets. (Some fifty Cuban security advisers were among the Sandinista forces that captured Managua in July 1979.) Subsequently the Soviet Union and other Communist states discreetly but steadily increased their military and intelligence support for the Sandinistas. The first arms agreement with the Soviet Union was probably signed during the visit of FSLN officials to Moscow, East Berlin, and Prague in March 1980. Some of the transfers resulting from this agreement were eighteen ZPU light antiaircraft guns, six SAM-7 surface-to-air missile launchers, 100 RPG-7 antitank weapons of Soviet make, and ninety-six W-50 trucks from East Germany, all of which were displayed in Managua during celebration of the revolution's first anniversary in July 1980, well before the election of Reagan as president of the United States.

As U.S.-Nicaraguan relations deteriorated over the issue of FSLN aid to the guerrillas in El Salvador, shipments of military supplies to

Managua increased. By the summer of 1981 the first T-54 and T-55 tanks arrived (on Algerian ships). On a second visit to Moscow, in November 1981, Humberto Ortega met with Soviet Defense Minister Dimitriy Ustinov and Chief of the Soviet General Staff Nikolay Ogarkov, presumably to sign a new arms transfer agreement. As the anti-FSLN insurgency intensified, Communist arms transfers (now on Soviet-bloc ships) again increased, totaling some 20,000 tons of material in 1983 (double the amounts for 1981 and 1982). In addition to dozens of tanks were other weapons specifically suited to counterinsurgency operations, including twenty-five to thirty armored personnel carriers and several MI-8 helicopters.

Moscow soon added An-26 transport planes, jeeps, field ambulances, and thousands more AK-47 rifles to the Nicaraguan arsenal. There were also reports of some eighty MiG fighters being held in Cuba for future delivery—and reports that dozens of Nicaraguan pilots were completing MiG training in Bulgaria and Cuba. By late 1984 Nicaragua had acquired more than 100 Soviet T-54 and T-55 medium tanks, over twenty light amphibious PT-76 tanks, 120 armored vehicles, more than 1,000 military trucks, 120 antiaircraft missiles, 120 antiaircraft guns, and 700 shoulder-fired surface-to-air missiles.

The Soviets and Cubans are assisting in various construction projects with immediate or potential military and intelligence applications. Cubans, using Soviet equipment, are helping to upgrade facilities at Puerto Cabezas, Estelí, La Rosita, and Bluefields. For the moment the construction of a large military airport in Punta Huete has been suspended; however, construction of a U.S.$80 million deep-water port at El Bluff on the Caribbean coast continues, financed largely by the Soviet-dominated COMECON. Tomás Borge described the new port as "undoubtedly a strategically important project." The Soviets are also helping to build a satellite communications earth station.

U.S. and Caribbean sources estimate that Cuban military and security advisers in Nicaragua today number 3,000, although President Daniel Ortega admits to only 800. In addition, there are some 100 Soviet military-security advisers and twenty-five Bulgarian, forty to fifty East German, and approximately twenty-five Palestine Liberation Organization specialists. There are also Libyan personnel and members of the Spanish Basque separatist organization ETA.[22]

Before 1979 and at least as early as 1976, many FSLN guerrillas—including Borge and Humberto Ortega—were being trained in Cuban schools or camps and in the Soviet Union. This pattern was continuing in 1985 when dozens of Nicaraguan security personnel were being trained in two-year and shorter courses in Cuba and in three-year security courses in the Soviet Union.

There appears to be a rough division of labor among the Communist states that give security assistance to Nicaragua—a pattern also observed in Soviet-bloc dealings with such "vanguard socialist-oriented" countries as Angola, Ethiopia, and (formerly) Grenada. The Soviets appear to be responsible for overall command and control; the Cubans provide manpower and serve as military and counterintelligence advisers; the East Germans provide trucks, police specialists, and highly qualified communications technicians; the Bulgarians aid the processing of information in security matters; and Bulgaria and Czechoslovakia both provide weapons, explosives, and ammunition.

Economic relations. In keeping with its gradual approach toward restructuring the mode of production, the Sandinista government has been measured in its expansion of economic cooperation with Communist states, though not necessarily or completely of its own volition. So far the primary objective of Soviet-bloc assistance seems to be the reinforcement of the FSLN in political, ideological, and security aspects. During the two and one-half years following the visit of a high-level Soviet technical mission to Managua in January 1980, however, a variety of trade, technical, and economic agreements were signed, and various commissions for trade and economic assistance were established. Since this time the Soviets and their allies have further stepped up their economic aid to the Sandinista regime. By June 1985 the total economic aid of Communist nations to Nicaragua (including annuities, credits, and machinery but not goods for development projects) had reached U.S.$600 million. Soviet-Nicaraguan trade has also grown steadily. Though not dramatic, such trade now exceeds in volume that of the Soviets with Mexico or Peru. To facilitate increasing commerce, a regular maritime link was established between Leningrad and the Nicaraguan port of Corinto in early 1985.

Still, Moscow appears hesitant to take on another Cuba, which has cost the Soviets "two tankers [of oil] a day for 20 years."[23] Nicaragua is less populous than Cuba, however, and expansion of Soviet and COMECON aid to Managua cannot be excluded. Indeed, by 1985 Moscow had become Nicaragua's major oil supplier. Other signs also indicate a projected increase in Soviet aid and possible Nicaraguan participation in COMECON.

Domestic politics and foreign policy. While rapidly becoming a dictatorship of a Leninist-oriented party, Nicaragua is still not a full-fledged Leninist state like the East European countries, Cuba, and Vietnam. At home the FSLN has been engaged in a gradual, skillful process of socialist transformation, benefiting from earlier Soviet, East European, and Cuban experiences and the awareness that too rapid a Leninization of the country would overly alarm the dominant power in the region—the United States. The FSLN government is prepared to make superficial, tactical concessions (which can later be revised) as long as it exercises complete control over the real power base—the party, the state security, and the army. On these matters the FSLN closely follows the Soviet and Cuban models and will never compromise.

In regional politics the FSLN appears prepared to follow the Bolshevik example—that is, to forgo full-scale internationalism (aid to revolutionaries in the region) until circumstances permit its resumption. Meanwhile, the flow of small arms to the Salvadoran guerrillas evidently continues. In the long run, as a former Sandinista told us in Costa Rica and as the 1969 program of the FSLN testifies, the Sandinista revolution will necessarily spread throughout the region or perish.

As in Cuba much earlier, Moscow (now with Havana's help) has made guarded political, security, and economic commitments to the FSLN. Yet, as the Grenada case demonstrates and various Soviet signals suggest, the FSLN can count on nothing more than "political" support from the Soviet Union in case of a direct conflict with the United States. In such an event, the Cubans could only provide insufficient support, lacking—as they admit—the air- and sea-lift capabilities to bring in adequate reinforcements.

Struggle in Nicaragua. The FSLN contends that the oppositional insurgency (the "contra" movement) owes its existence to the United States, ignoring evidence that the anti-Sandinista insurgency, like the insurgencies in Afghanistan, Angola, Ethiopia, and Mozambique, is symptomatic of conditions created by most Leninist-oriented regimes in the third world. In every socialist-oriented country with an elitist vanguard party a significant resistance movement exists, with strong popular support that has multiplied in response to forced socialist transformation of the society by the ruling party.

Outside players cannot buy into such a large insurgency, which, in Nicaragua, draws major impetus from the FSLN military buildup, enforced recruitment, ideological mobilization by the elite vanguard party (with its arbitrary Leninist rules of the political game), the economic ineptitude of the government and growing national penury, the vigilant and often coercive control of the masses, and the blatantly pro-Soviet stance of the government. Witness three days of official national mourning following the death of Soviet leader Chernenko and the government's refusal to establish diplomatic relations with China until the fall of 1985, when there was a visible thaw in Soviet - Chinese relations.

Grenada. The NJM regime's interest in cultivating close ties with foreign Communist states was fully reciprocated by the Soviet Union and Cuba, as the documents captured in Grenada demonstrate.[24] Soviet and Cuban involvement in Granada gradually increased and in some areas went far beyond what was indicated in published Soviet, Cuban, Grenadian, and other Caribbean sources, in spite of the country's minuscule size and repeated Soviet statements that the Caribbean Basin was very distant and not a priority area. Soviet ties with Grenada served three kinds of objectives: political-ideological, military-security, and, to a much lesser extent, economic.

Ideology and politics. The Soviet Union's most important objective in the Caribbean Basin is political, that is, to encourage and support "anti-imperialist" (anti-American) forces. The most vigorous forms of support are given to regimes classified as revolutionary: fully developed Leninist regimes like Cuba or those following the path toward socialism, such as Grenada before October 1983 and Nicaragua. The extent of Grenada's political-ideological ties with the Soviet Union and its allies was manifest in the relatively large number of officials from the Soviet Union and other Communist countries discovered in Grenada at the time of the U.S. intervention. The Soviets alone numbered about forty-seven, a considerable number given that the Soviet embassy had been established in Grenada only in November 1981. (Installation of wire services by the official Soviet news agency TASS took place at the same time.)

Shortly thereafter the Soviet press spoke of Grenada's "progressive social transformation" and referred to the NJM as Grenada's "political vanguard." Other Soviet spokesmen, exercising habitual caution, referred to the NJM regime (along with the regimes in Nicaragua, Angola, Ethiopia, and Afghanistan) as "progressive," "anti-imperialist," "national-democratic," and, at most, "on the path toward socialist orientation"—that is, evolving but still not fully Leninist. The generally tentative terminology probably reflected Moscow's guarded expectations—conditioned by unpleasant experiences with other radical third world regimes and by Cuba's arduous though finally successful path toward Leninism. It also denoted a desire to set apart the regimes that embody socialism's most mature form, described as "developed socialism": the Soviet Union, the countries of Eastern Europe, Mongolia, Vietnam, and Cuba. Although Grenada was not yet considered a part of this elite "socialist commonwealth," by 1982 some Soviet officials had begun to treat the NJM as a "fraternal" (Marxist-Leninist) party, even calling it a Communist party in private conversations.[25]

The NJM, however, was not given the same high-level treatment accorded the Nicaraguan junta. The Soviets' excuse was that their relations with the NJM should be played down publicly so as not to provide the United States with a pretext to "further squeeze Grenada." Soviet support for Nicaragua had to be expressed on a higher political level since Nicaragua was already under attack from the United States. But Grenadian diplomats detected additional reasons such as Grenada's smaller size and lesser importance and perhaps some residual confusion on the part of CPSU officials about the ideological orientation of the NJM. Such confusion was fostered by the NJM's continued membership in the Socialist International, among other factors.

Formal relations between the NJM and the CPSU began with the visit of Deputy Prime Minister Bernard Coard to the Soviet Union in May–June 1980, in the wake of supportive lobbying by the PCC and the Workers' party of Jamaica. After gathering considerable information about the NJM and observing indications that the revolution was taking hold, the Soviets decided to make a formal commitment to Grenada during the Moscow visit of Prime Minister Maurice Bishop in July 1982. In a secret agreement of July 27, the CPSU and the NJM agreed to cooperate along lines similar to those pursued by the Soviets in dealing with other "anti-imperialist," "socialist-oriented" third world countries. The agreement states that "inter-party cooperation is the most important basis" for the development of relations between Grenada and the Soviet Union. Accordingly, six of the seven main points in the accord delineate the prescribed manner of carrying out Soviet-Grenadian relations, that is, through party channels. Party-to-party relations were paramount, although the agreement also provides for the "all around development of inter-state relations and ties between mass organizations." The agreement required the CPSU and the NJM to "extend and deepen" cooperation "at all levels" and to "exchange experience" on the social, economic, and cultural development of their countries, as well as on international matters. This party-to-party format for Soviet-Grenadian relations was adhered to in subsequent dealings between the two countries.

(Given their express emphasis on party supremacy, the Soviets were "bewildered" that by 1983 no work had yet begun on construction of an NJM party headquarters. They immediately made plans to build one. The Soviets also agreed to supply office equipment and cars. This transaction, in which the Soviets were to reimburse the Cubans for material and technical support, offers a good example of the close Soviet-Cuban cooperation in Grenada as well as the significance placed on party structure by the Soviets.)

According to the agreement, both parties (the CPSU and the NJM) were to cooperate in "training party and government cadres." Subsequently the Soviets "pressed" the NJM into accepting a number of scholarships for Grenadian party officials (fifteen in 1982 alone). Other NJM members "with a higher cultural level" were to study at the Higher Party School of the CPSU Institute of Social Sciences in the company of counterparts from other revolutionary third world parties. Fourteen Grenadians were enrolled there in May 1983. Soviet officials also recommended that the NJM give top priority to establishing their own party school and that, in anticipation, they start sending teacher trainees to the Soviet Union.

Still other Grenadians were trained in Cuba, where the course of study included propaganda and foreign relations, particularly vis-à-vis other Caribbean nations. In 1983 Cuba was scheduled to receive eighteen Grenadian party cadres for study and training in political indoctrination and propaganda techniques. Those selected for such training constituted but a small fraction of dozens of Grenadians said to be studying in Cuba at the time of the U.S.-OECS invasion. Other Grenadians studied at the Karl Marx Party College in East Berlin, and ten were enrolled at the Academy of Social Sciences of the Central Committee in Sofia, in accordance with agreements between the NJM and the parties of East Germany and Bulgaria.

The Soviets established other organizational ties with the NJM through a newly established Grenada Peace Council (GPC), which became an integral part of the World Peace Council (WPC)—an organization supervised by the International Department of the Central Committee of the CPSU. Such ties were reinforced by the appointment of a number of Soviet civilian consultants and advisers to various Grenadian ministries, including the Ministry of Education, and other agencies. Formation of a Grenadian-Soviet friendship society further advanced cooperation.

Military assistance. According to former Chief of the Soviet General Staff Marshal Ogarkov, Moscow seeks to develop military and intelligence ties with revolutionary regimes in the Caribbean Basin so as to raise "the combat readiness and preparedness" of progressive forces facing a threat from imperialism. In a 1983 conversation with his Grenadian counterpart, Major Einstein Louison, Ogarkov specified the conditions favoring this goal: "Over two decades ago there was only Cuba in Latin America; today there are Nicaragua and Grenada, and a serious battle is going on in El Salvador." Although the Soviets have proceeded very cautiously, they probably desire in the long run to develop additional military and intelligence facilities of the sort they now have in Cuba.

The captured Grenada documents demonstrate a program of gradually upgraded Soviet military assistance to Grenada. Military aid, which preceded any Soviet ideological recognition of the NJM, began even before the first formal arms agreement, signed in Havana on October 27, 1980. This "top secret" agreement, valued at 4.4 million rubles, specified the type, manner, and payment of arms deliveries that were to occur between 1980 and 1981. Like two subsequent agreements, for which it served as the prototype, it provided for deliveries of "special and other equipment," "free of charge of delivery." Originally Cuba was to act as the almost exclusive intermediary in the Soviet transfers of weapons and ammunition. These were delivered by sea to Cuban ports, transported on Cuban ships to Grenada, and then carried by night to hidden depots throughout the island.

The "special equipment" listed in this first agreement included twelve mortars, twenty-four antitank grenade launchers, fifty-four machine guns, 1,000 submachine guns, eighteen antiaircraft mounts, and other weapons, communications devices, ammunition, logistical equipment, and spare parts. The agreement provided that Grenadian servicemen be trained to handle the new equipment and further stipulated that Grenada not sell or transfer the arms to third parties without Soviet consent or divulge the terms and implementation of the accord.

A second major Soviet military aid agreement was signed in Havana on February 9, 1981, for arms shipments to take place between 1981 and 1983. The Soviets again employed the euphemism of "special and other equipment," whose value this time was calculated at 5 million rubles. The agreement provided for the delivery of eight armored personnel carriers, two armored reconnaissance and patrol vehicles, 1,000 submachine guns, and a variety of other armaments and munitions; engineering, communications, and transport equipment; and other materials. Included were 12,600 complete sets of uniforms, apparently designed for an army of 6,300 men. Also included were spare parts and training and auxiliary equipment valued at nearly 1 million rubles.

A third "top secret" agreement, valued at 10 million rubles, was concluded in Moscow on July 27, 1982, for the period 1982–1985. Its contents included an additional fifty armored personnel carriers, sixty mortars, sixty antitank and other heavy guns, fifty portable rocket launchers, fifty light antitank grenade launchers, 2,000 submachine guns, other small arms, communications and engineering workshops, and other equipment.

This agreement also included, for the first time, "civilian" equipment for Grenada's expanding Ministry of the Interior. The ministry and the People's Militia were to receive twenty light antitank rocket launchers, fifty submachine guns, and "special instruments" such as infrared viewers, videotape recorders, tape recorders, cameras, PTU-47 television systems, and other equipment designed for clandestine intelligence gathering.

Another interesting feature of the 1982 agreement was that it provided for the training of Grenadian servicemen not only at Soviet military schools but also in Grenada by specially assigned Soviet military and security "specialists and interpreters." The government of Grenada was to provide these Soviet specialists with "comfortable living accommodations," "all municipal utilities, medical services, transport facilities for the execution of their duties," and "meals at reasonable prices at the places of their residence," all without "any taxes and duties."

Future plans for greater Soviet military involvement in Grenada are suggested by Article 4 of the 1982 agreement, whereby the Soviet Union would periodically send a group of Soviet advisers to Grenada to plan technical assistance for a vehicle repair shop, a command-staff school, storage facilities, and roads. A corollary agreement, reached in November 1982, provided for a team of Soviet specialists to assist with these tasks. Marshal Ogarkov was probably referring to this agreement when he spoke of sending a team of military experts to Grenada in 1983 to "conduct studies related to the construction of military projects."

U.S. forces found yet another secret agreement, still unsigned and dated 1983, for the delivery of "special and other equipment" valued at 5.4 million rubles during the period 1983–1986. Included were two patrol gunboats, spare parts, tools and accessories, 3,000 more uniforms, and 12,000 rounds of ammunition.

In accordance with the agreements Grenadian officers were sent for military training to the Soviet Union. In late 1982 fifteen were studying at Soviet military schools; twenty more were expected to arrive in 1983. Officials of the Ministry of the Interior were sent to the Soviet Union for training in intelligence and counterintelligence. Cuba also granted training scholarships to Grenadian military personnel (twelve in 1982).

By secret written agreement Cuba maintained twenty-seven permanent military advisers in Grenada, supervised by a Cuban official working within the Grenadian Ministry of Defense, and a dozen or so additional advisers sent for short terms of two to four months. By 1982 the Cuban presence in Grenada consisted of a small contingent of military advisers, a varying number of overt and covert agents and civilian workers, and several hundred construction workers (many of them armed) assigned to building the runway at Point Salines.

The controversial Point Salines airport was designed for tourism but probably also had some planned military application. The nearby, double-fenced facilities occupied by the Cubans, sometimes called Little Havana, were indeed operated like a military camp. The complex, which contained oil and water storage tanks, barracks stocked with guns and ammunition, and a hospital, had direct access to the airport and was off limits to Grenadians. Plans for a second Little Havana were in the making at the time of the intervention. That the airport was to have some military purpose after its official opening, scheduled for March 13, 1984, is suggested, among other things, by an entry in the diary of Lieutenant Colonel Liam James dated March 1980 (the "airport will be used for Cuban and Soviet military"). Initially it would probably have served as a facility for Soviet reconnaissance aircraft and as a refueling stop for Soviet and Cuban transports bound for Angola. The captured documents show that Moscow was eager to have the Grenadians begin work on yet another militarily important project—a Soviet-sponsored satellite station—in 1983. Like the airport, the station was ostensibly designed for civilian use.

The division of labor in Communist security assistance to Grenada was similar to the pattern seen in Nicaragua and established earlier in Africa. The Cubans provided the manpower; the East Germans, technical and military or internal security equipment and highly qualified technicians; and the Czechoslovaks, explosives, ammunition, and automatic rifles. Among their duties, the East Germans upgraded Grenada's telephone system. After Bishop's trip to Pyongyang in April 1983, North Korea agreed to supply arms worth U.S.$12 million (including thousands of rifles and fifty rocket launchers), two coast guard boats, and uniforms. There were also military agreements with Bulgaria and even Vietnam, which agreed to train twenty Grenadian military officers.

The documents suggest that the security aid to Grenada was designed to build by 1985 a sizable Grenadian army consisting of four regular and fourteen reserve battalions.[26] At the time of the U.S.-OECS invasion in October 1983, the total arms requirements for supporting such a force were not yet in place, since the deliveries stipulated in the three arms transfer agreements were scheduled to occur through 1986. The weapons recovered, however, were sufficient to equip about 10,000 men.

Economic assistance. Economic objectives played a relatively minor role in Soviet strategy vis-à-vis Grenada. There, as in Nicaragua, economic aid was aimed primarily at reinforcing Soviet political and security objectives. Soviet-Grenadian economic cooperation between 1979 and 1983 was subservient to and lagged behind military-security relations. Economic aid to Grenada was clearly not proportionate to the aid extended to Cuba.

Still, Grenadian officials sought economic cooperation and consulted with Soviet State Planning Committee (Gosplan) officials, who offered a training course to several NJM officials, and with COMECON experts. In response to the NJM's active search for long-term markets in COMECON countries, the Soviet Union, East Germany, and Bulgaria agreed to purchase at stable prices and at steady intervals such vital Grenadian export commodities as cocoa, nutmeg, and bananas. The Soviets granted Grenada several million dollars' worth of foodstuffs and contruction materials, supplied dozens of vehicles and machines on deferred payment terms, and offered other miscellaneous credits and donations. They also upgraded Radio Grenada from a one-kilowatt to a seventy-five kilowatt station capable of broadcasting to foreign audiences and pledged to outfit by 1983 a Soviet An-26 transport aircraft for special use by the Grenadian party leadership. The East Germans delivered dozens of trucks and other vehicles to Grenada, mainly for use by various government ministries. The North Koreans, in addition to military assistance, agreed to provide some agricultural equipment and fishing boats and to construct a national sports stadium for 15,000 people beginning in late 1983. Not all the equipment received from Communist sources was of great value, because of poor quality, mismanagement, or both.

There is no evidence that the Soviets provided funding for the controversial Point Salines airport complex. Most of the grants and loans for this and several other public works projects came from Libya, Cuba, Canada, Iraq, Syria, the OPEC fund, and the European Economic Community. There was likewise no indication that Moscow would fully finance water supply or seaport development projects recommended by Soviet technicians. Nor, apparently, did the Soviets commit themselves to supply 20,000 tons of fertilizer requested of them by the Grenadians.

Setback in Grenada. By mid-1983 the Soviet Union and its allies had accumulated a substantial political and security, if not economic, investment in Grenada that they hoped to safeguard and eventually to exploit. The internal power struggle on the island and its violent outcome seemed to work in Moscow's favor until the joint intervention by the United States and Grenada's immediate neighbors.

There is still no clear evidence about the extent of Soviet or Cuban involvement in the NJM power struggle of September–October 1983. We have at our disposal crucial NJM documents, but we obviously lack the archives of the CPSU and the PCC. What evidence we do have suggests that Soviet officials knew about the Bishop-Coard rivalry and, unlike the Cubans, made no move to help the embattled Bishop. The Soviets appeared to be suspicious of Bishop's independence and his poor Leninist credentials, suggested by his belated attempts (apparently not coordinated with Moscow) at rapprochement with the United States and by his unwillingness to abide by Leninist democratic-centralist rules. The Soviets undoubtedly would have felt more at ease with the ideologically more compatible apparatchik Coard.

Unlike the Cuban missile crisis of 1962, Soviet and Cuban involvement in Grenada did not present an immediate threat to U.S. interests. The Soviets had made a significant, though guarded, commitment to Grenada, according it a special revolutionary status. They had also sent a considerable number of weapons to strengthen the NJM against internal and external threats. There is no conclusive evidence, however, that Grenada had become a depot for large concentrations of Soviet arms designed for future use in Latin America. Nevertheless, in the years ahead this was likely to become a reality, at which time it would have been very difficult to effect a reversal.

Already the existing arsenal had made the Grenadian armed forces a factor to be reckoned with in the West Indian environment. That they were a potential threat to Grenada's small neighbors was the overwhelming consensus of OECS members. Some of the countries in question have no armed forces at all, while others have armies of less than a few hundred. Even the much larger Jamaica had a smaller army than the one being contemplated in Grenada, although Jamaica's population is twenty times as large. Furthermore, although Grenada did not have Soviet military bases at the time of the U.S.-led invasion, one cannot exclude the possibility that it might eventually have become a component in Soviet military planning and a bridge to revolutionary forces elsewhere in the region, as Cuba has been in the past quarter-century.

Despite the active Soviet and Cuban role in Grenada, the NJM crisis of October 1983 derived initially from internal problems. Newly installed Leninist regimes, with their emphasis on military buildup, ideological mobilization, economic controls, democratic centralism, and "Bolshevik staunchness," tend to produce the kind of popular disenchantment and factional bloodshed witnessed in Grenada.

In Grenada "proletarian internationalist" ties with the Soviet Union and Cuba were useless in containing the internal crisis and subsequent power struggle. On the contrary, arms supplied by the Soviet Union and other Communist countries became a destabilizing factor, serving to destroy rather than to defend the revolution and its original leaders.

The Grenadian episode demonstrates that third world leaders dependent on the Soviet Union, much like leaders of Communist countries at the Soviet periphery, cannot rely on continuing Soviet support. Deviation or perceived offense can serve as a pretext for Soviet attempts to remove them. Outside the immediate Soviet sphere, moreover, even a mortal challenge from "imperialism" does not automatically ensure Moscow's protection. The Soviet Union is much less able or willing to support pro-Soviet regimes in the American "backyard"—particularly when Washington is determined to protect its interests—than in its own periphery or in remote regions of Africa.

Soviet Policies toward "Progressive" Regimes: Mexico and Panama

Mexico. Mexico has traditionally been viewed by the Soviets as one of the friendliest countries in Latin America and also one of the most important owing to its independence, large size and population, and location at the southern frontier of the United States. Because of U.S. hegemony in the area and Mexico's vulnerable position vis-à-vis its powerful northern neighbor, Mexico has habitually pursued friendly relations with counterbalancing powers outside the Western Hemisphere: Germany during World War I and World War II and the Soviet Union thereafter.

The main channels of the Soviet involvement in Mexico are diplomatic and, to a lesser degree, economic. The Soviet Union first established diplomatic relations with Mexico in 1924. Relations were severed in 1930 but were reestablished in 1942 and have not been interrupted since. The largest Soviet embassy in Latin America outside Cuba is in Mexico City. Before the Cuban Revolution, it was the main base for expanding Soviet influence in the Caribbean Basin and South America.

Because of Mexico's history of revolution and traditionally independent posture with respect to U.S. foreign policy, the Soviets see Mexico as a progressively oriented country that should be treated in a special fashion. A foreign policy independent of the United States has been recurrent throughout Mexico's history. For example, Mexico was one of the few countries not to break diplomatic relations with the Soviet Union in 1947 and the only Latin American country not to cut off diplomatic ties with Cuba in the 1960s (although Mexico did demonstrate support of the U.S. embargo by halting most of its trade with Cuba in 1962). Mexico was also critical of U.S. policies in Guatemala in 1954 and the U.S. intervention in the Dominican Republic in 1965. These policies and others convinced the Soviets that Mexico was not only independent of the United States but also occasionally even "anti-imperialist." Consequently they have allowed the Soviet and East European embassies in Mexico City to function as centers of liaison for the coordination and support of Communist parties and guerrilla activities in the Caribbean Basin. (One example of this was an important meeting between the Salvadoran guerrilla leadership and Soviet and East European officials that reportedly took place in the Hungarian embassy in March 1981.) For these reasons both the Soviets and the Cubans have so far refrained from encouraging revolutionary struggle by the Mexican left against what they see as the bourgeois yet independent Mexican regime. Thus the Soviets have always stressed the democratic orientation of the Mexican Communist party, and they applauded López Portillo's 1978 decision to facilitate its legalization.

The Soviets have consistently tried to promote closer economic cooperation with Mexico through bilateral economic, technical, and scientific agreements concluded by the Mexico–Soviet Union Joint Commission for Consultations and through multilateral cooperation with COMECON. Indeed, Mexico is the only Latin American country aside from Cuba to have signed a formal agreement with COMECON. Bilaterally Mexico has signed a number of scientific agreements with the Soviet Union, such as an agreement on data bank access and the maritime agreement of December 1985, which provided for cooperation between the two countries' merchant marines and the training of a professional Mexican staff in that field. In 1986 the Soviet Union extended an invitation to a Mexican astronaut to participate in a Soviet space mission. In spite of Soviet efforts, Soviet-Mexican economic cooperation and trade remained relatively low in volume throughout the 1970s and the first half of the 1980s.

The Soviets and the Cubans seem to have made a conscious effort to develop cordial relations with the Mexican armed forces during the 1970s and the first half of the 1980s. Military leaders exchange visits, and some scholarships are offered, but no nondiplomatic Soviet or Cuban military and security personnel are stationed in Mexico. Furthermore, Mexico's armed forces do not depend on the Soviet Union for arms.

Cuban-Mexican relations improved considerably in the 1970s as the Soviet Union responded with interest to the Mexican oil boom and the increasing tendency of Mexican leaders to become involved in the regional politics of the unstable Caribbean Basin independently of the United States. Mexico's traditional autonomy was reaffirmed repeatedly during the wave of revolutionary activities in the basin following the Nicaraguan revolution of 1979. In 1981 the Mexican government offered immediate and future financial assistance to the new Sandinista regime. It also donated money to the guerrilla organization of the Democratic Revolutionary Front (FDR) and the FMLN of El Salvador; allowed the FDR-FMLN government in exile to operate out of Mexico; and, with France in the early 1980s, attempted to mediate between the government in El Salvador and the FDR-FMLN. Mexico also plays an important role in the Contadora mediations. These efforts were cautiously applauded by the Soviet ambassador to Mexico, Rostislav Sergeiev, who in 1982 described Mexico's foreign policies as a "great contribution to peace in the world."[27] Sergeiev said that Mexico has "ample resources to forge ahead" despite the difficult economic situation. The Soviets are not so enthusiastic about the policies of current Mexican President Miguel De la Madrid as they were about the policies of his two predecessors. The grave economic crisis in Mexico, however ($100 billion in foreign debts, 100 percent inflation, and 50 percent unemployment), aggravated by the effects of the Mexico City earthquake of 1985, may encourage unforeseen shifts to the radical right or left, with corresponding opportunities for Moscow.

Panama. For the Soviets Panama is an important country because of its strategic location and its nonaligned, at times even "progressive," orientation. In Panama, as in Peru in the 1970s, the armed forces are responsible for determining what the Soviets consider the basically anti-imperialist foreign policies of the country. This was certainly true until the death of General Omar Torrijos in 1981. Torrijos had been the real power in Panama since 1968. He was perceived by the Soviets and the pro-Soviet People's party of Panama (the Communist party) as a "patriotic officer," an ardent patriot, and, most important, a leader of "the national liberation" process aimed at liquidating the colonial enclave at the canal.[28] (Torrijos had supposedly given orders for the National Guard to attack and blow up the canal if the U.S. Senate rejected his agreement with President Carter.)[29] Under Torrijos Panama and Cuba also maintained cordial relations (reflecting Castro's and Torrijos's close personal relationship) and cooperated to some extent in helping Nicaragua's Sandinistas overthrow the dictatorship of Somoza. Shortly before his death, however, Torrijos apparently had become concerned about what he saw as increasing Cuban and Nicaraguan interference in Central America.

In 1986 there was no indication of Soviet or Cuban support for radical elements inside Panama, probably because the People's party has been able to operate legally and because of the good relations of the party both with Torrijos's "anti-imperialist" regime and, after Torrijos's death, with the ensuing military and civilian governments in Panama. There are other reasons for the current Soviet-Cuban constraint. In Panama the Cubans maintain their second largest embassy, and it has served as a vital point of liaison for Soviet-Cuban coordination of revolutionary activities in other countries of the region.[30] Although some Panamanian revolutionaries are possibly being trained in Cuba for future eventualities, none have yet been observed conducting revolutionary activities in Panama. The Soviets may also be on their good behavior because of their desire to establish diplomatic relations with Panama, an opening that Torrijos was reluctant to pursue until the completion of canal negotiations with the United States.

The post-Torrijos leadership has expressed a wish to conduct diplomatic relations with the Soviet Union "eventually," but in the early 1980s this was still not apparently "a priority."[31] In the meantime the Soviets continue to court Panama by promoting commerce, cultural ties, and a notable educational exchange program. (Between 1980 and 1982 the Soviet Union gave thirty-five scholarships to Panamanian students; Cuba, twenty-nine.)[32]

The death of Torrijos created political uncertainties, confirmed by the subsequent power struggles and government reshufflings leading to President Aristides Royo's resignation and replacement by Vice President Ricardo de la Espriella and, later, the forced resignation of President Nicolás Arditto Barletta. Arditto Barletta was succeeded by Erick Arturo del Valle, who is dependent on the present commander of the Panamanian Defense Forces, General Manuel Noriega. Panamanian Communists perceived Arditto Barletta as a protégé of the oligarchy whose government was "prepared to abide by the model proposed by the International Monetary Fund." They perceive General Noriega, however, as having been "closely associated with Torrijos." Continuing political problems in the post-Torrijos era and a worsening of Panama's economic difficulties may destabilize the country and lead to a new eruption of the battle for national independence, this time against "World Bank plans." This could call into question implementation of the canal treaty negotiated with the Carter administration in 1977 and lead to unforeseen changes in Soviet and Cuban perceptions and policies regarding Panama.

Soviet Policies toward "Bourgeois-Liberal" Regimes: Venezuela, Costa Rica, and Colombia

Venezuela. Venezuela is a democratic country run by what the Soviets see as a liberal-bourgeois regime that nevertheless displays some independent features, though not to the same extent as Mexico. The Soviets established relations with Venezuela in 1970, and since then they have exhibited a growing interest in the country because of its ever-increasing importance in the third world and specifically in the Caribbean Basin, where, along with Mexico, it is a primary oil producer. One minor success of negotiations between the two countries was the 1976 agreement by which Venezuela supplies Cuba with determinate amounts of oil (formerly designated for Spain) while the Soviet Union fulfills Venezuela's obligations to Spain. In the 1970s Venezuela shared the Soviet and Cuban interest in pursuing better ties, hoping thereby to strengthen its bargaining position vis-à-vis the United States, as Mexico had previously done by using the same tactics. Thus in 1975 Venezuela played a key role in the process that led the Organization of American States (OAS) to lift most sanctions against Cuba; in the late 1970s it gave substantial financial support to the Sandinista revolutionaries in Nicaragua.

Unlike Mexico and Panama, however, Venezuela is not viewed by the Soviets as a progressive country, particularly since the administration of President Luis Herrera's Comité de Organización Política Electoral Independiente (COPEI). The Soviets are obviously displeased by Venezuela's deteriorating relations with Cuba (Cuban diplomats were ordered to leave Venezuela in 1980; later Venezuelans accused of bombing a Cuban airliner were acquitted) and with Nicaragua, where Venezuela is increasingly critical of the Sandinista junta. Venezuela's foreign relations have not undergone any substantial change during the present social democratic government led by President Jaime Lusinchi. Yet the Soviets and Cubans so far have discouraged support for leftist guerrillas who would violently oppose the democratically elected government. Such a policy obviously takes into consideration Venezuela's economic and commercial significance to the Soviet Union and Cuba as well as the absence of a serious guerrilla movement and sufficiently ripened revolutionary conditions in Venezuela. Another Soviet consideration is to safeguard and facilitate valuable embassy operations in Caracas. The Soviets have succeeded in building a large embassy staff in Caracas (ninety-three as opposed to the fifty-five at the U.S. embassy), many of whom, according to Venezuelan sources, are engaged in gathering intelligence information in the region. (The number of Soviet diplomats far exceeds the needs of the foreign trade and the Soviet communications media in Venezuela.)[33]

Costa Rica. The Soviets and Cubans established diplomatic relations with Costa Rica in the early 1970s when it was viewed as a tranquil exception to the right-wing dictatorships of Central America. And until 1979 the small, pro-Soviet Costa Rican Communist party, the Popular Vanguard party, favored only peaceful means for coming to power. There were various reasons for this. Costa Rica is the only Central American country with a long democratic tradition and, in comparison with its neighbors, an insignificant military tradition. (Costa Rica had a democratically elected government in 1948 and has had no army since that year.) Since 1974 the Soviets have been developing a small trade relationship with Costa Rica, based primarily on the importation of small amounts of coffee and other agricultural products. Overall, however, the Soviets view Costa Rica as only marginally important because of its small size, lack of economic resources (unlike Mexico and Venezuela), and nonstrategic location (unlike Panama). Furthermore, Costa Rica has been traditionally friendly toward the United States and never sufficiently "anti-imperialist" to attract great interest on the part of the Soviets.

This picture of Costa Rican tranquility changed in the late 1970s and early 1980s. The high cost of oil imports and the falling world prices for coffee, sugar, and other agricultural commodities contributed to Costa Rica's most serious economic crisis in thirty years. Costa Rica's problems have been complicated by the Cuban- and Nicaraguan-supported network of guerrilla activity throughout Central America and terrorism inside Costa Rica.

In May 1980 the Costa Rican legislature concluded in a published inquiry that the Cubans had been conducting a very extensive covert network in 1978–1979, supplying arms and other aid from Venezuela through Costa Rica to the Sandinistas in Nicaragua. When the civil war ended in Nicaragua, the arms traffic network was redirected. Now originating mainly in Cuba, it was routed directly or indirectly through Honduras to El Salvador, all under the supervision of Cubans and facilitated by the Costa Rican left.

Until recent terrorist acts against the police and U.S. embassy personnel in San Jose, terrorism was virtually unknown to Costa Rica. The ideological and military training of the group of urban terrorists responsible for these acts appears to have been provided by the Cubans. Two of the accused terrorists were trained in the Soviet Union, others in Cuba and Nicaragua.[34] Some of those arrested belonged to the Revolutionary Movement of the People (MRP), a Leninist group with close ties to Cuba that implicitly approves the antigovernment terrorism. (This group is not to be confused with the Popular Vanguard party, which is still less inclined to favor violent means for coming to power.)

The Soviet connection in these activities is seriously implied, though difficult to trace. The arms transfer through Costa Rica was originated by the Cubans, but they could not have accomplished it without the knowledge of Soviet embassy personnel in San Jose. The Soviets probably did not initiate the terrorist attacks inside Costa Rica. Yet they must have known of the plans, and if they did not approve them, they at least did not oppose them. (After the terrorist attack on personnel of the U.S. embassy, the Soviet embassy asked the Costa Rican police for protection.) The sporadic Soviet-Cuban-sponsored terrorist activities in Costa Rica have cost the Soviets, though not so dearly as the Cubans, whose diplomatic mission was shut down after the investigation by the Costa Rican legislature. Cuban requests to reopen offices in San Jose were granted, but only at the level of a Cuban chargé d'affaires. Because of this interference and Soviet involvement in local labor problems, including support for the Communist labor union (some Soviet diplomats were linked to a banana strike), diplomatic relations have cooled, and a technical and economic aid agreement concluded earlier with the Soviet Union has been renounced. Costa Rican officials do not plan to increase trade with the Soviet Union, and, if more evidence of Soviet involvement in terrorism in Costa Rica becomes available, relations with the Soviet Union may be broken. In the fall of 1982 the number of officials at the Soviet embassy in San Jose was reduced from twenty-five to eight, and Soviet–Costa Rican relations were at a low ebb. The post left vacant by Soviet Ambassador Vladimir Chernishov in June 1981 was left unfilled for sixteen months. Two men proposed for the post by the Soviets were supposedly rejected by the Costa Rican government, and only in December 1982 was Yuri Pavlov accredited as the new Soviet ambassador. In 1985 seventeen other Soviet officials were ordered to leave. Although the staff at the Soviet embassy was limited to eight, the actual number of Soviet diplomats, according to Costa Rican sources in 1985, was said to be nearly forty.[35]

The Soviets, while complaining about recent Costa Rican hostility, did not view their losses in Costa Rica as significant ones; the previous Costa Rican government of President Luis Alberto Monge was always viewed as subservient to the United States, and Costa Rica does not have substantial economic benefits to offer the Soviet Union. President Oscar Arias, elected in 1986, is not viewed by the Soviets as either progressive or anti-imperialist. Visiting Soviet officials like Vladimir Kazimirov—chief of the first Latin American Countries Department of the Soviet Ministry of Foreign Affairs—have expressed the intention of improving Soviet–Costa Rican relations. The Soviets, however, like the leaders of the Popular Vanguard party, perceive Costa Rica as being under U.S. rule.

Colombia. In Soviet calculations, Colombia, though larger than Costa Rica, is probably not a very significant country in resources or location, even though Soviet trade with Colombia has been growing. More important, Colombia in the first half of the 1980s was hardly a country the Soviets could characterize as having "anti-imperialist" policies on important international issues. Thus in terms of economics, security, and politics, the Soviets have little to lose by antagonizing the Colombians; and by not opposing Cuba's support to Colombian terrorist and guerrilla operations, the Soviet Union can deny responsibility and minimize costs.

Cuba has had excellent contacts with Colombian revolutionaries, who have been training in Cuba since the 1960s. Leaders of some of the guerrilla groups in Colombia have also attended schools in Moscow. During the 1970s, when Cuba established diplomatic relations with Colombia, Cuba limited its contacts with these groups— the urban April 19 Movement (M-19), the People's Liberation Army (ELN), and the Revolutionary Armed Forces of Colombia (FARC). But after 1979, when Colombia ran against Cuba for the Latin American seat on the United Nations Security Council, Cuba, with Soviet backing, renewed its assistance to the Colombian guerrillas. The seizure of the Dominican Republic's embassy in Bogotá in February 1980 was followed by a sharp increase in leftist guerrilla activities. (The guerrillas responsible for this were later flown to Cuba.)[36] In the summer of 1980 Cuba made efforts to unite these organizations or at least to ensure their practical cooperation. Although a united strategy was not achieved, the groups did agree to cooperate.

Moreover, there is some evidence that Cuba played a prominent role in organizing and providing intensive training for some of the M-19 guerrillas (who came to Cuba via Panama) and, beginning in 1979, provided them with money for the purchase of arms (via Panama) to be used in the 1981 spring offensive. This offensive was to coincide with a scheduled civil strike and was supposed to help initiate a nationwide insurrection. A number of guerrillas from a large group, sent by ship to Colombia in February 1981, were intercepted while attempting to land on Colombia's Pacific coast. One member confessed that they had been trained and armed in Cuba. Another ship carrying weapons for guerrillas was intercepted and sunk by the Colombian navy in Colombia's territorial waters. In response to this attempt, Colombia broke diplomatic relations with Cuba in 1981. Until the amnesty of 1982 these guerrilla groups continued to engage in a number of ambushes and terrorist operations against military units. According to Colombian authorities, Nicaragua was the source of many of the weapons captured from the guerrillas. The same authorities allege an indisputable link between the Communist party of Colombia and at least one of Colombia's guerrilla groups, FARC.[37]

The Colombian offensive—like the guerrilla operations in Costa Rica and most important, as we shall see, the large guerrilla offensive in El Salvador—was apparently planned to coincide with the U.S. presidential election in November 1980 and the period shortly thereafter. The motive was to put the United States and its allies on the defensive in the U.S. strategic backyard during a delicate transition period. The timing and implementation of all these operations appear to betray a large element of planning and preparation. Although not in charge of the training and military operations on a daily basis, the Soviets must have kept abreast of and certainly must have approved these operations.

The Colombian administration of President Belisario Betancur, elected in 1982, generally played down Cuban and Nicaraguan support of revolutionary activities in the Caribbean Basin, in part to demonstrate independence from the United States but also because insurgency activities had temporarily subsided in Colombia in 1982–1983. Betancur also refused to isolate Cuba and Nicaragua from the OAS during President Reagan's visit in November 1982 and in a rather surprising move proposed instead that Colombia join the nonaligned group of nations. Perhaps he hoped thereby to dissuade the Soviets and Cubans from promoting further havoc, or perhaps he was retaliating against the Reagan administration for slighting his country in the Caribbean Basin Initiative. The Colombian leadership, however, was unable to buy continuous immunity from the guerrillas. This was suggested by a daring attack of M-19 guerrilla commandos on Bogotá's Palace of Justice in November 1985. It left dozens of dead and wounded and seriously jolted the Colombian government. Since then the new president of Colombia, Virgilio Barco, of the Liberal party, has assumed an aggressive posture vis-à-vis the guerrillas.

Soviet Policies toward "Reactionary" Regimes: El Salvador, Guatemala, and Honduras

El Salvador. The Sandinista victory over the forces of Somoza in 1979 prompted the Soviets to anticipate a chain reaction of leftist upheavals and revolutions throughout Central America and contributed to a corresponding shift in Soviet policy toward reactionary regimes. After Nicaragua the Central American country singled out by Soviet writers at that time as being most pregnant with revolutionary opportunities was El Salvador, a country that the United States perceives as having an important strategic position.[38] Perhaps even more than Nicaragua, El Salvador has a strong heritage of instability caused by a rigid class structure, unequal distribution of wealth, and high unemployment (30 percent). In El Salvador, the smallest yet most densely populated country in Latin America, socioeconomic and political conditions have traditionally been determined by an oligarchy of wealthy families protected by military strong men. The recent civil war, in which at least 20,000 have died, has ravaged that country.

Cuban assistance to the Salvadoran guerrillas increased sharply after 1979 when the Cubans helped to unite the various revolutionary groups under the Farabundo Martí National Liberation Front (FDR-FMLN). At that time the Cubans also substantially increased their training of Salvadoran guerrillas. Though originally very cautious, the Soviets decided to back the Cuban plan and help supply weapons after a meeting of the various guerrilla groups organized by Castro in Havana in December 1979.[39] In the spring of 1980 the Soviets also agreed to provide for the training of a few dozen Salvadoran youths.

This change in tactics was reflected when the pro-Soviet Communist party of El Salvador (PCES) endorsed violent revolution at its seventh national congress in May 1980. This was a very important shift from the early 1970s, when PCES leader Shafik Jorge Handal broke with some of his colleagues who had advocated revolutionary tactics and was critical of violent means in the Soviet press. Up to that time the PCES had participated in several presidential and legislative elections and had opposed armed struggle and terrorism in favor of peaceful tactics. (Because of this Handal was labeled "a caviar Communist" by guerrilla leaders.) In the fall of 1979, though jubilant over the victory in Nicaragua, Handal was still cautious about commenting on the prospects for revolution in El Salvador. In April 1980, however, he unexpectedly became much more optimistic and, according to Soviet sources, expressed "confidence" in the "defeat of internal reaction, despite the fact that the latter is backed by imperialist forces."[40]

The fact that this important shift in Handal's line was well advertised in the Soviet press means that the Soviets fully supported it.

The example of Nicaragua and the changing relationship between the superpowers, however important, were not the only motives for the shift in tactics by the PCES and the Soviets in the spring and fall of 1980. Both the Soviets and the Cubans probably feared that if the PCES did not use violence to implement its anti-imperialist strategy, it would soon be overtaken by more radical rivals, who were quickly gaining popular strength. The PCES, they probably reasoned, should not be suddenly surprised by successes of non-Communist guerrillas and thereby be deprived of credit for the victory. To this end Cuban and Soviet tactics after the spring of 1980 were conceived so as to transform the numerically small PCES into a leading force in the guerrilla struggle.

It appears that Soviet support of Cuban involvement in El Salvador, though not the main cause of civil war in that country, did significantly strengthen the guerrillas. A passive line was exchanged for one of organized violence around the time of the seventh congress of the PCES in 1979, which coincided with Handal's search for arms in the East. The latter is well documented in the U.S. administration's white paper.[41] After the congress, as Castro later admitted, the Cubans took charge of coordinating the delivery of weapons to the guerrillas, and Castro actively brokered unification of the various revolutionary groups. (The Cuban involvement in the Salvadoran civil war is well documented by Jorge Domínguez.)[42] In June and July 1980, with the assistance of Soviet officials responsible for third world affairs in the Soviet Secretariat (K. Brutents and M. Kudachkin), Handal visited the Soviet Union and several East European countries to obtain American-made weapons (M-14 and M-16 rifles, M-79 grenades); he secured other U.S. equipment during similar trips to Vietnam and Ethiopia. The Soviets were "helpful" in arranging Handal's visits. In fact, without Soviet sponsorship the East Europeans and very likely the Vietnamese and Ethiopians would probably not have cooperated. By proceeding with caution, however, the Soviet Union could deny its involvement if later accused.

The Soviets' East European allies (except Poland and Romania) promised to provide additional weapons, communications equipment, uniforms, and medical supplies, while the Soviets helped to arrange for their transport, with Cuban assistance, to Nicaragua and from there directly by ship, air, or land (through Honduras) to El Salvador. After the U.S. presidential election Cuban experts, with cautious yet active Soviet backing, played a key role in the arms transfer and preparations for the "final" guerrilla offensive, originally scheduled to coincide with the leadership transition in Washington in January 1981.

The Soviet-backed, Cuban-coordinated arms transfer to guerrillas in El Salvador was not the only source of support for the guerrillas, perhaps not even the most important one. They also received arms from sources inside El Salvador, including deserters and disloyal troops. Although precise numerical evidence about the Soviet and Cuban arms transfers and support for revolutionary forces in the Caribbean Basin is incomplete, the evidence is more solid than some critics would like to acknowledge. Costa Rican and other Central American sources, as well as Colombian sources, have reconfirmed the basic premises of the U.S. white paper (as do the Grenada documents discovered in 1983). The flow of arms in March–April 1981 declined temporarily but then increased again before the new August offensive.[43] Arms transfers continued in 1984–1985, though apparently at a minimal level.

To be sure, the Soviets' original optimism about rapid revolutionary advances following the general offensive in El Salvador was mistaken. In a subsequent reappraisal the Soviets determined that the difference between the situation in El Salvador and the comparable prerevolutionary situation in Nicaragua was that in El Salvador the bourgeoisie were stronger than their Nicaraguan counterparts; thus the Salvadoran left, although it enjoyed some mass support, was unable to exploit that support fully.[44] This led to a necessary postponement of the "final" offensive.

In 1983–1986 the Soviets became aware that the government of José Napoleón Duarte had managed to consolidate political power in two elections and that the Salvadoran military had substantially increased its qualitative and quantitative strength with the help of military aid from the United States. Subsequently the FMLN guerrillas suffered some crushing defeats, including the desertion and surrender of 3,545 guerrillas to Salvadoran army units between January 1, 1982, and September 6, 1985. Moreover, in 1985 there were signs of division between the political arm of the FMLN-FDR and some of the FMLN military commanders.

These new conditions prompted a change in the strategy and tactics of the FMLN between 1984 and 1986. Basically, the PCES and the FMLN have shifted from the tactics of popular insurrection to prolonged guerrilla warfare, aimed primarily at harming the consolidation of Duarte's regime. Their actions have included kidnappings (of city mayors but also of President Duarte's daughter), sabotage, economic destabilization through national transportation bans, destruction of electric power plants and coffee fields, and the like. The FMLN and the PCES have also begun to consolidate their political gains in the trade unions.[45] To constrain the Reagan administration, the FMLN has targeted U.S. advisers in El Salvador and has sought to evoke fear of a "new Vietnam" in letters addressed to the U.S. Congress.[46] The Soviets still support the FMLN guerrillas in El Salvador, although they are cautious and much more guarded in their optimism about short-run successes. A likely and realistic goal is to help the FMLN survive the Reagan tenure and dramatically increase support for the guerrillas again after 1988. At that time the FMLN could actively augment the scope and intensity of its activities.

Guatemala. Since the overthrow of the "progressive" government of Jacobo Arbenz in 1954, the Soviets have viewed each successive Guatemalan regime as reactionary.[47] As they continued to observe the Guatemala scene in the early 1980s, their sources indicated an awareness of deteriorating socioeconomic conditions. The agricultural economy of this most populous Central American country, like that of its neighbors, was in serious disarray because of the recent worldwide decline in coffee, cotton, and sugar prices. Economic conditions worsened after the loss of transport routes through Nicaragua (whose use was denied Guatemala by a hostile Nicaraguan regime) and the destruction of the Pan American Highway in El Salvador. The industrial sector, though growing, is still weak and unable to incorporate the impoverished and ever more radicalized Indian population (particularly in the northwestern part of the country), which constitutes a majority of the Guatemalan population.

The worsening socioeconomic conditions and the effects of guerrilla warfare in neighboring countries have contributed to the radicalization of Guatemalan society. Incredible violence by factions right and left, which goes back to the mid-1950s, intensified with the upsurge in guerrilla movements in the 1970s. Under the oppressive rule of General Romeo Lucas in the late 1970s and early 1980s, violence on the part of the extreme right (the famous death squads) and extreme left further harmed the country. Still, conditions in Guatemala in the first half of the 1980s were even less ripe for a popular revolution of the Nicaraguan style than conditions in El Salvador.

While the United States suspended arms transfers and military advisory assistance to the Guatemalan government in the late 1970s, the Cubans, with Soviet backing, stepped up military aid to the guerrillas, whom they have supported cautiously since the 1960s. Their pattern for providing aid resembled the scheme followed in

Nicaragua and El Salvador. First, the Cubans insisted on unification of the four leading guerrilla groups, one of which has close ties to the Guatemalan Communist party. The unity agreement was signed in Managua in November 1980 in the presence of highly placed Nicaraguan officials. (The Guatemalan guerrilla leaders have headquarters in Managua.) Later the agreement was presented to Castro. Although the revolutionary groups did not at first agree to establish a unified political front, they did agree on a joint military strategy, including increased insurgency activities.

Their political unification, apparently modeled on the Nicaraguan and Salvadoran examples, was achieved in Cuba in March 1981 under the banner of the Guatemalan Nationalist Revolutionary Union. At that time the Guatemalan Labor (Communist) party, which in the past had advocated cautious resistance to military rule, also began to advocate "clandestine methods" in the struggle, heeding, as their leaders observed, that "all the legal ways are closed."[48] This was followed by an increase in Cuban training and military assistance to the revolutionaries. Soon at least several hundred guerrillas were being trained in Cuba. Meanwhile the arms transfer from Nicaragua via Honduras continued, though on a smaller scale. There is also some collaboration between the Salvadoran and Guatemalan guerrillas, although the actual insurgency in Guatemala is conducted on a smaller scale than in El Salvador. The guerrillas admit to having suffered several setbacks between 1982 and 1985.

Subsequent developments in Guatemala may be decisive in the outcome of the guerrilla war in that country. Given the succession of rapid political turnovers in the past five years (Aníbal Garcia, elected in March 1982, was overthrown by General Efraím Ríos Montt, who in turn was overthrown by General Oscar Humberto Mejía Victores in August 1983), the political violence, and continuous guerrilla war, it seems likely that the trend toward instability and political polarization will not be easily reversed. Surely this was the belief of the guerrilla leaders in Guatemala. For them and for the Cubans and Soviets, no Guatemalan president will have the capacity to introduce meaningful reforms in the face of the powerful, status-quo-oriented Guatemalan military. The democratic election of Christian Democrat Vinicio Cerezo in November 1985, an extraordinary exception in the Guatemalan experience, may yet become a turning point in Guatemalan history, leading to the introduction of serious reforms and an end to violence. Meanwhile the Cubans, with tacit Soviet support, are expected to try to continue at least moderate support for revolutionary forces in Guatemala.

Honduras. Honduras, one of the poorest countries in the Caribbean Basin, is also going through a dramatic economic and financial crisis, with a foreign debt of almost $1 billion. The army has played an important role in this country's government, which the Soviets have described as a "soft dictatorship."

The Cubans have sought to encourage a degree of revolutionary activity in Honduras, providing the guerrillas in 1981 with arms and instruction in Cuba and Nicaragua and urging the unification of revolutionary groups, which are much smaller than in El Salvador and Guatemala. Although the guerrilla insurgency is still very limited, Honduras's strategic position bordering Nicaragua, El Salvador, and Guatemala makes it an important element in Soviet-Cuban tactics. In the early 1980s, with Soviet and Cuban support, the small, pro-Soviet Communist party of Honduras organized the Committee for Solidarity with the Struggle of the Central American Peoples.[49] Whereas the pro-Chinese Marxist-Leninist Communist party of Honduras urged Hondurans to participate in the November 1985 election, the pro-Soviet party urged electoral abstention.

Regional Conflict in the Caribbean Basin

Although we have limited ourselves primarily to examining how Soviet and Cuban foreign policies promote instability in the Caribbean Basin, we have also tried to show the internal sources of instability. But there is also a regional dimension of the problem that is rooted in old territorial disputes and more recent political and security problems.

For example, Nicaragua refused to recognize the 1919 treaty acknowledging Colombian sovereignty over the Caribbean islands of San Andrés (where Colombia is building a naval base), Providencia, Roncador Cay, Quitasueño, and the Serrana Keys. Nicaragua also disputes the Cañas Jerez Treaty of 1858, ratified by the Cleveland Resolution, which gives Costa Rica freedom in perpetuity to navigate the San Juan River on Nicaragua's borders. Venezuela's claim to two-thirds of Guyanese territory goes back to the 1899 Treaty of Washington, which involved Great Britain as arbiter. (Guyana has declared its readiness to accept military aid from Cuba should Guyana be attacked by Venezuela in any attempt to seize this territory.) A serious problem of demarcation also exists concerning portions of the borders between Venezuela and Colombia. A significant part of the new state of Belize (former British Honduras) is claimed by Guatemala. Guatemala, which professes to need a large port on the Caribbean coast, has claimed this territory almost since it became an independent state in 1821. In the future, strong pressure from Guatemala against Belize may cause this small country, with a population of only 140,000, to move closer to Cuba and Nicaragua in search of allies and protection.

In the recent past some countries of the Central American isthmus were invaded by their neighbors. In 1954 the CIA financed and backed an intervention in Guatemala simultaneously from Honduras and El Salvador. An old border dispute between Honduras and El Salvador led to the so-called Soccer War in 1969. There are also a number of trade disagreements among various countries in the basin, including those with ideological or political affinities, like Honduras and Guatemala.

The new, revolutionary policies of the Sandinistas in Nicaragua have compounded existing regional problems. This is manifested in the Central American arms race, which began with the Sandinistas' planned military buildup and was publicly announced in the spring of 1980. The Nicaraguan buildup, which predated the Reagan administration's tough line on Nicaragua, has destabilized the region more than any other factor. In particular, the supply of heavy tanks, which are not included in the inventory of Nicaragua's neighbors Honduras, El Salvador, and Guatemala, has fueled this race. While by the end of 1985 the Nicaraguan forces could count at least one hundred T-54 and T-55 tanks in their arsenal, the other Central American nations combined possessed approximately thirty small Sherman and Scorpion tanks. True, the Honduran air force, which includes *super mystères*, is better than that of Nicaragua, but its primary role is to deter Nicaragua's preponderance on the ground.

The large-scale deliveries of sophisticated weapons to Nicaragua from the Soviet Union and its allies but also from France and Algeria are intended to equip what the Sandinistas hope will be one of the largest standing armies in the region. (The goal is 50,000 men, which would make it larger than all other armies except those of Cuba and Mexico.) The Nicaraguan armed forces have grown from 14,000 under Somoza to 75,000 active duty armed forces, making it the largest military force in Central America. (The others are as follows: El Salvador, 49,000; Guatemala, 43,000; Honduras, 22,000; and Costa Rica, 8,000 civil/rural guards.)

In response to their internal problems—but also to what they perceive as the threat from Nicaragua—Honduras, El Salvador, and Guatemala have begun making large-scale arms purchases, particularly to upgrade their air forces but also including antitank missiles and helicopters. Even Costa Rica, which has no army, has plans to form special antiterrorist units and is trying to better the training of its civil and rural guards.

A third source of regional instability is the forced migration from Nicaragua of various large groups that have settled close to the Nicaraguan borders in Honduras and Costa Rica and are intent on resisting the regime in Managua. These include a few thousand supporters of the former dictator Somoza, mainly members of his national guard. In 1981–1982 some former guardsmen began to cooperate with the growing anti-Sandinista organization of exiled Nicaraguans known as the Nicaraguan Democratic Force, which operates both in Honduras and inside Nicaragua. It is made up of a wide spectrum of opponents of the Managua regime, consisting of former Somozistas, former Sandinistas (including supporters of Edén Pastora), and apolitical deserters from the Sandinista army.

Although the migration of Somoza's supporters was clearly an aftereffect of the civil war that preceded the Sandinista victory, the migration of other groups has been caused by the Sandinistas' antagonistic postrevolutionary policies. This migration concerns 100,000 mostly English-speaking Miskito, Sumo, and Rama Indians, 8,000 to 10,000 of whom have already been forcibly removed by Sandinista troops from border areas adjacent to Honduras. The Sandinista government claims that the eviction was necessary because of intrusions into Nicaragua by former Somoza guardsmen. During the removal about 100 Indians were killed. Afterward some 3,000 fled to Honduras. Others have since been murdered by the Sandinistas.[50] The flight of Indians from the border areas and of thousands of other Nicaraguans from areas throughout the country has exacerbated tension with Honduras, which has had to receive these people.

The Sandinistas have also contributed to regional instability by supporting insurgency and terrorism, primarily in El Salvador but also in Honduras, Costa Rica, and even Colombia. Because of a long common frontier with Nicaragua and because of mutual accusations and hostilities on both sides, the threat of war is greatest between Honduras and Nicaragua, each of which has accused the other of numerous border violations. Nicaraguan leaders have spoken about "a real state of war" along the borders with Honduras. This led to the imposition of martial law in border areas with Honduras between 1982 and 1983 and to an increased military presence along both sides of the border, with Honduras deploying substantial portions of its armed forces in these areas. Honduras, which had been receiving Argentine military aid before the Malvinas crisis, is now receiving U.S. aid to upgrade its military capability and airport facilities. Meanwhile, since 1982 U.S. military advisers and Honduran troops have been conducting joint military training exercises near the borders with Nicaragua. The growing fear of war between Nicaragua and Honduras nearly climaxed several times during this period.

There is also border unrest on the Costa Rican–Nicaraguan frontier. Costa Rican officials, who originally supported the Sandinista revolution, share the concern of their Honduran counterparts about the tense border situation. In their view it was created by continual Nicaraguan incursions into Costa Rican territory in pursuit of anti-FSLN guerrillas. In 1982–1985 there were approximately 100 border incidents between Costa Rica and Nicaragua, including violations of Costa Rican airspace and attacks by FSLN units on Costa Rican territory that resulted in the death of Costa Rican civil guards. Nicaraguan infiltration of Costa Rica and support for terrorism there are other concerns.

Conflict in the Central American isthmus may further polarize the countries of the region. In early 1982 Honduras, El Salvador, Costa Rica, and Guatemala formed the Central American Democratic Community (CDC)—a political alliance aimed at isolating the Sandinista regime in Managua. (Costa Rica had objected to establishing an economic or military alliance within this group.) By 1980 Mexico had also become concerned over the widening Central American conflict. After the influx of thousands of Guatemalans into Mexico, Mexico created a 4,000-man quick reaction force to cope with unrest on its borders with Guatemala. As feared by some Central American leaders, tension in the region has reached a dangerous level at which any incident can transform the conflict, with uncontrollable consequences. Should the conflict between Honduras and Nicaragua suddenly escalate, the regime in El Salvador, if not incapacitated by its own guerrillas, would very likely come to the political and military aid of Honduras. (Already units of the Salvadoran army occasionally cross into Honduran territory to conduct attacks against Salvadoran guerrilla sanctuaries.) Costa Rica, although it has no regular army, would probably also be dragged into the conflict in some limited way. Meanwhile Nicaragua might call for aid from Cuba, while Honduras and El Salvador would seek increasing military assistance from Israel and the United States. This in turn could aggravate tensions between the superpowers and ultimately precipitate a dangerous widening of the conflict.

Future Soviet-Cuban Strategy in the Caribbean Basin

We have outlined at least four major factors that in the past have visibly affected Soviet and Cuban policies in the Caribbean Basin:

(1) the presence of opportunity, (2) the degree of Soviet and Cuban concurrence on strategy, (3) the dynamics of Soviet and East European internal politics, and (4) U.S. ability and willingness to counter Soviet-Cuban strategy. At times in the past the absence of exploitable opportunities, disagreement with Cuba about overall strategy, unfavorable internal conditions in the Soviet Union and Eastern Europe, or a firm U.S. response has hindered the successful implementation of Soviet strategy. Soviet success or failure in the future will depend on these same variables.

Opportunities for Exerting Influence. In the English-speaking Caribbean islands, where it was early feared that a chain reaction of revolutionary coups would follow the 1979 coup in Grenada, Soviet and Cuban prospects appear rather unfavorable. In the early 1980s a series of democratic elections in Dominica, St. Lucia, St. Vincent, and St. Kitts–Nevis rejected the radical, leftist orientation. The Soviets and Cubans, as well as Western observers, apparently underestimated the efficacy of the parliamentary tradition and the system of legitimate self-government in some of these countries. Another electoral setback recognized by the Soviets was the defeat of Jamaica's socialist Prime Minister Michael Manley, who in October 1980 lost to the more pro-Western Edward Seaga. (After his election Seaga expelled a host of Cuban diplomats, including some intelligence operators.)

The U.S.-OECS intervention in Grenada in 1983 was a watershed in the history of the Caribbean Basin, comparable only to the victory of the Caribbean's Western labor movements over the pro-Soviet labor movement in the 1950s. The failure of Leninism in Grenada can be interpreted as a general failure of the Leninist temptation in the democratic, parliamentarian environment that prevails in the eastern Caribbean.

The Grenada affair must have had an alarming effect on the perceptions of Communist and radical third world leaders. The intervention indicated that Soviet allies outside the immediate Soviet periphery are not automatically assured of Moscow's protection, even when faced with a mortal challenge from imperialism. These are troubling implications for socialist-oriented Nicaragua, Angola, and Ethiopia but also for Communist Cuba.

Castro must question the ambiguous Soviet commitment to Cuba should Cuba come into direct conflict with the United States. In contrast to their behavior in their own periphery (or even in remote regions of Africa), Soviet leaders are less able or willing to support pro-Soviet regimes in America's backyard, particularly when Washington is willing to protect its interests forcibly. After Grenada the

Caribbean may have assumed a lower priority on Castro's agenda. At the same time Castro appears to have rededicated his efforts to expanding Cuban influence in Central America.

Initially the intervention in Grenada created a bunker mentality among the Sandinistas, who saw the intervention as a final rupturing of U.S. patience. The intervention, U.S. military exercises in the Caribbean and Central America, and U.S. sponsorship of anti-FSLN revolutionary activities in the region were seen as the preamble to a Grenada-style intervention in Nicaragua. In its aftermath one could observe a noticeable weakening of Nicaraguan support for guerrillas in El Salvador and temporarily increased pressures for negotiations with the Duarte government. The sobering effect of the intervention should not be overestimated, however. Ultimately it sharpened Managua's obstinacy and played into the hands of hard-liners such as Minister of the Interior Borge. For Borge the intervention in Grenada served as the sought after proof of a forthcoming U.S. intervention in Nicaragua.

Some residual effects of the intervention were evident elsewhere in the Caribbean Basin, particularly in Suriname. Under pressure from Brazil but also because of the intervention, Suriname expelled Cuban advisers only hours after the U.S. intervention and subsequently reduced diplomatic ties with Cuba to a minimum. The decision to expel the advisers appears to have been made after the October 19 coup, for which the Surinamese held the Cubans responsible, but the U.S. intervention may have accelerated the disengagement. Recent developments, such as improved relations between Nicaragua and Suriname, suggest that the effect of the intervention has since dissipated.

In the late 1980s a slow economic recovery in the industrial world will continue to be accompanied by seriously deteriorating socioeconomic conditions in the Caribbean region. As in the past, a worsening of these conditions might lead to radicalization and thereby make conditions propitious for Soviet and Cuban activity. Such changes cannot be excluded, even in Jamaica and the Dominican Republic, which have democratically elected governments. Both face severe economic problems. With the possible exception of Haiti, however, where poverty is coupled with the unpredictable consequences of the abdication of Jean-Claude Duvalier, possibilities for revolutionary upheaval in the late 1980s seemed less abundant in the Caribbean islands than in Central America.

There are several reasons for this. First, the Central American political culture, in contrast to that of the English-speaking Caribbean, is deeply affected by Catholic and Hispanic traditions, including a ruling tradition of powerful caudillos and often violent authoritarianism. Second, in the 1980s deteriorating socioeconomic conditions have reached a critical point throughout Central America, including once prosperous Costa Rica. The political and economic dynamics of these countries have often been characterized by violence, and this has been aggravated by outside interference.

The revolutionary success in Nicaragua may have led the Soviets and Cubans to overestimate Central America's overall revolutionary potential. Certainly in the mid-1980s there appears to be much less Soviet optimism about El Salvador and perhaps also Guatemala. The guerrilla offensive in El Salvador, at least up to 1986, failed to spark a popular insurrection of the kind seen in Nicaragua, in part because of some rather significant differences in political developments. Nicaragua's revolution was genuine in that it expressed the will of a majority of the people in overthrowing the hated Somoza dictatorship. El Salvador's revolution is much less so. Until recently both the Soviets and the Cubans have committed their resources to the Salvadoran cause without considerable returns. Meanwhile, in countries such as Costa Rica and Colombia, Cuban support for the guerrillas has had damaging consequences for diplomatic relations. Overall, Soviet sources indicate less enthusiasm about the prospects for revolution in Central America in 1983–1986 than in 1979–1982.

Yet, because of continuously deteriorating socioeconomic conditions combined with a shift to the antireformist right in El Salvador or unrelenting violence and insurgency in El Salvador and Guatemala, unforeseen opportunities may arise for Soviet-backed Cuban activity. Deep socioeconomic cleavages, which are the main source of the continuing crisis, are especially pronounced in countries located in the northern tier: El Salvador, Guatemala, and, to a lesser degree, Honduras. Costa Rica and Panama do not have such marked social problems, but they do face severe economic difficulties that make them candidates for social upheaval in the future.

Mexico and Panama, where so far little or no violence has occurred, are nonetheless worrisome. The mounting economic crisis in Mexico, coupled with the effects of the 1985 earthquake, imposes additional hardships on the already impoverished masses and could lead to great unrest, radical shifts in Mexican policy, and massive new waves of emigration to the United States. Meanwhile in Panama the forced resignation of President Arditto Barletta in 1985 makes that country's future still more unpredictable. New revolutionary upheaval in Suriname on the South American coast may yet be exploited by the Soviets and Cubans. The most immediate and critical problem in 1986, however, remains the warlike situation on Nicaragua's borders with Honduras and Costa Rica and the accompanying arms race in that region.

Relations between the Soviet Union and Cuba. The state of relations between the Soviet Union and Cuba is central to the implementation of Soviet strategy in the Caribbean region. Their joint strategy for dealing with third world countries in the late 1960s and 1970s was designed not necessarily to create Leninist regimes but rather to achieve a variety of anti-imperialist ideological, political, security, and economic objectives. Soviet and Cuban strategies have not always been identical and, in fact, were a subject of contention in the 1960s. As recent Soviet-Cuban policies in Africa and Central America attest, however, most of these differences and disagreements have been overcome in favor of a unified third world strategy. Although Cuba is not subservient to the Soviet Union, its foreign policies in both areas depend on Soviet support. The Soviets are newcomers, but with Cuban help they have been able to exploit the socioeconomic malaise and characteristic anti–United States sentiment in Central America. Their tactics have been violent or peaceful or both.

It is very unlikely that the late 1980s will witness the serious differences or fissures evident in the Soviet-Cuban alliance in 1962–1968. One cannot exclude some disagreements on day-to-day tactics, but differences in strategy are unlikely. This forecast would preclude any meaningful rapprochement between Cuba and the United States, which Cuba sees as its natural enemy. Past moderation or a conciliatory approach by the United States did not lead to appreciable changes in Soviet and Cuban policies. In response to two overtures from U.S. policy makers, the Cuban leaders clearly indicated the impossibility of forgoing the alliance with their Soviet friends. The U.S. overture of 1975 preceded the Soviet-Cuban intervention in Angola; a similar overture in 1977 was followed by the intervention in Ethiopia; and U.S. acceptance of the Sandinista regime in Nicaragua in 1979 was followed by more assertive Cuban policies in El Salvador.

The Soviet-Cuban alliance has produced tangible benefits for both countries. Moscow has made significant ideological, political, security, and economic investments in Cuba. In return Moscow has gained an indispensable ally, a true proletarian internationalist who is willing to coordinate insurgency and deploy troops in strategic areas of the third world in support of Soviet policy. Soviet strategy in Africa and Central America would be seriously handicapped should Moscow now turn its back on Castro's regime.

At the same time Soviet security, economic, and political support has become essential to Cuba. This dependence and Cuba's continuing commitment to revolutionary change preclude any effort by Castro to alter the Soviet-Cuban relationship. Pursuit of the revolution, furthermore, helps Castro to compensate for failed domestic experiments and mishandled Cuban internal politics. To forgo the alliance with the Soviet Union and move closer to the United States would undermine the regime's very rationale.

Short of an unlikely anti-Castro coup, little possibility exists for radical change in the Soviet-Cuban alliance in the 1980s. Even Castro's death would probably not precipitate profound changes in Cuban policy. His replacement by the number two man, his brother Raúl, would probably result in Cuba's greater integration in the Soviet alliance system.

Soviet and East European Internal Politics. Soviet strategy and tactics in the Caribbean Basin in the 1980s will also be influenced by Soviet domestic politics and economic conditions internal to the Soviet Union and Eastern Europe. In the early 1980s overall economic conditions in the Soviet Union and Cuba were apparently not propitious for large economic commitments or revolutionary undertakings. Similar economic problems in the 1970s, however, did not deter the Soviets and Cubans from becoming involved in various African and Caribbean Basin countries. Despite serious economic problems, Cuba has not only maintained but also extended these commitments. Throughout, the Soviets have backed Cuba's pivotal role while also giving significant and direct economic support to new client regimes in Nicaragua and (before 1983) Grenada.

Given the domestic constraints on the Soviet Union and Cuba, it is unlikely that they can afford to take on new revolutionary clients in the late 1980s. Unlike Cuba, the Soviet Union is a superpower with global responsibilities and obligations not only to clients in Asia, Africa, and the Caribbean but also and primarily to a hard core of allies in Eastern Europe, where economic conditions in the 1980s are rapidly going from bad to worse. Bankruptcy in Poland, economic difficulties in other East European countries and the Soviet Union, the continuing war in Afghanistan, and the leadership problems resulting from three political successions between 1982 and 1985 may force the Soviets in coming years to refocus their attention on their own "strategic backyard," as they did in the mid-1950s and late 1960s.

The cumulative effect of these conditions may be forced Soviet constraint in the Caribbean Basin, for at least a few years. It would be optimistic, however, to expect the Soviets to cease the arms transfer and economic support necessary for the survival of existing revolutionary regimes in the region. Accordingly, Soviet support for Cuba and Nicaragua has intensified, even during the succession years (1982–1985). In years to come, however, the regime of General Secretary Gorbachev will very likely be more cautious about increasing support for struggling revolutionaries because of necessarily increasing preoccupation with problems internal to the Soviet Union and at the Soviet periphery. The Soviets, who determine the limits of Cuban assertiveness, may also exert a moderating force on Cuban activities while waiting for new, low-risk opportunities to arise.

The Correlation of Forces between the Superpowers. The final and most crucial variable in the formulation of Soviet strategy and tactics in the 1980s will be the perceived balance of power between the Soviet Union and the United States, in part determined by U.S. willingness and ability to respond to Soviet ventures in the Caribbean and elsewhere. In the wake of the Vietnam War, the American public and Congress were basically unwilling to constrain Cuban and Soviet assertiveness. Thus the Soviets and Cubans had a free hand in Angola and Ethiopia and in the Caribbean Basin, where in 1979 President Jimmy Carter suddenly classified as "acceptable" what was first an "unacceptable" Soviet brigade in Cuba.

The election of Ronald Reagan to the presidency in 1980 indicated a shift in the American public mood. Rightly or wrongly, both the Soviets and the Cubans view President Reagan as unpredictable and a hard-liner. President Carter, though also perceived as unpredictable, was thought to be softer and less dangerous than his successor. President Reagan revealed his stance during the campaign of 1980, when he threatened to retaliate against the Soviet invasion of Afghanistan by blockading Cuba. For the Cubans, this was tantamount to throwing down the gauntlet. In response they made every effort to coordinate and time the guerrilla offensives of 1980–1981 in El Salvador and Colombia for the period shortly following the transition from President Carter. The success of this offensive would have placed President Reagan in what could have been an embarrassing defensive position during the delicate period initiating his tenure.

Although the Reagan administration has not woven its Caribbean Basin policies into a coherent strategy, it has made the basin a major issue in the East-West context, and there has been some resulting moderation in Soviet and Cuban revolutionary tactics in the region. The Reagan administration wisely did not rule out the use of a blockade or other military force against Nicaragua or, as former Secretary of State Alexander Haig put it, "going to the [Cuban] source" to prevent further Cuban involvement in El Salvador. Unfortunately, before Haig's departure the administration unwisely engaged in some unnecessary confrontational talk that lost some of its intended effectiveness when appropriate actions were not forthcoming.

In the 1980s the Soviets have increased their military and economic aid to existing revolutionary regimes while continuing to cultivate anti-imperialist trends in Mexico. U.S. support for Great Britain in the Falkland Islands war in 1982 served the ends of both the Soviets and the Cubans, who supported the Argentines and skillfully exploited the heightened anti-Americanism on the Latin American continent. U.S. efforts to work with the Argentines to moderate the situation in Central America were thwarted as a result of this war.

The intervention in Grenada sent reverberations throughout the Soviet alliance system. It came as a surprise especially in the Soviet Union, where it was taken as an important signal that America might be recovering from the Vietnam syndrome and might again be prepared (as in the 1950s and 1960s) to use military force to defend its interests. In the months following the intervention, the Soviets appeared to be reassessing the costs and benefits of their support for revolutionary forces in the Caribbean Basin. Although the intervention added a dimension to the policy-making process in Moscow, it did not trigger a wholesale reappraisal of Soviet foreign policy. The operation was too small and too simple to be compared with what Vietnam demanded or what Nicaragua might require. Among other things, the long-term effects will depend on follow-up U.S. policies concerning other aspiring Leninist forces in the third world in general and in the Caribbean Basin in particular.

Although the Grenada intervention raised the costs of Soviet and Cuban support for revolutionary activities in geographically remote regions, its effect on third world revolutionary regimes is still unclear. If followed by a long-term U.S. strategy to curb Soviet-Cuban influence in the third world and successfully to stabilize Grenada and the Caribbean Basin, the effect of the intervention may be more important than some observers anticipated.

Toward a New U.S. Strategy. Since the late 1950s superpower competition in the third world, with its potential for igniting global conflict, has been a central issue for U.S. policy makers. Then and now prevention of superpower confrontation and the escalation of such conflict is given highest priority in U.S. strategic planning.

A successful and sensitive U.S. policy toward the Caribbean Basin is very important to this objective, and it necessitates an understanding and appreciation of the third world's historical, political, economic, and social diversity. It is simplistic to attribute conflict in these countries solely to Soviet and Cuban policies. Equally naive is the notion that poverty is the sole cause of the problem. What is undeniable is the volatile interaction between the two, the penchant for the Soviet Union, its allies, and its proxies to take advantage of economic, social, and political instability or crises in developing nations. This has been particularly true over the past decade, during which the Soviets invaded Afghanistan and, along with Cuba and other proxies, became active in Angola, Ethiopia, and South Yemen. Meanwhile, the Soviets and Cubans provided substantial weapons and advisers to revolutionary forces in Nicaragua, El Salvador, and Grenada. Given the centrality of the Soviet-American competition in third world areas, U.S. policy makers must abandon short-term strategies that address short-term crises for consistent, long-term strategies designed to avoid conflict and manage future crises effectively.

The Caribbean Basin is extremely important to the United States. It is immediately contiguous to U.S. territory, and it constitutes a vital passageway for petroleum and other important raw materials. It would assume an even more critical strategic importance if the United States were to be involved in an overseas conventional war. In that event a growing Soviet-Cuban military presence in the Caribbean might endanger U.S. logistical support for NATO forces in Europe, as well as the delivery of strategic materials to the United States. The United States also has compelling economic interests in the Caribbean by virtue of large private business investments. U.S. domestic stability and the prospering of U.S. and regional interests require the prevention of abrupt economic dislocations, massive immigration, and hostile radicalization of Caribbean political life.

The Reagan administration has fully recognized the importance of Central America and the Caribbean Basin to the United States, directing much-needed attention to this long-neglected region. Formation of the National Bipartisan Commission on Central America (chaired by Henry Kissinger) was a significant step toward devising long-term, viable policies. In its aftermath U.S. officials should be much more visible and vocal in their support and implementation of legislation based on recommendations of the bipartisan report.

There is an urgent need to anticipate long-term challenges to the United States, not only in Central America (the only region dealt with by the bipartisan commission) but also in the Caribbean Basin, South America, and other parts of the third world. An analysis of the NJM strategy in Grenada suggests links among the revolutionary forces of Central America, the Caribbean, and South America. These links are very much a part of Soviet and Cuban strategic thinking and must not be neglected or overlooked by U.S. policy makers.

An equally urgent need is to study the dynamics of political and economic challenges in Peru, Argentina, Brazil, and Uruguay, the volatile situation in Chile, and the possible political and economic destabilization of Mexico. It is also necessary to study the strategies and tactics of communist and radical third world regimes that affect these Central and South American countries and to examine their ties with the Soviet Union and Cuba. Given the revolutionary experience in Grenada and elsewhere in the third world, Soviet and Cuban perceptions and policies deserve special attention by U.S. policy makers. We should be better prepared to anticipate and prevent crises in the third world and manage those that are unavoidable.

Policy makers need to substitute for ideological rigidity the resilient frame of mind necessary to understand radical third world regimes. They should avoid indiscriminate labeling of all radical forces as Marxist or Marxist-Leninist, since these terms tend to confuse the political and ideological orientation of these groups. It is ludicrous to call Suriname's Lieutenant Colonel Desire Bouterse a Marxist. Careless use of the Marxist-Leninist label (even in documents such as the distinguished report of the National Bipartisan Commission on Central America) indicates a misreading of the complexity and differences existing among Communist and radical third world parties. National Communist parties such as those of China and Yugoslavia fear Soviet imperialist ambitions, while others such as Italy's Eurocommunist party are of pluralist or semipluralist orientation and refuse the Leninist label. Some radical regimes in the third world are not Leninist. As suggested by the Grenada documents, radically nationalist forces can coexist or struggle with Leninist factions within radical third world regimes. The distinction between Leninist and non-Leninist forces should not be blurred. Because "Leninist-oriented" clearly means having both a vanguard party and a pro-Soviet foreign policy, U.S. policy makers and their advisers should avoid stereotyping and classifying all third world radical parties with this label.

Politically, U.S. policy makers must support democratic processes in third world countries that resist oppression, be it of the left or the right. We must continue to exercise pressure on El Salvador to curb and eliminate right-wing death squads. Experience indicates, however, that the extreme left cannot be defeated by wiping out the political center; nor can we endorse the guerrillas' violent approach. Moreover, we must avoid creating a double standard by insisting on progress toward democracy in El Salvador but not in Nicaragua, where the Sandinistas are establishing a regime similar to that in Grenada before 1983.

Political and economic aid should be extended to friendly third world regimes to the extent that they observe basic human rights and in amounts that each nation can absorb effectively. The most prudent way to prevent a future Grenada or Nicaragua is to strengthen existing ties and encourage more capable democratic institutions in developing nations. In the Caribbean Basin in particular, we must help democratic forces resist attempts by the parties in power to subvert legal and constitutional procedures, as happened in Grenada under Eric Gairy and in Guyana under Forbes Burnham. The projected work of the National Endowment for Democracy is an important step toward these goals.

The United States should promote friendly ties with third world radical regimes, excluding only those aligned with the Soviet Union and its allies. Meanwhile, through diplomatic exchange programs, we should attempt to cultivate political ties with opposition parties of various persuasions, while becoming better acquainted and more knowledgeable about their leaders. The Carter administration erred by failing to do this in 1979 in Grenada. It is imperative that we understand various elites and counterelites in radical third world nations. Heeding the British example, we must upgrade, expand, and stabilize our diplomatic representation in each of the Caribbean nations, no matter how minuscule.

Inadequate U.S. intelligence concerning the developments in Grenada points out that intelligence gathering and evaluating in the area must be upgraded. According to east Caribbean sources, in 1980 there were no experts on Grenada in U.S. intelligence agencies. Within U.S. government structures efforts must be made to strengthen and disseminate appropriate intelligence evaluations. Moreover, we must train and prepare credible and dynamic diplomatic personnel with adequate linguistic abilities to cope with new challenges in radical areas of the third world.

The main problems of the Caribbean Basin are miserable living conditions, hunger, and unemployment, which in turn invite violence and revolution. If unresolved, the socioeconomic problems in the Central American isthmus, exacerbated by current U.S. economic difficulties, might sooner or later engulf the United States in a conflict of overwhelming dimensions. The Soviets and Cubans count on the continuation of these economic and social difficulties to provide heightened opportunities for their own self-serving role in the Caribbean Basin. It would be a tragic failure of the Western democracies to allow the Soviets ostensibly to champion the cause of political and economic justice—the traditional undertaking of the democracies—while in the long run furthering the political, military, and social objectives of totalitarianism. Military concerns about arms levels in the region alone will not lead to resolution of the systemic social and economic crisis visited on those least able to bear the burden. Successful containment of Soviet initiatives in the Caribbean Basin depends on the equitable distribution of wealth and burdens among all nations of the region. What is required finally is a balanced approach to the problems that can prevent the widening of the conflict in the basin and its exploitation by the Soviet Union and Cuba.

We need to allocate greater resources to encourage economic growth in developing nations, particularly those on the periphery of the United States. The Caribbean Basin Initiative and the Central American Project are the basis for formulating economic assistance packages and improving the flow of credit and investment in Central America and the Caribbean islands. Immediate economic aid, from both the private and the public sectors, is imperative—even before political solutions are found.

Immediate emergency aid should be followed by the five-year economic assistance programs recommended by the bipartisan commission. The success of this approach will require not only American resources but also bipartisan public support and above all patience, since there will be no quick results. Financial aid alone, however, is not the answer to all the problems of the Caribbean Basin. In fact, economic assistance to some Caribbean islands is relatively high now and may be at the upper limit of what these nations can absorb for the time being. Other, more urgent needs include concentrated assistance in developing a technical infrastructure (roads, ports, communications), advice on planning and budgeting programs, and the education of economic and financial experts. We should use both the private and the public sectors to provide this assistance.

The United States must not entertain unrealistic expectations for Central America and the Caribbean Basin. We must recognize that despite the best efforts, at least some of the Caribbean nations may never achieve self-sustained economic growth and will therefore continue to depend on economic aid from the United States, Canada, and other industrialized nations.

U.S. security assistance must be an integral part of U.S. strategy vis-à-vis third world nations. Whereas security threats in some parts of Asia and most of Africa tend not to affect vital U.S. interests, threats in the Caribbean Basin do. In the Caribbean Basin, threats to a given nation's stability might be caused not always by deteriorating socioeconomic conditions or by Soviet-Cuban interference but by coup attempts organized by North American gangsters, as in Dominica, or by bands of modern-day buccaneers, as in Barbados.

Therefore, we cannot separate diplomacy from force in the Caribbean Basin. Although exact recommendations cannot be given about how or under what circumstances force should be used, only extraordinary circumstances (such as those that existed in Grenada in October 1983) and the high probability of effecting a favorable outcome would be a justification for these means. The indirect application of force (military exercises, for example) is to be preferred in most instances. In peacetime and whenever prudent, the United States should continue to use indirect military force to further its foreign policy objectives, particularly regular and irregular bilateral and multilateral exercises in the Caribbean Basin and Central America. To be effective, joint military exercises and other forms of military activities in the Caribbean Basin and elsewhere require sensitivity to and consideration of the pride and self-respect of U.S. friends and allies. Responsible arms transfers and other forms of security aid to friendly third world nations (taking into account the reasonable security needs of each country and each country's record on human rights) are another option.

The Grenada experience suggests that one of the most complex challenges facing the United States is to counter the activities of Soviet junior partners such as Cuba, Vietnam, North Korea, and some of the East European countries. This has been the most serious security problem faced by the United States in the past decade. An important lesson of the Grenada experience is that the United States needs to develop an effective counterstrategy to multiply and intensify the constraints on the Soviets and their allies in strategic regions of the third world.

Inducements and pressures need to be exercised on the Soviet Union, Cuba, Libya, the Warsaw Treaty Organization nations, and other countries whose policies toward the third world purposely serve Soviet security and political interests. The indebtedness and other serious economic problems facing nations such as Cuba and Nicaragua may provide the United States with some opportunities to employ negative incentives to curb their revolutionary activities. Accordingly, the U.S. government should do its utmost to coordinate Western credit policies toward Cuba, Nicaragua, and other Soviet junior partners.

In addition to various forms of pressure and indirect use of force, the United States should not discourage allies (such as former Egyptian President Anwar Sadat) from actively pursuing policies aimed at hampering the subversive activities of Soviet allies. While exerting pressure on Soviet allies, we should also not discount proposals for negotiation when offered by regimes such as those in Nicaragua and

Cuba. We should, however, guard against naiveté. Given the Cuban and Nicaraguan expressed commitment to revolution, any negotiated solution must be based on reciprocity, verifiable agreements, and careful monitoring. Soviet and Cuban military ties with Nicaragua should be unacceptable and therefore nonnegotiable.

Occasional tactical differences persist between the Soviet Union and Cuba, as well as between various competing factions in a number of radical third world countries. Using new and imaginative tactics, the United States can act on existing and future tactical differences to undermine Soviet partnership policies. In some cases we might consider furnishing aid to insurgents fighting against recognized oppressive governments. Other means can be devised to co-opt non-Leninist insurgents who might otherwise develop close ties with the Soviet Union through Leninist elements in the region, such as Coard's group in Grenada or the Communist party of El Salvador, led by First Secretary Handal. Such a strategy might have been quite effective in both Nicaragua and Grenada before 1979.

The experience of Nicaragua and Grenada should have dispelled any existing misperceptions regarding socialist-oriented revolutions in the third world. We should neither exaggerate nor underestimate the ties of some of these revolutionaries with the Soviet Union and its allies. We must judge each revolution independently, distinguishing between Soviet-Cuban–fomented strife and revolutionary situations indigenous to third world countries.

No American foreign policy can be successful without the bipartisan support of the American people. Implementing policy over a period of time is difficult in the American political system. Effective implementation of policies recommended by the National Bipartisan Commission on Central America will require strong domestic support and enduring commitment, as will any effective U.S. counterstrategy to Soviet-Cuban involvement in the third world.

Every effort should be made to develop long-term policies for coping with the Soviet-Cuban threat to U.S. security interests. The Soviets and their allies place great importance on reaching and even influencing public opinion in the United States. Indeed, one of the captured documents in Grenada was a telephone book listing sympathetic media contacts and other useful persons in the United States.

Much has been written about the need to educate the American public concerning Soviet-American arms control and the strategic balance, but little has been done to generate public interest in revolutionary situations in the third world and Soviet-Cuban attempts to exploit them. It is up to U.S. government agencies and private organizations to foster more research and increase public awareness about third world revolutions as they relate to Soviet, Cuban, and allied proxy strategies and tactics.

It is also necessary to demonstrate to the American people how the Soviets try to reduce the U.S. capacity to respond to and challenge their strategy. A reduction in the U.S. capacity to respond has been achieved not only by the impressive Soviet military buildup of the last decade but also by indirect political maneuvering and propagandizing. These latter efforts are aimed at distorting the nature of local third world conflicts, presenting each as a new Vietnam and a menacing prelude to general war.

An extensive effort must be made to bridge existing divisions on these issues through the education of the American public. This will significantly promote the consensus building needed to implement and sustain long-term foreign policies intended to counter Soviet-Cuban strategy in the third world.

Notes

1. For the most convincing interpretation of this kind, see Richard Feinberg, "Central America: The View from Moscow," *Washington Quarterly*, vol. 5, no. 2 (Spring 1982), pp. 171–75.

2. Even sophisticated and well-prepared reports and policy papers like *Cuba's Renewed Support for Violence in Latin America* (Special Report no. 90) and *Strategic Situation in Central America and the Caribbean* (Current Policy no. 352), both published by the U.S. Department of State, Bureau of Public Affairs, Washington, D.C., December 14, 1981, did not adequately integrate Cuban strategy in the Caribbean Basin with that of the Soviets. (In 1983–85, the quality of U.S. government reports improved considerably.) The same was true of some otherwise good scholarly analyses. See, for example, Max Singer, "The Record in Latin America," *Commentary*, vol. 74, no. 6 (December 1982), pp. 43–49.

3. Feinberg, "Central America," p. 174.

4. *New York Times*, March 12, 1982.

5. It is interesting that Marx and Engels favored the United States in the war against Mexico in 1848. Later Marx wrote a very unflattering essay on Simón Bolívar, which was based on the recollections of the French soldier of fortune Ducoudrey Holstein. This negative evaluation of Bolívar colored Soviet writings on Latin America until the 1950s.

6. President Kennedy himself formed this impression while negotiating with Khrushchev in Vienna in 1961 after the Bay of Pigs invasion attempt. As James Reston, who interviewed Kennedy after the summit, reported: "Khrushchev had assumed, Kennedy said, that any American president who invaded Cuba with inadequate preparation was inexperienced and a president who then didn't use force to see the invasion through was weak. Kennedy admitted Khrushchev's logic on both points."

7. For a more detailed discussion of the formulation of Soviet-Cuban strategy, see Jiri Valenta, "The USSR, Cuba, and the Crisis in Central America," *Orbis*, vol. 25, no. 3 (Fall 1981), pp. 715–46.

8. An interview conducted by *Yomiuri Shimbun* (Tokyo), April 13, 1980, as reported in *Foreign Broadcast Information Service* [hereafter cited as *FBIS-USSR*], April 16, 1980. See also an analysis of candidate Politburo member and CPSU Central Committee Secretary Boris Ponomarev, "Joint Struggle of the Workers and National-Liberation Movements against Imperialism and for Social Progress," *Kommunist*, no. 16 (November 1980), pp. 30–44.

9. *TASS* (Moscow), July 12, 1960. For an elaboration of Soviet strategy, see M. F. Kudachkin, *Velikii Oktiabr'i Kommunisticheskie partii Latinskoi Ameriki* [The great October and Communist parties of Latin America] (Moscow: Progress Publishers, 1978). Soviet anti-imperialist strategy has also been put forward in numerous articles published in *Latinskaia Amerika* (Moscow) in the 1960s and 1970s.

10. See an important essay of Yu. N. Korolev, "The Timeliness of the Chilean Experience," *Latinskaia Amerika* (Moscow), September 1980, pp. 5–14 (author's emphasis).

11. U.S. Department of State, *Cuba's Renewed Support for Violence*, p. 3.

12. Feinberg, "Central America," p. 173.

13. Ibid.

14. Viktor Belenko, in John Barron, *MiG Pilot: Final Escape of Lieutenant Belenko* (New York: Readers' Digest Press, 1980), p. 65.

15. See *U.S. Naval Institute Proceedings*, May 1973, p. 351.

16. The Cuban dictator Fulgencio Batista had broken relations with the Soviet Union in 1952 after his *coup d'état*.

17. Figures on COMECON economic credits were reported by CANA (Bridgetown) on September 1, 1981, in *FBIS-Latin America*, September 2, 1981; and in Katushev's speech on Radio Havana, *FBIS-Latin America*, November 1, 1982.

18. Jimmy Carter, *Keeping the Faith: Memoirs of a President* (New York: Bantam Books, 1982), p. 480.

19. Rodriguez's statement was reported by Radio Madrid, April 7, 1982, *FBIS-Latin America*, April 8, 1982. Raul Castro's statement was reported in *Prela*, November 8, 1982.

20. For more extensive documentation of Soviet-Nicaraguan relations, see Jiri and Virginia Valenta "Sandinistas in Power," *Problems of Communism* (September–October 1985), pp. 1–28.

21. For more extensive documentation and a look at the Grenada documents themselves, see Jiri Valenta and Herbert Ellison, eds., *Grenada and Soviet-Cuban Policy: Crisis and the US/OECS Intervention* (Boulder, Colo.: Westview Press, 1986); and Jiri Valenta and Virginia Valenta, "Leninism in Grenada," *Problems of Communism* (July–August 1984), pp. 1–23.

22. Valenta and Ellison, *Grenada and Soviet/Cuban Policy;* and Valenta and Valenta, "Sandinistas in Power," p. 24.

23. Valenta and Valenta, "Sandinistas in Power," p. 25.

24. Valenta and Ellison, *Grenada and Soviet/Cuban Policy.*

25. Ibid., p. 12.
26. Ibid., p. 15.
27. *Notimex* (Mexico City), September 16, 1982.
28. An interview with Ascanio Villalaz, national executive member and second deputy of the general secretary of the Revolutionary Democratic party of Panama, by Felix Dixon, member of the People's party of Panama in the Soviet-sponsored *World Marxist Review* (Prague), vol. 23, no. 11 (November 1980), pp. 49–50. Dixon is the party's representative on the *World Marxist Review*.
29. In Torrijos's words, "We would have started our struggle for liberation, and possibly tomorrow the Canal would not be operating anymore." Carter, *Keeping the Faith*, p. 178.
30. *La Republica* (Panama City), October 16, 1981.
31. Foreign Minister Juan Amado III, *Critica* (Panama City), August 24, 1982.
32. *La Estrella de Panama* (Panama City), September 10, 1982.
33. See *El Diario de Caracas* (Caracas) October 16, 1984, p. 15.
34. U.S. Department of State, *Cuba's Renewed Support for Violence in Latin America*, p. 8; and *La Republica* (Panama City), February 7, 1982.
35. *La Nacion* (San Jose), May 9, 1981, and September 23, 1982. An interview with President Luis Alberto Monge, Radio Reloj (San Jose), April 6, 1982, *FBIS-Latin America*, April 7, 1982, p. 1; and *La Republica* (San Jose), August 21, 1985, p. 8.
36. Curiously, diplomats from the Communist countries left the embassy party en masse before the seizure, leaving the diplomats from other countries to be taken hostage. It appears that the Communists were warned beforehand. At least that is the impression of the former U.S. ambassador to Colombia Diego Asencio. See his and Nancy Asencio's *Our Man Is Inside: Outmaneuvering the Terrorists* (Boston: Little, Brown, 1982), p. 7.
37. *El Tiempo* (Bogota), February 21, 1982; *El Espectador* (Bogota), November 19, 1981; *Latin* (Buenos Aires), August 26, 1981, and November 1, 1980; and Bogota Radio Sutatenza Network (Bogota), October 10, 1981, *FBIS-Latin America*, October 21, 1980, p. F2.
38. V. Korionov, "El Salvador: The Struggle Sharpens," *Pravda*, December 30, 1981, p. 4; and Y. Korolyov, "El Salvador: The 'Hot Spot' in Latin America," *International Affairs* (1981), pp. 58–66.
39. U.S. Department of State, *Communist Interference in El Salvador*, Special Report no. 80, February 23, 1981.
40. For a more extensive discussion, see Jiri Valenta, "The USSR, Cuba and the Crisis in Central America."
41. Having carefully analyzed the white paper, we agree with Mark Falcoff that all errors therein—and several have been pointed out by critics—are irrelevant to the document's authenticity and its political significance. See Mark Falcoff, "The El Salvador White Paper and Its Critics," *AEI Foreign Policy and Defense Review*, vol. 4, no. 2 (1982), pp. 18–24. The Soviet and Cuban role in El Salvador was further confirmed by captured guerrillas who were trained in Cuba (*El Mundo* [San Salvador], March 20, 1981) and by American news-

papermen (*Washington Post*, September 21, 1983). A captured FMLN military plan described the "socialist countries of Nicaragua, Cuba, and the USSR" as the FMLN's "strategic rear guard." See Department of State, *News Briefing Intelligence Information on External Support of the Guerrillas in El Salvador* (August 8, 1984), app. A.

42. See Jorge Dominiguez's essay in A. Adelman and R. Reading, eds., *Confrontation in the Caribbean Basin: International Perspectives on Security, Sovereignty and Survival* (Pittsburg: Pittsburgh University Press), p. 165.

43. *El Mundo* (San Salvador), April 3, 1982.

44. Feinberg, "Central America," p. 172; and private interviews.

45. See a summary of the confession of Handal's deputy commander Hugo in *La Prensa Grafica*, September 5, 1985, pp. 12–28.

46. Not all FMLN propaganda efforts aimed at the U.S. public and Congress are skillful. This is suggested by an FMLN statement expressing "happiness" at the loss of the Challenger space shuttle in January 1986.

47. Rusland Tuchin, "Guatemala: Reign of Terror," *New Times* (Moscow), no. 14 (April 1980), pp. 9–10.

48. Antonio Castro and Guillermo Toriello, "Guatemala: A Step toward Unity," *World Marxist Review*, vol. 24, no. 3 (March 1981), pp. 66–68. Castro is a Central Committee Political Commission member of the party of Labor; for a report on the unification of the Guatemalan guerrilla movement, see AFP (Paris), December 11, 1981, *FBIS-Latin America*, December 14, 1981.

49. Milton R. Paredes, "Solidarity with Revolutionary Peoples," *World Marxist Review*, vol. 23, no. 8 (August 1980), p. 15; *La Prensa* (Tegucigalpa), September, 25, 1981; *Voz de Honduras* (Tegucigalpa), April 20, 1981, *FBIS-Latin America*, April 20, 1981.

50. *La Nacion* (San Jose), July 11, 1982; and the *Daily Telegraph* (London), September 15, 1982; an interview with Roberto Guillen, who before his defection served as deputy chief of military counterintelligence for the Ministry of Defense under the Sandinistas, in *Time*, January 24, 1983, pp. 46–51.

5
Cuba's Strategy in Exporting Revolution
Mark Falcoff

Although the relationship between Cuba and the Soviet Union since 1959 has been the source of considerable debate and controversy, few deny that the advent of the Castro regime has been one of the three or four most important events in the history of Soviet foreign policy. Unlike the puppet governments of East Germany, Poland, or the Baltic countries, the Castro dictatorship aligned itself voluntarily with the Soviet Union. In this sense it could be said that Cuba, alone of all the states in the Soviet community of nations, is a genuinely dependable Soviet ally. In addition, the acquisition of a Spanish-speaking client state—an opportunity lost with the collapse of the Second Spanish Republic in 1939—has opened vast cultural horizons to the Soviet Union; in some ways, it amounts to the linguistic equivalent of the acquisition of a warm weather port.

Because most Spanish-speaking states lie to the south of the United States and maintain with it a relationship at times heavily charged with acrimony, envy, and resentment, the Soviets have been able to introduce their own agendas under the guise of irredentism. More practically, the Cuban regime has acted as an important adjunct of Soviet political, diplomatic, propaganda, and intelligence activities in Latin America. It has also functioned as an active Soviet proxy in far-off theaters of war (in Angola and Ethiopia) and as the principal broker, with Moscow, of like-minded political forces and governments in the Caribbean region.[1] Fidel Castro himself has actively worked to push the "nonaligned" movement into "anti-imperialist" (that is, pro-Soviet) channels. In addition, for over twenty-five years the Soviet Union has incrementally developed a military position on the island of Cuba, "strengthening the image of Soviet power in an overall East-West context, reinforcing the impression of a Soviet counterweight to the United States in Latin America," and—what is perhaps most important—"potentially providing a physical capacity for Soviet access to other areas of the continent as well as to the United States."[2]

Theories of Revolution: Conflict and Convergence

Before 1959 Soviet commentators regarded Latin America as a "semi-feudal" region inevitably consigned to the U.S. sphere of influence. This perception was amply reflected in the actual conduct of Communist parties throughout the region, which was far from revolutionary. Typically, in each country the Communists labored to build broad fronts with "progressive" elements of the so-called national bourgeoisie, laying the presumptive groundwork for a confrontation with this same class at some later (higher) stage of economic and social development.[3] Operating from so primitive a base of social theory, these parties were ill-equipped to deal with many of the developments of postwar Latin America, and in some countries they paid dearly for their ignorance. In Chile, for example, having supported the election of President Gabriel González Videla (1946–1952), they found themselves promptly outlawed and driven underground, and in Argentina and Bolivia—two countries that experienced something akin to a social revolution in the 1950s—they found themselves firmly on the side of the counterrevolutionaries. But in countries like Mexico, Venezuela, and Guatemala (before 1954), even in Cuba itself, the popular-front strategy paid rich dividends, as it influenced the labor movement, education, the media, and the development of full-blown parties with a professionally trained bureaucracy. Without taking these facts into account, one simply cannot appreciate the influence of the Cuban revolution on Soviet thinking or the ambivalent attitude of entrenched Communist leaders throughout the hemisphere who were, perforce, required to rethink their strategies.

By their actions, and later by the explicit theories drawn to rationalize them, the Cubans challenged the two assumptions upon which Soviet thinking about Latin America had rested.[4] First, Castro and his confederates had apparently demonstrated that the "objective conditions" for revolution were present in all Latin American countries and that such tactical alliances as had been forged with non-Communist parties, movements, and governments were unnecessary when not counterproductive. Second, Castro's success in defeating a U.S.-backed exile expeditionary force convinced the Soviets they should abandon the "geographical fatalism" that historically had consigned the entire region to a position of extreme marginality in their strategic planning.

Since 1959 serious differences have arisen between Moscow and Havana over the degree to which the Cuban experience is immediately applicable to other Latin American countries and over what risks are worth running with the United States. But the increasing

Soviet commitment to the Cuban regime—in arms, credits, and strategic raw materials—strongly suggests that Moscow is in the Caribbean region to stay. There is no other way to explain the transfer of resources which, according to the most conservative estimates, amounted in the early 1980s to some $3 billion a year, approximately 25 percent of Cuba's gross domestic product and five times the present level of U.S. aid to all Latin American nations combined.[5] It requires no specialized knowledge of the current state of the Soviet economy to conclude that these contributions to the Castro regime are far from gratuitous.

What they indicate above all is a growing convergence of Cuban and Soviet policies and perceptions of the situation in Latin America. During the 1960s, Castro's insistence upon sponsoring guerrilla warfare in countries such as Venezuela, Colombia, Brazil, Argentina, and Peru (with whom the Soviets maintained or wished to maintain normal state-to-state relations) nearly broke the Cuban-Soviet alliance. But judicious application of Soviet economic pressure in 1967–1968, combined with the signal failure of Cuban-sponsored insurgencies on the ground, eventually brought Castro around; in 1968 he endorsed the Soviet occupation of Czechslovakia, and also the Brezhnev Doctrine, which asserts the right of the Soviet Union to define the limits of permissible behavior for Communist countries.

Since the mid-1970s, the center of theoretical gravity has moved somewhat back in the Cubans' direction. First, their role in Africa as proxy forces for the Soviets underlined their uniquely practical value on third world battlefields and as such increased Castro's leverage, both ideological and political, with the Kremlin. Second, the success of the Nicaraguan revolution in 1979, the New Jewel coup in Grenada, and the spectacular growth of the FDR-FMLN (the combined politico-military leadership of the Salvadoran guerrilla movement) in El Salvador 1979–80 all suggested that the Cuban perception of revolutionary opportunities in the Caribbean Basin had been far more accurate than the Soviets were inclined to think. Meanwhile, a shift in the international posture (or posturing) of a number of Latin American states within the context of the nonaligned movement gave Castro sufficient ideological cover to establish correct diplomatic relations with a number of countries, including those that in the past he had characterized as dominated by "oligarchical" governments—Venezuela, Colombia, Ecuador, Argentina, and Costa Rica. By 1980 the gap between the Soviets and the Cubans on matters of Latin American policy had, for all practical purposes, been closed.

Differences remain, of course. The Cuban objective in the Caribbean Basin and indeed in Latin America as a whole, is the creation of regimes in its own image and likeness. Castro sees himself as a latter-day Bolívar, destined to liberate the continent from North American "domination," indeed obligated to do so, not only to justify his own revolution, but also to prevent any alternative from challenging his fundamental assumptions. No doubt he would pursue this policy in any case; however, in the absence of Soviet assistance, it would constitute little threat to the United States or to Cuba's neighbors. The Soviets have a more cold-blooded attitude toward the region: while they would welcome the emergence of Leninist regimes, they would be satisfied with far less. For the moment their purposes would be served equally by "progressive" anti-American governments to whom no important commitments need be made, but who would offer them opportunities to legitimize their naval, maritime, and intelligence presence in the area.[6] Such regimes could be used to distract the United States from concerns elsewhere, opening, in effect, a "second front" in what they like to call America's "strategic rear."[7]

It is important not to exaggerate the practical significance of these differences. A long debate on whether Cuba is a Soviet puppet or pawn, or whether it acts independently, has already consumed far more scholarly energies than it deserves.[8] It is important for the short- and possibly mid-term future that Cuban and Soviet objectives be fully coherent, even if—as in El Salvador—Castro's efforts prove less than successful. One could even argue that in Central America conflict, rather than its definitive resolution, best serves Soviet interests, since the victory of revolutionary forces would probably confront Moscow with some hard decisions on the deployment of increasingly scarce resources.

Cuban-Soviet Military Links

Since 1960 the Soviet Union has donated more than $2.5 billion in arms to Cuba, much of it since 1975, when Moscow undertook to support a major modernization of all branches of Castro's armed forces. The effect of this program has been to transform a fundamentally defensive body into one with significant offensive capability, increasing airborne-trained forces to 3,000–4,000 troops and improving the Cuban army's airlift and sealift capability. Moreover, since January 1981, Soviet merchant ships have delivered some 66,000 tons of military equipment to Cuba, roughly five times the *annual* average for the previous ten years. Some have chosen to rationalize this support as a response to fear of invasion following the election of a conservative Republican administration in the United States, but is more likely part of a new five-year program of upgrading and replacement of exhausted stocks, which was already on the boards at the time of President Reagan's first inauguration. Nor can this development be separated from Cuba's active support of the new revolutionary regime in Nicaragua or the insurgency in El Salvador: substantial portions of materiel from these shipments are meant to replace items—particularly small arms and ammunition—already shipped to Central America.

The Cuban army is the largest in the Caribbean Basin and the second largest in Latin America after Brazil's, a country with roughly ten times Cuba's population. At this point it is also the only Latin American military institution to have participated since World War II in combat overseas, giving both its army and its air force personnel recent experience in operating many of the sophisticated weapons in their inventory. In particular, the Cuban air force is one of the largest and probably the best equipped in Latin America, boasting some 200 MiGs and two squadrons of Floggers; the MiG-23s have a capacity to operate throughout the Caribbean Basin, so that in Nicaragua, for example, they could be employed in either a ground attack or an air superiority role. They could have played a smiliar role in Grenada after the completion of the 9,000-foot runway there, had not the regime of Maurice Bishop come to an end in late 1983.[9]

The armed forces are among the most reliably pro-Soviet elements in the Cuban power structure. Armed Forces Minister Raúl Castro, the dictator's brother, has long been known as Moscow's man in Havana, and his views are reinforced by a cadre of officers who are graduates of the M. V. Frunze Military Academy in the Soviet Union. By 1972, some 275 Cubans had successfully completed training at this institution, and at this writing they hold most of the important posts in the military and administrative structure. The missile and radar bases are under their absolute control. It is not uncommon for the graduates of an elite military institution such as West Point to dominate an armed forces establishment; what is remarkable in the Cuban case is the degree to which those trained abroad have come to constitute their own political class. Unique, too, is the interpenetration of party and army. As Irving Louis Horowitz, arguably the leading student of the subject, has written, not even the Soviet Union has "so close an identification of party and military. Raúl [Castro] himself has provided the one hundred percent isomorphism between Communist party activities and Cuban military activities of the officer corps."[10]

The Soviet military presence in Cuba is not limited to proxies. At present it includes a ground forces brigade of 2,600 men comprising one tank battalion and three motorized rifle battalions as well as various combat support units. The Soviets have also stationed on the island a military advisory group of 2,000, an intelligence collection facility—the largest outside the USSR—and a complement of 6,000–8,000 civilian advisers and technicians. The combat brigade is a symbolic commitment to Castro, implying a readiness to defend Cuba if invaded and also presumptively raising for the United States the diplomatic and strategic costs of such a course. In all likelihood it provides security for Soviet personnel and key Soviet facilities, particularly the intelligence-gathering unit. And in the event of a power struggle within the Cuban leadership, the brigade is there to ensure the victory of the pro-Soviet faction, should the possibility of international realignment (or even neutralism) ever arise.[11] The military advisory group provides technical advice and training with sophisticated weaponry, and particularly MiGs, surface-to-air missiles, and FOXTROT submarines; some members are attached to Cuban ground units. The intelligence unit monitors U.S. military and civilian communications.

Cuba has also been the site of an extensive naval ship visitation program. Some twenty-one Soviet naval task groups have been deployed in the Caribbean since 1961, virtually all of them visiting Cuban ports. The most recent visit (April–May 1981) included a Kara-class cruiser, the largest Soviet combat vessel ever to visit the island. In addition, Soviet intelligence collection ships operating off the Eastern coast of the United States call there, as do hydrographic research and space-support ships operating in the region. Since 1975, Soviet Tu-95 Bear D reconnaissance aircraft have been deployed periodically to Cuba, generally during times of international tension or during U.S., NATO, or Soviet exercises. In addition, the Soviets have apparently sent a considerable number of their own pilots to augment Cuba's air defense during such periods as 1976 and 1978, when many Cubans were posted to Angola and Ethiopia. This allowed the Cuban Air Force to operate abroad without diminishing its capacity to fulfill its primary mission.

Cuban Contributions to Soviet Expansionism: Methodologies

During the early 1960s Cuba's insistence on replicating its own experience in the Sierra Maestra elsewhere in Latin America provoked serious tensions with the Soviet Union, divided the regime from the urban-based Latin American Communist parties, led to the island's expulsion from the organized community of American states and, most important, brought about the collapse of movements it sponsored in Venezuela, Peru, Argentina and Bolivia.[12] Since the late

1970s, however, the Cubans have devised a far more sophisticated approach to armed struggle. First, the distinction between urban and rural bases has been abolished; the Cubans have finally come to understand their own revolution (which in spite of assiduously cultivated myths was never exclusively rural), and the explosive potential of Latin American cities, one of whose characteristics is a plethora of adolescents of school-leaving age with quite literally nothing to do. Second, the Cubans have discarded the rigid ideological sectarianism that hindered their earliest efforts to export revolution; their front organizations have learned to incorporate a variety of non-Marxist, Catholic, and independent left groups without relinquishing control to them. Third and most important, they have devised a strategy of unification that has finally overcome the chief obstacle to the growth of Latin American Marxist movements—the tendency to splinter and divide along personalist and ideological grounds, or both.

The strategy of unification is a gradual one that may vary slightly according to circumstances. Its main lines are reasonably clear, however.[13] Havana first allies itself with a target country most nearly in tune with its (and Moscow's) ideological goals. Quite often such groups have already received Cuban training and equipment. Other formations or organizations are persuaded to come aboard (and to subordinate their leadership to a unified command, typically called a directorate) in exchange for an assured flow of arms, training, and intelligence, as well as an international "solidarity" network that reaches deep into Western countries.[14] In Nicaragua, the Cubans conducted their efforts through the Frente Sandinista de Liberación Nacional (FSLN); in El Salvador through the local Communist party (PCES), the Armed Forces of National Resistance (FARN), and the Popular Liberation Forces (FPL).

The most successful application of this strategy has been in Nicaragua. Though the FSLN had a long history of opposing the Somoza regime, it was but one of many such organizations and by no means the most numerous or broadly representative. Given its discipline, unity of purpose, and ready access to foreign assistance, however, it was well-situated to take advantage of the divisions among genuinely democratic forces and, after a final breakdown of communication between the FSLN and the dictatorship in 1978, to achieve hegemony over the forces of the opposition. Of critical importance, too, was the care the Sandinistas took to hide both their ties to Cuba and the Soviet Union and their Marxist-Leninist ideological commitments.[15] Even after victory, the Sandinistas masked the degree to which "unification" was achieved through manipulation, until complete control of the country could be established through a new army, police, and domestic surveillance apparatus, and also to secure as much financial aid as possible from the United States and Western countries.[16]

The same tactics were used under slightly different circumstances in El Salvador in 1979–80. There a democratic revolution had already overthrown the dictatorship of General Carlos Humberto Romero, but had failed to consolidate itself against forces of the extreme left and right. While the provisional government struggled to achieve some mastery of the forces of order and to enact sweeping social and economic changes in the face of considerable public resistance, the four main armed formations of the Salvadoran left met in Havana in May 1980. There, in exchange for (and as a precondition to) Cuban aid, these groups consolidated into a Unified Revolutionary Directorate (DRU). Later, a unified political propaganda front (the Democratic Revolutionary Front [FDR]) was established, with formal links to the Socialist International, to make the directorate's case for aid in Western Europe and to neutralize attempts by the Reagan administration to counter its challenge on the ground in El Salvador. Though a carefully planned "general offensive" by guerrilla forces in early 1981 failed to achieve its objective, for most of 1982 and 1983 the fate of El Salvador hung in the balance at the U.S. Capitol, where FDR operatives, allies, and sympathizers came within a hair of achieving their objective—a cutoff of U.S. military assistance to the beleaguered Salvadoran government.[17]

Central to the strategy of unification is deception—that is, the techniques used to successfully deny the ideological goals and external links of a revolutionary directorate. This deception is critical not only to disarm foreign opinion, but also to achieve what appears to be a genuine coalition between Marxist and non-Marxist elements in the target country. In the case of Nicaragua, for example, the critical moment in Sandinista fortunes came when firmly anti-Marxist elements of the opposition (including leaders of the business community) were finally persuaded to join them in 1979; this convinced many doubters, including a number of Latin American countries and finally the United States, to abandon Somoza. Deception allows the Soviet Union to maintain an apparent aloofness from developments in target countries, since the Cubans are willing to play a more active and visible role.[18] It also allows the Soviets to refuse to discuss Central American issues in the context of general East-West negotiations.[19]

Cuban Contributions to Soviet Expansionism: Resources

Institutional Capabilities. In 1974 the Americas Department of the Cuban Communist party was given responsibility for directing unification strategies.[20] Its director, Manuel Piñeiro Losada, is a former chief of Cuban intelligence and one of the most important party functionaries on the island. He coordinates the efforts of a wide range of agencies, including the armed forces, the intelligence services (DGI), and the Ministry of Interior (MININT), as well as various supporting elements. Representatives of the department are well placed in Cuban embassies abroad, particularly in the Caribbean, where they sometimes serve as ambassadors or chargés d'affaires. They also serve overseas as employees of the Cuban news agency, Prensa Latina, or Cubana Airlines.

Within Cuba itself, a network of guerrilla camps, including the party's Nico López Training School, offers instruction on guerrilla warfare, propaganda, and agitation to prospective revolutionaries. The military curriculum includes sabotage, explosives, military tactics, and weapons use. Since 1979, several hundred trainees at a time have come from El Salvador, Nicaragua, Guatemala, Costa Rica, Honduras, Colombia, Grenada, the Dominican Republic, and elsewhere in Latin America. The Cubans also operate training schools for their own nationals—carefully selected intelligence personnel selected for clandestine operations in Latin America, Africa, and the Middle East; there the instructors are not merely Cuban, but also Soviet, East German, and Czech. Other selected groups are trained in Libya and in some of the Eastern European countries.

Greater Manpower and Trained Resources. One of the paradoxes of the Cuban Revolution has been its overproduction of technicians and professionals who cannot be absorbed into the local economy, whose absorptive capacities have actually decreased since 1959.[21] The inability of the old regime to resolve this contradiction—in the view of some observers—is what imparted a peculiarly radical flavor to Castro's movement once in power.[22] In contrast, the present Cuban government deals with unemployment and underemployment by exporting skilled laborers and technicians to third world countries, an imperative that has grown all the more acute as the proportion of young adults in the population grows rapidly. In Africa, for instance, in addition to combat troops, tens of thousands of Cuban civilians operate as economic functionaries, administrative and political technicians, public health officials, teachers, and doctors. Some 6,000 of the doctors work in Nicaragua alongside the estimated 3,000 military and security personnel Castro has dispatched to that country. In Grenada, before the fall of the Bishop regime, some 800 Cuban construction workers were on the island helping to build, among other things, a new international airport, and another 100 Cuban technicians were in Suriname before being expelled in October 1983.

Greater Logistical Capabilities. Cuba still lacks sufficient transport aircraft to support long-range, large-scale troop movements and would have to turn to the Soviets—as they have in their African involvements—to achieve such capability. As noted earlier, in the Caribbean Castro has sufficient aircraft to transport large numbers of troops and supplies. Particularly important in this connection is the recent acquisition of AN–26 short-range transports. These planes are capable of airdropping troops in portions of Florida and Belize, Haiti, Barbados, and the Dominican Republic. If based in Nicaragua, the AN-26s could reach all of Central America in either a transport or an air-drop role. In addition, more than thirty smaller military and civilian transport planes, including those used in Angola, could fly troops and munitions to neighboring countries.

Increased Soviet and Bloc Cooperation. The most important recent development in Cuban and Soviet overseas activities, particularly in the Caribbean Basin, has been the orchestration of bloc support for revolutionary movements and regimes. Thus, after the arrival of the first high-level Nicaraguan delegation to the USSR and the establishment of party-to-party relations with the CPSU, the FSLN concluded similar accords with East Germany, Bulgaria, and Czechoslovakia. Shortly after that, East German police and intelligence advisers showed up in Nicaragua alongside their Cuban and Soviet counterparts. Likewise, after a party-to-party agreement was reached between the CPSU and the victorious New Jewel Movement in Grenada, similar accords were reached with East Germany, Bulgaria, and North Korea. The captured documents of Grenada indicate that if concrete economic assistance from this quarter was extremely meager, some $40 million in assorted munitions, military equipment, uniforms, and training materials was in the process of being delivered to the Bishop government from the Soviet Union, Cuba, and North Korea.

Access to Other Global Resources. The Cubans have acted in some ways as a broker between the Soviet Union and its allies on one hand and revolutionary forces and governments in the Caribbean Basin on the other. Captured documents assembled with the State Department White Paper, as well as those uncovered in Grenada, show how Havana provided entrees for the Salvadoran FMLN-FDR in bloc embassies in Mexico City and in the Soviet Union itself, and from there in Vietnam, Ethiopia, Libya, and to other covert sources of assistance.[23] The Cubans were also of critical importance in orienting Grenadians to the labyrinthine world of international organizations, particularly to the Socialist International.[24] In Nicaragua, Libya has extended economic assistance and supplied Managua with military equipment; and the Palestine Liberation Organization (PLO), which provided "volunteers" to fight in Sandinista ranks during the civil war, has provided pilots and mechanics for the Nicaraguan Air Force.

Cuba's Role: The Case of Nicaragua

Though many countries contributed to the overthrow of Nicaraguan dictator Anastasio Somoza in 1979, the Cubans undoubtedly maintained the closest relationship with the FSLN. Havana forged the critical unity agreement among the various leftist factions (much as Castro was to do later in El Salvador) and provided the arms that tipped the military balance in the final months. Once the new regime was installed, Cuban diplomats, intelligence agents, military officers, and assorted political operatives assumed a major role in the consolidation of power. According to Miguel Bolaños Hunter, a former counterintelligence officer for the Sandinista regime, the present director of Nicaraguan intelligence is actually a Cuban who goes by the *nom de guerre* of Renán Montero, under whose direction both Cuban and Soviet operatives function in something approaching a tandem relationship. "In the counterintelligence unit where I worked," he stated, "there are two Soviets and a Cuban advisor. There can be at least seven to ten Cubans at any given time; the Soviets only come occasionally to review and brief the F-2 section," that is to say, the division responsible for surveillance of foreign embassies. In the same document he reported that some seventy Soviet advisers were involved in all aspects of Nicaraguan state security, along with four hundred Cubans (as well as forty to fifty East Germans and twenty to twenty-five Bulgarians). The structure of the new security system, including its methodology, has been lifted almost without alteration from Cuban and Bulgarian handbooks, and the Soviets have built a school for state security in Nicaragua.[25]

The Cuban presence is most apparent, however, in the military establishment. There are some 3,000 Cuban soldiers (not counting high-level advisers) presently in Nicaragua and a covert team of some 2,000 soldiers working as technical advisers, building roads, and handling heavy machinery. Much of this effort goes toward training recruits to the new army and developing all aspects of army security and defense. The Cubans are also instructing the Nicaraguan soldiers in the use of a plethora of Soviet weapons, which they and Moscow have unloaded on Managua since 1979, including bazookas, machine guns, mines, and handguns, as well as "Katsuka" rocket launchers and .45 caliber recoilless rifles, 100 Soviet tanks, armored transport vehicles, artillery, and heat-seeking SAM-7 missiles.[26]

Cuba's primary influence on Nicaragua is, of course, political. Between the two regimes there is, as Antonio Jorge has written, "a noticeable convergence in ideological persuasion, structures, modus operandi, and even in intangibles such as political and revolutionary style," so that in the end an "intense political-ideology affinity and shared *Weltanschauung* will finally impose itself."[27] Cuba represents the successful transition of a Hispanic-American country from a client-state of the United States to a similar relationship with the Soviet Union, a consummation that from many points of view is the desideratum of the Nicaraguan leadership. That this imposes a special role upon Cuban advisers in Managua is not, therefore, to be wondered at.

Cuba's Role: The Case of Grenada

The capture of a huge cache of documents relating to the rule of the New Jewel Movement in Grenada has permitted an even more thorough evaluation of the Cuban role in "revolutionary" praxis in the Caribbean.[28] The documents illustrate that the Cubans were active in setting up "parallel" organizations to compete with established trade unions, farmers' associations, youth and women's groups; to provide military training; to ease access to international organizations and the non aligned movement; to funnel economic and military aid from the Soviet bloc; and most important, to provide guidance in dealings with the Soviet Union.

Of particular importance was the Cuban role as advocate for the Grenadians in the highest circles in Moscow. From the lengthy reports sent back by W. Richard Jacobs, Maurice Bishop's ambassador to the Soviet Union, it is clear that the Soviets were reluctant to make commitments to Grenada beyond their power to fulfill them and had only responded, he wrote, "because Cuba has strongly championed our cause."[29] Grenada's relations with Cuba were thus roughly similar to those of Castro with the Soviet Union—indicative of a kind of subcontracting of Soviet influence in certain areas of the third world, where Moscow lacks experience, knowledge, and geographical proximity, but possesses a reliable surrogate.

Cuba's Role: Nonrevolutionary States

The autonomous aspects of Cuban foreign policy—those that do not appear to respond, at least immediately, to Soviet influence or interests—are apparent in Castro's relations with Caribbean governments, which by no stretch of the imagination could be regarded as revolutionary. Probably the best example is Michael Manley's Jamaica from 1976–1980, where the socialist aspects of the regime were more apparent in rhetoric and international posturing than in substance, and where the Cuban presence was apparent largely in economic and technical assistance projects (agriculture, tourism, sports, and so forth). A similar policy was followed with Forbes Burham's Guyana, where the links were principally commercial (agreements to purchase rice, lumber, and other goods in exchange for Cuban assistance through trained personnel to health and education programs). Both Jamaica and Guyana tended to sacrifice the interests of local Communist parties that had little chance of coming to power in order to break out of diplomatic isolation in the region and also to allow foreign policy to be guided by a curious zero-sum notion of Cuban–U.S. relations. As Jorge notes, in the Caribbean region the Cubans are prepared to do business with any regime that declares itself to be anti-American, "informed by the principle that any net loss inflicted on the United States automatically constitutes a gain for Cuba." What Castro seeks to do, he adds, "is to multiply the geographical loci of confrontations with the United States in the hopes of creating new allies and simultaneously debilitating its main adversary."[30]

Future Prospects

It seems highly unlikely that at any point in the foreseeable future the Cuban regime will redefine its international mission in terms different from, or incompatible with, the Soviet Union's. This is true not only for simple reasons of economic necessity, but also because Castro and his associates are highly ideological and call upon Marxism-Leninism to explain and justify the entire course of Cuban history since 1959. Questioning their relationship with the Soviet Union would be tantamount to questioning the Cuban revolution itself, since the only concrete accomplishment Castro can point to over twenty-five years is international realignment. Whether his successors will define their nation's destiny in these terms or feel free to act upon their changed perceptions remains to be seen.

For the Soviet Union, the special relationship with Cuba imposes serious and weighty economic obligations, but if twenty-five years and $4 billion have not caused them to rethink their priorities, it is difficult to imagine under what circumstances they might do so in the future. A more interesting question is the degree to which the Soviets might be willing to assume a similar obligation with respect to Nicaragua or some other client-state in Latin America. In the past those who wished to minimize the security threat of Marxist regimes insisted that the Soviets could not afford "another Cuba," and perhaps indeed they cannot, at least on the terms known to conventional bankers. Yet their willingness to provide 45 percent of Nicaragua's petroleum (requiring an annual extension of some $250 million in credit) does raise questions about how Moscow goes about making cost-benefit analyses. Moreover, as measured by the degree to which Western countries can be persuaded to subsidize such regimes, Soviet resources seem to be less thinly stretched. This may explain why, among other things, Castro reportedly advised the Sandinistas after their victory not to alienate the United States and why he challenged Washington to provide the new revolutionary government with large amounts of economic aid.

No doubt for the United States Cuba is a bigger problem than is the Soviet Union in Latin America and particularly in the Caribbean Basin. This is so because public perceptions of the Soviet threat generally are well developed in the United States; the Cuban threat, less so. To comprehend the sophisticated way the Soviets develop and use proxy assets requires more study than most ordinary citizens can take the time for, even if they are careful readers of the quality press. And, of course, the Cubans' genuine wish to do what they are doing creates an aura of **independence** and even quasi-legitimacy to their actions. In addition, Castro's repeated offers to American journalists to settle his differences with the United States—which, however, discount from the very start any serious consideration of the outstanding foreign policy and security issues that divide us—impart an element of great confusion to the discussion of U.S. Cuban policy.

Notes

1. Mark Falcoff, "Bishop's Cuba, Castro's Grenada: Notes toward an Inner History," in Herbert Ellison and Jiri Valenta, eds., *Soviet and Cuban Strategy After Grenada* (Lexington, Mass.: D. C. Heath, 1985), pp. 67–76.

2. Morris Rothenberg, "Latin America in Soviet Eyes," *Problems of Communism* 32, no. 5 (September–October 1983): 1–18.

3. Rollie Poppino, *International Communism in Latin America: A Brief History of the Movement* (Glencoe, Ill.: Free Press, 1964).

4. Of course, these theories were not fully descriptive of the events

themselves. Wrapped in a mythological mantle, they proved a poor guide for others in the late 1960s. See Luigi Einaudi, "Changing Concepts of the Cuban Revolution," Rand Corporation Paper, 1966.

5. Jiri Valenta and Virginia Valenta, "Soviet Strategies and Policies in the Caribbean Basin," in Howard J. Wiarda, ed., *Rift and Revolution: The Central American Imbroglio* (Washington, D.C.: American Enterprise Institute, 1984), p. 213. (See chap. 6.)

6. Ibid., pp. 204–11.

7. R. Bruce McColm, "Central America and the Caribbean: The Larger Scenario," *Strategic Review* 11, no. 3 (Summer, 1983): 28–42.

8. The best summary of different views is Robert A. Pastor, "Cuba and the Soviet Union: Does Cuba Act Alone?", in Barry B. Levine, ed., *The New Cuban Presence in the Caribbean* (Boulder, Colo.: Westview Press, 1983).

9. U.S. Department of State, Bureau of Public Affairs, "Cuban Armed Forces and the Soviet Military Presence" Special Report No. 103, August 1982.

10. "Military Origins and Outcomes of the Cuban Revolution," *Armed Forces and Society* 1, no. 4 (August 1975) and 3, no. 3 (May 1977). See also Marta San Martín and Ramón E. Bonachea, "The Military Dimension of the Cuban Revolution," in Irving Louis Horowitz, ed., *Cuban Communism*, 5th edition (New Brunswick, N.J.: Transaction Books, 1984).

11. Doubtless the Soviets have learned from their experiences in Egypt and Peru, where there was no such force present to protect their investment.

12. The *foco* theory of a peasant-based guerrilla insurgency is discussed in Einaudi, "Changing Concepts of the Cuban Revolution."

13. "Cuba's Strategy of Unification at Work," in *Western Hemisphere Security: The Latin American Connection* (Pittsburgh, Pa.: World Affairs Council of Pittsburgh, 1983).

14. For some notion of how the Soviets assist such groups internationally, see the document book released with the State Department White Paper, *Communist Interference in El Salvador,* U.S. Department of State, Special Report No. 80, February 23, 1981. Of particular interest also is the diary of a trip through the United States by Salvadoran Communist functionary Shafik Handal, described in Mark Falcoff, "Central America as a U.S. Domestic Issue," in Wiarda, ed., *Rift and Revolution,* pp. 369–70.

15. A recent study establishes beyond reasonable doubt that at no point did the Sandinistas seriously consider abandoning their ideology or modifying it in meaningful ways. They modified only some of the methods to disguise its fundamental nature. David Nolan, *The Ideology of the Sandinistas and the Nicaraguan Revolution* (Coral Gables, Fla.: Institute of Inter-American Studies, University of Miami, 1984).

16. These developments led to a massive defection of many leaders whose organizations had been "unified." This was predictable. Less predictable (and also less easy to explain), was the continued flow of Western aid in the face of patent betrayal of the Sandinistas' earlier declared principles.

17. Falcoff, "Central America as a U.S. Domestic Issue."

18. "Cuba's Strategy of Unification."

19. Robert Hunter, "Strategy for Central America," in *U.S. Policy for Central America: Consultant Papers for the Kissinger Commission*, special issue of the *AEI Foreign Policy and Defense Review* 5, no. 1 (1984): 61–70.

20. For a more general discussion, see Edward González, "The Cuban and Soviet Challenge in the Caribbean Basin," *Orbis* (forthcoming).

21. *World Development Report, 1981* (full citation to come)

22. James O'Connor, *The Origins of Socialism in Cuba* (Ithaca, N.Y.: Cornell University Press, 1970).

23. *Communist Interference in El Salvador.*

24. Falcoff, "Bishop's Cuba, Castro's Grenada."

25. "Inside Communist Nicaragua: The Miguel Bolaños Transcripts," Heritage Foundation *Backgrounder*, no. 294 (September 30, 1983).

26. Ibid., and Morris Rothenberg, "The Soviets and Central America," in Robert S. Leiken, ed., *Central America: Anatomy of Conflict* (New York: Pergamon Press for the Carnegie Endowment, 1984), pp. 131–49.

27. Antonio Jorge, "How Exportable Is the Cuban Model? Culture Contact in a Modern Context," in Levine, *The New Cuban Presence in the Caribbean*, pp. 211–22.

28. The most useful version is Paul Seabury and Walter A. McDougall, *The Grenada Papers* (San Francisco, Calif.: Institute for Contemporary Studies/ICS Press, 1985).

29. "Grenada-Soviet Relations: A Summary, 7/11/83," in *The Grenada Papers*, pp. 196–216.

30. Jorge, "How Exportable Is the Cuban Model?," p. 212.

6
Revolutionary Movements in Central America: The Development of a New Strategy

Ernest Evans

Introduction

The makers of American foreign policy have always had considerable difficulty in formulating effective policies to deal with revolutionary change in other countries. To be sure, responding to revolutionary change is a difficult foreign policy problem for any country, but in the case of the United States the difficulties inherent in this problem are magnified by a key characteristic of American political history. Since the end of the period of the Civil War and Reconstruction (1861–1877) the major issues in the American political system have been dealt with through procedures such as elections, lawsuits, demonstrations, and lobbying: that is, by procedures that do not directly involve the use of violence (though there can be and usually are acts of violence that are the indirect result of such procedures, such as the violence directed against many civil rights workers in the South in the 1960s). Put differently, in the past century there has not been very much explicitly political violence in the United States. Moreover, what political violence there has been has generally been "pro status quo" violence—violence against movements, such as the labor movement, the civil rights movement, and the Socialist party, that are attempting to make changes in the social, economic, and political structures of American society.[1]

A country such as the United States, which has had very little revolutionary violence in its own recent political history, will inevitably have major difficulties in understanding revolutionary change anywhere else in the world. In the specific case of revolutionary change in Latin America, this general lack of understanding is reinforced by a widespread lack of knowledge on the part of most Americans of the history, politics, and culture of Latin America.

The United States has been, therefore, poorly prepared to respond to the problems created for its foreign policy by the violent upheavals in Central America that began to take place in the late 1970s. For example, the merits of U.S. policy toward the Nicaraguan revolution of 1978–1979 have been hotly debated, but virtually all analysts of this policy would agree that the United States had a poor understanding of the major groups involved in the revolution and of the dynamics of the revolutionary process. Specifically, when the revolution began, the United States overestimated Somoza's strength and underestimated that of the Sandinistas; after it realized the weakness of Somoza's government, it overestimated the chances of creating a moderate (that is, non-Sandinista, non-Somoza) government; and in the final stage of the revolution it overestimated its ability to force the Sandinistas to moderate their proposed government and political program.[2]

The purpose of this article is to try to clear up some of the confusion and misunderstanding concerning contemporary revolutionary movements in Central America. The central arguments that will be developed in this article can be summarized as follows: The current revolutionary movements in Central America are significantly different from the earlier generation of Latin American revolutionary movements. The time frame of this earlier generation was 1960–1977. These earlier movements either were Guevarist in their strategy (that is, the "foco" theory) or were pursuing a strategy of urban terrorism. The new wave of revolutionary movements is pursuing a different strategy for seizing power. This new strategy has profound implications for the way that the revolutionaries engage in guerrilla warfare and terrorism, for the violence and terrorism engaged in by both the revolutionaries and the pro-status quo forces in the region, and for the ability of the United States to influence the course of events in Central America.

The Earlier Generation of Revolutionary Movements

The victory of Fidel Castro's guerrillas in Cuba in 1959 led to a number of attempts to duplicate his revolution elsewhere in Latin America.[3] In 1962–1964, radical groups in Venezuela tried unsuccessfully to overthrow the government of Rómulo Betancourt. In Peru in 1962–1965, there were a series of uprisings in rural areas that had to be put down by the Peruvian military. Guerrillas in Guatemala in the 1960s launched several unsuccessful campaigns in an effort to overthrow the Guatemalan government.[4]

The death of Che Guevara and the destruction of his guerrilla foco in Bolivia in 1967 was a major turning point for revolutionary movements in Latin America.[5] Guevara's defeat, together with the earlier defeat of rural guerrillas in Argentina, Brazil, Colombia, Guatemala, Peru, and Venezuela, convinced many revolutionaries that the countryside was not the best arena for revolutionary movements. The result was a shift toward urban guerrilla warfare.

The results of these urban guerrilla campaigns were often spectacular. In 1969, the U.S. ambassador to Brazil was kidnapped by Brazilian terrorists. In Uruguay, the Tupamaro guerrillas became world-famous because of a series of widely publicized political kidnappings and assassinations. In Argentina, the various urban guerrilla movements became so powerful that when the military took power in 1976, the country was in a state of civil war.

Yet these urban guerrilla movements also ended in failure. The Brazilian military successfully crushed the urban guerrillas in the early 1970s. In Uruguay, the military successfully destroyed the Tupamaros in an intensive campaign in the spring and summer of 1972. In Argentina, the military was able to destroy the urban guerrillas within two years of taking power.[6]

In assessing the reasons for the failure of the rural and urban guerrillas of the period 1960–1977, it must be remembered that the failures of these movements were not due entirely to their own mistakes. To a considerable degree, these movements failed because the governments that they were up against were more efficient, better prepared, and more determined than was Batista's government in Cuba. Put differently, the governments of Latin America and the U.S. government *also* learned certain lessons from the Cuban Revolution. And (like the losing side in many wars) they were often far more perceptive in assessing the lessons of the Cuban Revolution than the revolutionary movements of Latin America were.[7]

There can be no doubt, however, that the revolutionaries of the period 1960–1977 made a number of major mistakes. Before analyzing these mistakes, it is necessary to understand that the errors of these revolutionary movements stemmed from the pervasive belief among Latin American revolutionaries that Latin America was "ripe for revolution"—that is, that the oppressed classes in Latin America (peasants, workers, and the urban and rural poor) were ready and eager to support revolutionary change and that the ruling classes were divided and demoralized and hence incapable of halting the revolutionary wave that would soon sweep through Latin America.

The assumption that Latin America was soon to be radically transformed shows up repeatedly in manifestoes by revolutionary movements and statements by guerrilla leaders. In its first manifesto in February 1963, the Venezuelan FALN (Armed Forces of National Liberation) stated: "The situation is ripe and there should not be a moment's delay in bringing together all patriots. . . ."[8] In Peru, Hugo Blanco, a radical who was organizing peasants in the countryside, wrote a letter to friends in 1962 in which he stated: "I am writing to you with the happiness the combatant feels as he sees that triumph in the war is near after fighting in a hundred battles."[9] A 1965 communiqué by the Peruvian MIR (Movement of the Revolutionary Left) stated: "The armed MIR calls on all sectors of the people to fight. Victory is ours. The guerrillas are spreading. Armed fighting is sweeping the country. Liberation is at hand."[10] In 1964 the Guatemalan group MR13 (Revolutionary Movement of November 13) issued a declaration which began: "The year 1965 will be of great importance. The Guatemalan Socialist revolution will make an enormous leap forward. The conditions for it exist and are mature."[11]

The assumption that revolutionary change was imminent in Latin America led to five major errors on the part of the rural and urban guerrillas:

1. There was a lack of emphasis on building popular support. Since it was felt that popular support for the guerrillas already existed, the guerrillas put little emphasis on efforts to mobilize and organize the population. Instead, the guerrillas assumed that all that was needed to mobilize popular support was for the guerrillas to launch their campaigns against the established governments. As Che Guevara says at the beginning of his book *Guerrilla Warfare:*

> We consider that the Cuban Revolution contributed three fundamental lessons to the conduct of revolutionary movements in America. They are:
>
> 1. Popular forces can win a war against the army.
> 2. *It is not necessary to wait until all conditions for making revolution exist; the insurrection can create them.* [Emphasis added.]
> 3. In underdeveloped America, the countryside is the basic area for armed fighting.[12]

In his "Minimanual of the Urban Guerrilla," Carlos Marighella stated:

> The rebellion of the urban guerrilla and his persistence in intervening in public questions is the best way of insuring

public support of the cause we defend. We repeat and insist on repeating: *it is the best way of insuring public support.* As soon as a reasonable section of the population begins to take seriously the action of the urban guerrilla, his success is guaranteed. [Emphasis in original.][13]

When the Peruvian MIR launched its campaign in 1965, it issued a communiqué which closed with the following sentence: "What today is a spark, tomorrow will be a fire which will consume all false patriots, all liars, all hired thugs, all the torturers, all the hypocrites, all those who are behind the crimes and abuses our people have suffered."[14]

Put differently, these rural and urban guerrillas had a "militaristic" strategy. Because they assumed that popular support for them already existed, they concentrated their efforts and energy on the strictly military aspects of guerrilla warfare. In both Che Guevara's *Guerrilla Warfare* and Marighella's "Minimanual" the great bulk of the texts deal with the tactics and technical aspects of guerrilla warfare (care and use of weapons, staging ambushes, organization of guerrilla units, logistics, and so forth). As Marighella put it quite forcefully in the "Minimanual": "The urban guerrilla's reason for existence, the basic condition in which he acts and survives, is to shoot."[15]

2. Little effort was made to win support from existing political organizations (parties, unions, peasant movements, and so forth). The guerrillas regarded such organizations as lacking in any genuine popular support and as led by opportunistic leaders whose loyalty and commitment could not be counted on; and hence they saw no advantages in making an effort to get the support of such groups. Camillo Torres, a Colombian priest who had been radicalized, made strenuous efforts in 1965 to put together a broad coalition of student groups, unions, and left-wing political movements and parties to provide political support to the guerrillas fighting against the government of Colombia. Torres's efforts ended in failure, in large part because so many of the guerrillas saw no need for such a coalition.[16] One Colombian guerrilla group issued the following attack on Torres's United Front:

> A United Front cannot be set up by making flimsy alliances between the discredited heads of factions with revolutionary aspirations, nor by means of simply stirring up the masses, nor by defining as the masses sectors other than poor workers and peasants who attract other sectors by their seriousness and numbers. Working for alliances between individuals and not making a serious attempt to organize an alliance of the exploited classes which is the essence of the

United Front will only stimulate the ambitions and pretensions of many of the present unscrupulous and opportunistic leaders of left-wing factions.[17]

In his book *Revolution in the Revolution?* Régis Debray argued that while it was true that the Communist parties of Latin America were not willing to mobilize the population to support revolutionary change, this lack of support by the local Communist parties was not an insurmountable obstacle to successful revolutions. He pointed out that in Cuba Castro's and Guevara's guerrilla movement had been able to win despite the fact that it did not get any support from the Cuban Communist party until quite late in the struggle against Batista.[18]

In the diary he kept during his campaign in Bolivia, Debray's friend Che Guevara recorded his lack of concern at the refusal of the Bolivian Communist party to support his guerrilla movement: "The party is now taking up arms against us and I do not know what it will lead to, but it will not test us, and it may in the long run prove beneficial (I am almost certain of this)."[19]

3. The guerrillas adopted military strategies that isolated them from the population. The rural guerrillas of the 1960s were basically pursuing the strategy of the foco. As expounded by writers like Debray and Guevara, the foco theory held that the guerrillas should base themselves in a remote part of the country, gradually build up their military strength, and then come "down from the Sierra Maestras" and engage and defeat the regular army in a series of conventional battles.[20] (This theory was based on a very selective account of the events of the Cuban Revolution, an account that ignored the role played by the urban insurgents in the Cuban Revolution and instead gave virtually all of the credit for the victory over Batista to Castro and Guevara.)

A major problem with the foco strategy was that the remote regions where the guerrillas would try to establish focos were usually thinly populated (and often the population that was there was culturally very different from the guerrillas) and often quite inaccessible to the rest of the country. The result was that the guerrilla foco had enormous difficulties in expanding because it could not easily recruit from the local population, nor could it count on getting many recruits or supplies from the populated regions of the country.

The problems with the foco strategy often led to a vicious circle for the guerrillas. Because the guerrillas were seen as weak and hence as not likely to win, they had difficulty getting popular support, which would further erode their chances of success. In Guevara's Bolivian diary, he concluded each month with a summary of the progress of the campaign. The entries for July, August, and September (he was killed in October 1967) graphically illustrate the operation of this vicious circle:

> July 1967
> The most important characteristics are:
> 1. The total lack of contact [with other groups in the country] continues.
> 2. The lack of incorporation of the peasants continues to be felt. . . .
>
> August 1967
> The most important characteristics:
> 1. We continue without any contacts of any kind and without reasonable hope of establishing them in the near future.
> 2. We continue without any incorporation on the part of the peasants.
>
> September 1967
> The characteristics are the same as those of last month, except that now the army is showing more effectiveness in action, and the mass of the peasants does not help us at all and have become informers.[21]

The strategy of urban guerrilla war also resulted in isolating the revolutionaries from the population. An urban guerrilla group must operate in conditions of great secrecy. For the guerrillas to be known to too many people means that they are extremely vulnerable in the event of a major crackdown by the police and the military. For example, one of the reasons for the relative ease with which the Uruguayan military crushed the Tupamaros in 1972 was that in the previous year the Tupamaros had greatly expanded their membership and had built a number of sizable "people's prisons," weapons caches, and hiding places, thereby making it much more difficult to maintain secrecy. In other words, the Tupamaros were successful as long as they were a fairly small group that was isolated from the population; as soon as they tried to expand and break out of this isolation, they were quickly destroyed by the security forces.

The dangers of isolation from the population that are present in a strategy of urban terrorism and guerrilla warfare have been recognized by a number of major revolutionaries. In 1902, for example, Lenin wrote the following criticism of the terrorism carried out by the rival Socialist Revolutionaries: "No verbal assurances or invocations can disprove the unquestionable fact that modern terrorism as it is practiced by the Socialist Revolutionaries is not in any way linked with work among the masses. . . ."[22]

4. The guerrillas committed acts of terrorism that alienated public and international support. As Lenin's statement indicates, many revolutionaries have realized that terrorism is a tactic that if improperly applied can be counterproductive. In *Guerrilla Warfare,* Che Guevara stated:

> It is necessary to distinguish clearly between sabotage, a revolutionary and highly effective method of warfare, and terrorism, a measure that is generally ineffective and indiscriminate in its results, since it often makes victims of innocent people and destroys a large number of lives that would be valuable to the revolution.[23]

The terrorism practiced by Latin American revolutionaries frequently alienated the population from the guerrillas. For example, Abraham Guillen, a revolutionary theorist who wrote a book entitled *The Strategy of the Urban Guerrilla,* which was widely read in Latin America, argued that many of the acts of terrorism engaged in by the Tupamaros had cost them public support. He maintained, for example, that holding individuals for months in "people's prisons" merely served to convince the public that the Tupamaros were as capable of repression as was the government, that in executing hostages they had acquired the image of assassins, and that in demanding large ransoms for hostages they had acquired the image of a "political Mafia."[24]

The large number of diplomatic kidnappings engaged in by the urban guerrillas destroyed the chances of any significant international support for the revolutionaries. The countries whose diplomats were kidnapped were obviously not going to be sympathetic to the revolutionaries, and even those countries whose diplomats were not targeted could hardly be expected to be eager to support revolutionary movements that violated one of the key ground rules of international conduct—namely, the principle of the inviolability of diplomatic personnel.

5. Military recklessness was another major error. The rural and urban guerrillas often engaged in costly, counterproductive military operations because they were convinced that victory was imminent and hence that they should feel free to undertake very risky operations. After the defeat of guerrillas in Venezuela, one of the guerrilla leaders, Douglas Bravo, acknowledged that:

> From the military point of view, our most serious mistake was being too adventurous. Although we talked a lot about a prolonged, long-drawn-out war, at the time we were using shock tactics, as for a *coup.* We wanted to overthrow Betan-

court in a few hours, in one or two battles. This resulted in very far-reaching defeats, and prevented us from getting down to building a guerrilla army. We were throwing far too many forces into a hopeless struggle.[25]

Other revolutionary movements were equally reckless. The 1969 kidnapping of the U.S. ambassador to Brazil was a Pyrrhic victory for the Brazilian urban guerrillas. They undertook this kidnapping at a time when their organization was poorly prepared to survive intensive repression, and hence they suffered major reversals (including the death of Carlos Marighella) when the Brazilian government instituted harsh repressive measures in the aftermath of the kidnapping of the U.S. ambassador.[26] And the Tupamaros made a fatal mistake when they staged a series of spectacular assassinations in April 1972. These assassinations did not seriously damage the government or the military; what they did do was to provide the Uruguayan military with the rationale it needed to launch its all-out campaign against the Tupamaros. Soon after the assassinations, the parliament of Uruguay declared a "State of Internal War," thereby in effect giving the military the right to use "any means necessary" to crush the Tupamaros. By the end of the summer of 1972, the military had destroyed the Tupamaros.[27]

In sum, by pursuing policies that isolated themselves from both domestic and international support and by engaging in military strategies based on the delusion of a quick and easy victory, the rural and urban guerrillas in Latin America in the period 1960–1977 seriously eroded whatever chances they might have had to overthrow any of the governments that they were fighting against.

Contemporary Revolutionary Movements in Latin America

A number of catastrophic military defeats have been due to a tendency of militaries to "fight the last war"—that is, to assume that the sort of strategies, tactics, and military units that were successful in one conflict will be equally successful in the next conflict. After the brilliant military career of Frederick the Great, the Prussian military saw little reason to innovate, and this lack of any innovation was a major factor in its crushing defeat by Napoleon at the battle of Jena in 1806. In 1940, the French army felt that World War II would essentially be a repeat of World War I, and hence was totally unprepared for the sort of mobile armored warfare that the Germans unleashed against France in 1940. In 1943 at the battle of Kursk, the Germans themselves paid the price of the overconfidence born of their spectacular successes in 1939–1941. Failing to appreciate how much the Russians had improved their military capabilities since 1941, the German attack at Kursk resulted in massive losses that gravely weakened the German army.

Yet, although successful militaries often tend to "fight the last war," in many cases defeated militaries have been eager to innovate and try new ideas precisely because they do *not* want to "fight the last war." After the Prussian defeat at Jena in 1806, for example, there were a series of major reforms in the Prussian military. Karl von Clausewitz was called in to give a series of lectures designed to upgrade the Prussian army. These reforms produced a revived Prussian army that inflicted a series of defeats on Napoleon in 1813–1815. After the German defeat in World War I, the German military was significantly more open to suggestions for changes and reforms than was the French military; and hence it is not surprising that in 1940 the Germans were far more sophisticated in their use of tanks and aircraft than the French were.[28] (Not all of the French army was so unprepared; General De Gaulle had argued years before that France could be defeated by a nation using modern tank warfare.)

Revolutionaries are also inclined to "fight the last war." Specifically, there is a tendency among revolutionaries to try to duplicate in their own country the strategy that proved successful in another country. In 1919 and 1920, the German Communists staged a number of urban uprisings in an effort to duplicate the Bolshevik revolution of October 1917; social and political conditions in Germany, however, were quite different from those in Russia, and hence these uprisings failed.[29] In 1948, the Malayan Communists launched a guerrilla campaign in Malaya hoping to repeat the success of the Chinese Communists; here again the Communists were defeated because there were major social and political differences between Malaya and China.[30] At the time that they launched their campaign against Israel in the mid-1960s, the leaders of the Palestinian movement seriously underestimated the difficulties involved in destroying the state of Israel, because they modeled their strategy against Israel on that of the Algerian National Liberation Front (FLN) against the French. Hence, they were not sufficiently cognizant of the fact that in their struggle against Israel they suffered from many difficulties and problems that the FLN did not have in its struggle against France.[31]

Still, like military establishments, revolutionary movements are capable of learning from their own failures and from the failures of other revolutionaries. In China, Mao Tse-tung's strategy of peasant-based guerrilla warfare was adopted as the official strategy of the Chinese Communist party in the late 1920s after a series of unsuccessful urban uprisings made it clear that the Bolshevik strategy of concentrating on organizing among the urban proletariat would not work in the Chinese context.[32] In their post-mortems on their unsuccessful 1956–1962 guerrilla campaign in Northern Ireland, the leaders of the Irish Republican Army agreed that a key reason for their failure was a lack of support among the Catholic population of Northern Ireland. Hence, in 1969–1971 as they were laying the groundwork for their campaign to drive the British out of Northern Ireland, the Provisional IRA went to considerable lengths to build a significant base of support among the Catholic population of Ulster.[33] In planning his own revolution, Castro carefully studied the reasons for the overthrow of the Arbenz government in Guatemala. (Perhaps the single most important lesson he drew from Arbenz's downfall was that a revolutionary government must immediately destroy the old military and create a new revolutionary army, a policy he immediately undertook when he came to power in Cuba.)[34]

The changes in strategy on the part of contemporary revolutionary movements in Central America are in large part the outcome of a process of reassessment similar to that undertaken by a number of other revolutionary movements that have suffered repeated failure. In order to understand the changes in strategy that resulted from this process of reassessment, it is first necessary to discuss the specific case of the evolution of the strategy of the Sandinista movement in Nicaragua. Although this process of reassessment has been taking place elsewhere in Central America as well, the spectacular victory of the Sandinistas has made them, in effect, the new "model" for a successful revolution, and hence the debates on strategy among Central American revolutionary movements have been massively influenced since 1979 by the victory of the Sandinistas over Somoza.

At the time of the Sandinista National Liberation Front's (FSLN) victory in 1979, it had been in existence for eighteen years. During these years, the FSLN went through what can be called three "learning processes" whereby it gradually evolved the revolutionary strategy that led to its victory in 1979:

• *The heritage of Augusto Sandino.* The Sandinistas studied the political ideas and military tactics of Augusto Sandino in his campaign against the U.S. Marines in 1927–1933. Sandino was fundamentally a nationalist rather than a radical leftist, and hence he was willing to work with anyone who was opposed to the American military occupation. Moreover, Sandino was a shrewd guerrilla commander: After an early defeat in which he tried to storm a U.S.-held strongpoint, he adopted the classic hit-and-run tactics of guerrilla warfare. In other words, Sandino avoided two of the major mistakes of the

Latin American rural and urban guerrillas of the period 1960–1977—loss of popular support because of an extremely radical political program and military recklessness.[35]

- *The aftermath of Guevara's defeat in Bolivia.* The Sandinistas felt that one of the key lessons to be learned from Guevara's defeat in Bolivia was the disastrous consequences for a rural guerrilla movement lacking any support from the peasantry and not having any contacts with the urban areas. So in the period 1967–1974, they deemphasized military activities and instead concentrated on organizing among the urban and rural population.[36] In the rural areas the organizers were the Guerra Popular Prolongada (Prolonged Popular War, GPP); in the urban areas the organizers were the Tendencia Proletaria (Proletarian Tendency, TP).

- *Their own set of experiences.* The fact that by the late 1970s the Sandinistas had been an ongoing movement since 1961 and that there were individuals (such as Tomás Borge) who had been members of the movement since its founding meant that, unlike the earlier revolutionary movements, most of which were quite short-lived, many of the leaders of the Sandinistas had learned through personal experience the problems associated with various types of strategies and tactics. Tomás Borge, for example, recalled after the revolution that the FSLN's first attempt in 1963 to wage rural guerrilla warfare failed because of lack of proper political and military preparation: "We committed the error of moving into the zone without first undertaking preparatory political work, without knowing the terrain, and without creating supply lines."[37]

From these various learning experiences, the Sandinistas developed a strategy for taking power that differed quite markedly from the strategies pursued by the early Latin American revolutionary movements:

- The Sandinistas were quite cautious in their military operations. As was noted previously, after Guevara's disaster in Bolivia in 1967, they essentially pulled back from military operations and concentrated on building their rural and urban popular base. When it became clear that they did not have sufficient arms to prevail in the September 1978 insurrection, they withdrew from the urban areas to build up their military strength for their successful offensive in the spring and summer of 1979.[38]

- Although the core elements of the FSLN were quite radical, they felt that victory over Somoza required a broad coalition of organized support. The political program of the FSLN that was put forward during the insurrection demanded many far-reaching social and political changes, but it had little of the Marxist-Leninist ideology and rhetoric that was so pervasive in the statements and manifestoes of the earlier generation of rural and urban guerrillas.[39] Moreover, the Sandinistas went to considerable lengths to get support from organized groups such as unions, political parties, and professional associations. They did not ignore or belittle such groups the way the guerrillas of the period 1960–1977 had tended to do.

• The Sandinistas made strenuous efforts to get a broad array of international backing. The earlier generation of Latin American revolutionaries had tended to feel that support from non-Communist countries was unnecessary (since revolution all over Latin America was imminent) and undesirable (since the price of such support could be compromising the radical goals of their movements). The Sandinistas, on the other hand, felt that such broad international support was essential for two reasons. First, they realized that, given Castro's fear of provoking the United States and given his ongoing efforts to "normalize" his relations with Latin America, there were real constraints on his willingness to assist their movement.[40] Second, they felt that a major constraint against U.S. intervention against them would be if they were supported by a broad range of countries in Latin America.[41] Third, they believed that it was important to get as much support as possible from sympathetic groups in the United States; they felt that a badly divided American public would tend to immobilize U.S. policy toward Nicaragua.[42]

These efforts to secure international support paid off. The Sandinistas were actively supported by Costa Rica, Mexico, Panama, and Venezuela, as well as by Cuba. When in June 1979 the United States proposed that the Organization of American States (OAS) create a peace-keeping force for Nicaragua, the American proposal was not supported by a single other nation in the OAS.[43] In the United States the Sandinistas were supported by many Catholic organizations, by a number of the more liberal Protestant churches, and by many academics who specialized in Latin America. This support was reflected in the Congress: When in September 1978 a group of seventy-six congressmen sent a letter to President Carter calling on him to increase aid to Somoza, another group of eighty-six congressmen sent a letter to Secretary of State Cyrus Vance urging that all aid to Somoza be terminated.[44]

The two countries in Central America which currently have the largest revolutionary movements are El Salvador and Guatemala. In both countries, the effect of the "Sandinista model" is a very important factor in the sort of new strategies that these movements are pursuing. It must be recognized, however, that in both El Salvador and Guatemala the current revolutionary movements antedate the victory of the Sandinistas in 1979, and that the process of reassessment of strategy and tactics that went on among the FSLN also went on among the revolutionary movements in El Salvador and Guatemala. In other words, the modifications in strategy by these various revolutionary movements are not simply a result of slavishly imitating the Sandinistas. On the contrary, the various learning experiences that the Sandinistas went through have also characterized these other revolutionary movements. They are aware of certain key figures and events in their national histories, of the successes and failures of the various guerrilla campaigns of the 1960s and 1970s, and of the lessons that they have learned in the course of the guerrilla warfare campaigns that they have waged in recent years.

The combined effect of their own learning experiences plus the victory of the Sandinistas in 1979 have led the revolutionary movements in El Salvador and Guatemala to adopt a strategy of revolution that is broadly similar to that of the FSLN.

The first component of the strategy is military caution. The guerrillas in both El Salvador and Guatemala are much less likely to engage in the sort of military recklessness that characterized the earlier generation of revolutionary movements. Instead, many of these guerrillas are committed to a strategy of gradually building up their own strength while eroding that of the governments that they are fighting. For example, the largest of the guerrilla groups in El Salvador, the Popular Forces of Liberation—Farabundo Martí (FPL)—is pursuing a strategy it calls "prolonged people's war." (In adopting this strategy, the FPL was heavily influenced by the example of the Vietnamese revolution.)[45]

Like all armies, guerrillas can at times delude themselves that they are on the verge of victory and hence there is no longer any need to exercise restraint. In the war between the French and the Vietminh in Indochina, for example, the Vietminh inflicted some major defeats on the French in 1950 in the area of Vietnam just south of the Chinese border. Emboldened by this success, the Vietminh announced that they would soon drive the French out of Hanoi. In their attack on Hanoi in early 1951, the Vietminh were decisively defeated and suffered heavy losses. Their military forces were not yet strong enough to defeat the French in large-scale conventional battles. Another example of military overconfidence by a revolutionary movement was the so-called Battle of Algiers during the Algerian war for independence. In late 1956 the FLN launched a series of attacks against French targets in the city of Algiers. The initial results of this urban terrorism were spectacular; the French seemed to be on the verge of total defeat. The French reacted firmly, however: The French army was called into Algiers and given responsibility for restoring law and order; in a ruthless campaign the French succeeded in crushing the FLN urban terrorist network. The overconfidence of the FLN had led them to undertake an urban terrorist campaign when conditions were not yet ready for such a campaign.

Given this inherent tendency among revolutionary movements to develop delusions that they are on the verge of victory, it is not surprising that the contemporary generation of Latin American revolutionary movements occasionally abandons its policy of military caution. Witness, for example, the "Final Offensive" that the El Salvadoran guerrillas launched in early January 1981 in an attempt to defeat the government before the Reagan administration came into office. On balance, however, the contemporary revolutionary movements in Central America exercise much more caution and restraint in their military operations than did the early generation of Latin American revolutionaries.

The second component of the strategy of revolution is the building of broad-based opposition coalitions. In El Salvador the revolutionaries have tried very hard (not always with complete success) to build a broad, unified opposition coalition to the government of El Salvador. In April 1980 a number of unions, peasant organizations, and political parties that were opposed to the current government in El Salvador formed the Democratic Revolutionary Front (FDR). In October 1980 the various guerrilla armies formed the Farabundo Martí Front for National Liberation (FMLN); the military operations of this front are coordinated through the Unified Revolutionary Directorate (DRU). The FMLN and the FDR are linked by a seven-person diplomatic commission. The head of this commission is Guillermo Ungo of the Social Democratic National Revolutionary Movement (MNR).[46]

The Guatemalan revolutionaries have made similar attempts to build a broad opposition coalition. In January 1981 the major guerrilla organizations issued their first joint communiqué. The guerrillas have also made attempts to form alliances with unions, peasant organizations, student groups, and political parties.[47]

The third component of the strategy of revolution is international support. In addition to their ties to the Soviet Union and Cuba (which will be discussed later), the new generation of revolutionary movements has tried to get support from a number of nations and international organizations. The El Salvadoran MNR is that nation's member of the Socialist International (SI), and hence the leadership of the MNR has lobbied for support (with some success) among the other member parties of the SI. A number of these parties are now heading their governments: the ruling parties in Spain, France, Greece, Costa Rica, Austria, and the Dominican Republic are all members of the SI. Many Catholic clergy, religious, and laity from Central America have lobbied for support for the revolutionaries among Catholics in the United States, Latin America, and Western Europe.

In their campaign to get as much international support as possible, the revolutionaries in Central America have benefited from a series of reports by various human rights groups and humanitarian organizations that have been strongly critical of the governments of El Salvador and Guatemala. In 1982, for example, the American Civil Liberties Union (ACLU) and the Americas Watch Committee issued two reports on human rights in El Salvador that strongly criticized the human rights practices of the El Salvadoran government. Oxfam-America, a famine relief group, has published an unfavorable evaluation of the land reform program in El Salvador. Amnesty International has issued a number of quite critical assessments of the human rights record of the governments of Guatemala and El Salvador.[48]

A final respect in which the contemporary revolutionary movements in Central America differ from their earlier generation of revolutionary movements concerns their relationship with Cuba and the Soviet Union. In the late 1960s, Castro began to scale down his support of revolutionary movements in Latin America. This was partly because of a desire to concentrate on pressing domestic problems (in particular the weak Cuban economy) and partly because both Castro and his Soviet ally felt a need for Cuba to reduce its isolation in the hemisphere. So, without abandoning his support for revolutionary movements, Castro began according support for these movements a lesser priority than Cuba's domestic problems and the need to establish good state-to-state relations with other countries in the Western Hemisphere.[49]

This reduction of Cuban aid to Latin American revolutionaries was duly noted by the current revolutionary movements in Central America and significantly influenced their attitude toward receiving Cuban support. Specifically, the revolutionaries were quite willing to take whatever support Castro was willing to give them; what they were *not* willing to do is rely exclusively on Cuba (or any other country) as their only supporter. One point comes through quite graphically in Che Guevara's Bolivian diary—namely, the desperate position Guevara's foco found itself in once all chance of significant outside support was lost by the refusal of the Bolivian Communists to cooperate with him. So, although the contemporary revolutionary movements in Central America have received a significant amount of arms and training from Cuba, their dependence on Cuban support is less than was the case with the earlier rural and urban guerrillas of Latin America.[50]

The Soviet Union, in contrast to Cuba, has played a *more* important role with respect to the contemporary generation of revolutionary movements than it did with earlier generation of revolutionary movements. The Soviet hostility toward this earlier generation stemmed from four factors:

• Many of these revolutionaries were considered doctrinally unorthodox. Trotskyism has played a larger role in Latin American politics than in the politics of any region in the world, and hence it is not surprising that many Latin American revolutionary movements have been dogmatically Trotskyist or at least heavily influenced by Trotskyism. Many of the members of the revolutionary movements in Peru in the early 1960s were Trotskyists (including Hugo Blanco).[51] One of the major urban guerrilla groups in Argentina, the People's Revolutionary Army (ERP) was created by a group of Argentine Trotskyists.[52]

• The revolutionaries were often quite hostile to the local Communist parties, which they considered as fundamentally "reformist." Given that most of the Communist parties in Latin America are Moscow-line parties, the Soviets obviously were distrustful of movements that were hostile to these parties.[53]

• The Soviets were skeptical of the chances of success of the guerrillas. They were afraid that the only result of the violence by these guerrillas would be to bring very conservative, strongly anti-Communist governments to power that would repress the local Communist party and be hostile to the Soviet Union. In the period of the Allende government in Chile, for example, both the Soviet Union and the Chilean Communist party attacked the terrorism of the MIR (Movement of the Revolutionary Left) on the grounds (which, ultimately, proved to be quite correct) that such terrorism would lead to a military coup.[54]

• Finally, for reasons very different of course from those of the United States, the Soviets also desire to avoid "another Cuba." Specifically, as the Soviets told Allende quite bluntly, they have no desire to acquire another client state in the Americas that will require the sort of economic subsidies that Cuba needs.[55] Put differently, while the Soviets would like to have pro-Soviet revolutionary governments in the Western Hemisphere, their enthusiasm for revolutionary governments is constrained by fears of being put in a position of having to provide massive subsidies to the new government.

With respect to the new generation of revolutionary movements in Central America, many of these Soviet concerns have been mitigated. These new revolutionary movements are quite willing to include the local Communist parties in their broad opposition coalitions (the Communist parties of El Salvador and Guatemala are both currently supporting the guerrillas).[56] Moreover, these revolutionary movements have a number of international backers, and hence in the event of victory the new governments can look to sources besides the Soviet Union for assistance. Nicaragua has received considerable economic assistance from Brazil, Mexico, and Venezuela.[57] Finally, the Soviets feel that these revolutionary movements have a significant chance of success. Given their claims to be the world's leading revolutionary power, the Soviets obviously want to be able to claim at least some of the credit for any successful revolution. Moreover, the Soviets are aware that failure to support a revolutionary movement early enough can aggravate relations with the new government. The Soviet failure to support the FLN until late in the Algerian war has inclined Algeria to keep a certain distance from the Soviet Union in its foreign policy.[58]

As for the contemporary Central American revolutionaries themselves, they are much more inclined to seek Soviet support than were the earlier generation of revolutionaries. Feeling that they are faced with a long struggle to achieve and consolidate power, these current revolutionary movements are attracted by the "assets" (arms, training, propaganda, international support) that the Soviet Union has at its disposal. So the upshot of this limited "convergence" of the Soviets and the Latin American revolutionaries is that the Soviets have given some direct aid (arms and training) to these revolutionaries and have also used their extensive propaganda structure to help mobilize political support for the revolutionaries.[59]

Patterns of Violence

The new strategy and tactics of the contemporary generation of revolutionary movements in Central America have meant that the violence which has resulted from these movements' military campaigns differs in three key respects from that of the earlier generation of revolutionary movements:

1. The violence is much more prolonged. The delusions of easy victory that were so pervasive among the earlier guerrilla organizations meant that quite often these organizations were so militarily reckless that they were quickly destroyed. In the 1965 guerrilla upris-

ing in Peru the three separate focos lasted six months, four months, and one month, respectively.[60] Che Guevara's foco in Bolivia lasted eleven months.[61] And an Argentine foco set up in the spring of 1963 was destroyed in February 1964.[62]

The military caution that characterizes the contemporary Central American revolutionary movements reduces the chances that the governments of the region can score quick, crushing victories over them. Instead, what occurs are long, drawn-out insurgencies: the guerrillas in El Salvador began their campaign in the early 1970s; the guerrillas in Guatemala revived in the mid-1970s; and the FSLN's struggle against Somoza lasted from 1961 to 1979.[63]

2. The level of violence is much higher. In several of the earlier guerrilla campaigns there were large numbers of people killed and wounded in the course of the fighting. For example, both the Peruvian military's campaign against the 1965 guerrilla uprisings and the Guatemalan military's 1966–1968 offensive against the guerrillas resulted in thousands of people being killed and wounded.[64]

In the current guerrilla campaigns, however, the level of violence has been much higher than in these earlier campaigns. One reason for this increased violence is that, unlike in the foco period, the fighting now often takes place in populated areas rather than in thinly settled mountains and jungles. (In this connection, it should be mentioned that El Salvador has a population density of 600 people per square mile; it is the most densely populated nation in the Western Hemisphere.[65]) Also, the very fact that the current revolutionary movements are more powerful than their predecessors means that their capability of causing violence is greatly increased. And because those political forces opposed to the revolutionaries see them as more powerful (and hence more likely to seize power), they are quite prepared to increase repressive measures in an effort to defeat the guerrillas.

The grim "statistics of violence" powerfully illustrate the magnitude of the violence taking place in El Salvador. It is of course true that any figures on fatalities in a civil war must be treated with great caution, because many of those making the estimates are in no sense impartial. In El Salvador, however, there is complete agreement that thousands of people have died in the civil war. The disputes concerning these figures are chiefly over the degree of responsibility that different groups have for the violence. The State Department in its February 1981 White Paper estimated that 10,000 people had been killed in El Salvador in 1980.[66] There have been a variety of estimates of the total number of fatalities in 1981 and 1982; all of these estimates agree, however, that in these two years thousands more El Salvadorans were killed.[67]

3. A final difference concerns violence against foreigners. The urban guerrillas of the late 1960s and early 1970s often achieved spectacular publicity with their kidnappings and assassinations of foreign nationals and diplomats. Yet, there were also real political costs entailed in such kidnappings: The country whose nationals were victimized could hardly be expected to be sympathetic to the guerrilla organizations involved. In 1970, for example, the West German ambassador to Guatemala was kidnapped and later assassinated by one of the Guatemalan guerrilla organizations. The West German government was quite angry over the incident, their diplomatic establishment in Guatemala was reduced to a minimum, and the Guatemalan ambassador was asked to leave Bonn.[68] Given that the contemporary revolutionary movements have made major efforts to get support from the Socialist International (in which the German member party, the Social Democratic party, or SDP, plays a very important role), they would be most unlikely to victimize a West German national because they would be afraid of alienating public and government opinion in West Germany.

Interestingly, while the revolutionaries have de-emphasized terrorism against foreign nationals, individuals and groups on the extreme right have engaged in a significant amount of such terrorism in recent years. The targets have included foreign clergy (the most well-known case, of course, being that of the murder of three American nuns and a lay worker in El Salvador in December 1980), American government officials, and foreign journalists. The right is engaging in such terrorism because it believes certain foreign organizations and countries are the allies of their political opponents, and hence they retaliate by using violence against individuals from these organizations and countries. At one point in the war in El Salvador, for example, the extreme rightist White Warriors Union (UGB) warned all Jesuits to leave El Salvador on penalty of death for their alleged aid to the revolutionary movements.[69]

Conclusion: Implications for U.S. Foreign Policy

The most important implication for U. S. foreign policy of the strategies being pursued by the contemporary generation of revolutionary movements in Central America is that these strategies greatly increase the difficulties involved in any sort of U.S. military intervention in Central America. Put differently, there are four reasons why any U.S.

military intervention against these current revolutionary movements will involve much higher costs and risks than were involved in the U.S. military interventions against the earlier generation of revolutionary movements:

1. The weaknesses of the earlier generation of guerrilla organizations meant that small advisory teams and limited amounts of military aid were all that was required to help local governments defeat these guerrillas. When it became known, for example, that Che Guevara was in Bolivia, the United States sent down a small advisory team to retrain a Bolivian battalion in ranger tactics. When its training was finished, the battalion was sent out after Guevara's foco and fairly quickly located it and destroyed it.[70] (An evaluation of Guevara's diary reveals the effectiveness of this ranger unit; in the first few months of the time period covered by the diary Guevara's foco scores a number of easy victories over the Bolivian army, while in the diary's final weeks the foco is progressively destroyed by a series of crippling defeats.)[71] In Guatemala, U.S. military aid averaged close to $2 million annually between 1962 and 1969.[72] An evaluation of the effectiveness of this aid written in 1977 stated:

> Over the past twenty years, U.S. military aid to Guatemala, even in its comparatively small scope, has contributed to institutional improvements in the Guatemalan armed forces. These forces are now better organized, equipped, trained, and staffed; they are more capable of fulfilling their military function.[73]

The much stronger contemporary guerrilla movements mean that in order for the United States to carry out any sort of effective military intervention, it must be prepared to commit much higher levels of resources. In March 1981, for example, the Reagan administration sent $25 million in military aid to El Salvador; for fiscal year 1982 it requested $26 million in military assistance to El Salvador; and in February 1982 it requested an additional $55 million worth of military assistance.[74]

2. Effective military intervention will be more difficult. The "militarism" that was so typical of the earlier generation of guerrillas simplified the task of the U.S. military personnel sent to various Latin American countries. Basically, all that these advisers were required to do was to improve the technical competence of the local militaries in counterguerrilla operations and, as noted previously, were often quite successful in doing so. But although the U.S. military has proved quite capable in the strictly military aspects of counterguerrilla warfare, the war in Indochina showed that the U.S. military finds it much

more difficult to respond to the sort of wars now under way in Central America—namely, the sort of revolutionary warfare in which political and military factors are equally important and are inextricably enmeshed with each other.

For both doctrinal and organizational reasons revolutionary warfare goes deeply against the grain of the U.S. military. The doctrinal problem is that in the U.S. military there has always been a widely shared belief that military issues are and should be kept separate from political issues.[75] The organizational problem is that the U.S. military is a big-unit, high-technology military. Wars against guerrillas, however, for the most part, require small units and fairly simple technology. Although the U.S. military could, of course, modify its organizational patterns, the war in Vietnam demonstrated that the U.S. military is extremely reluctant to modify its big-unit, high-technology orientation.[76]

The "bottom line" of the U.S. military's problems with responding to revolutionary warfare can be summed up as follows: Unless and until the United States makes the effort to develop a significant capability to conduct counterguerrilla warfare, increasing the U.S. military presence beyond a fairly low level in a country combating an insurgency may well do more harm than good. As Robert Thompson, a British expert on guerrilla warfare, stated with respect to the American intervention in Vietnam: "The trouble with you Americans is that whenever you double the effort you somehow manage to square the error."[77]

3. Another factor is domestic American politics. The contemporary revolutionary movements are very skillful in building public support for their cause in domestic U.S. politics. They have learned how to use both the media and sympathetic groups in the U.S. to mobilize public opinion against any U.S. military intervention in Central America.

The revolutionaries' ability to mobilize U.S. public opinion against intervention is made easier by certain changes in American society in the past two decades. First, memories of the Vietnam War are still a significant factor in the political views and beliefs of large numbers of Americans. Tragically, even the memorial for the Americans who died in Vietnam became enmeshed in a bitter political controversy. Second, under the influence of the Watergate scandal, U.S. media today stress investigative journalism. Since wars always provide opportunities for such journalism, it is very doubtful that any U.S. military intervention in Central America would long remain a so-called secret war. (In the modern world, *very* few wars are genuinely secret; wars that are called such are almost always in the category of what used to be called forgotten wars. Apparently the term secret has caught on because it sounds mysterious and exciting, whereas the term forgotten can lead to the obvious assumption that maybe it was forgotten because it was unimportant and uninteresting.)

4. The United States must also consider the reaction of the international community. The contemporary revolutionary movements have made major efforts to gain support from other countries and international organizations. Hence, any U.S. military intervention in Central America will aggravate U.S. relations with a number of countries. Both Mexico and Venezuela, for example, are supporters of certain of the revolutionary movements in Central America; hence, the ongoing U.S. military intervention against these movements has caused strains in U.S. relations with these major oil producers.[78] Given the strength of the peace movement in Western Europe, the current U.S. military intervention in Central America has resulted in frictions between the United States and its European allies because these allies are very reluctant to aggravate their own domestic problems by supporting such intervention. Any large-scale U.S. military intervention would seriously aggravate these strained relations.

In conclusion, the difficult foreign policy problem that the United States must deal with in respect to the contemporary revolutionary movements in Central America can be summed up as follows: The strength of these movements increases the chances that they will eventually come to power; and at the same time this strength means that any sort of U.S. military intervention in Central America will have much higher costs and risks than was the case with the U.S. military interventions against the earlier generation of revolutionary movements.

Notes

1. Richard Hofstadter and Michael Wallace, eds., *American Violence: A Documentary History* (New York: Vintage Books, 1970), pp. 9–11.

2. William LeoGrande, "The United States and the Nicaraguan Revolution," in Thomas Walker, ed., *Nicaragua in Revolution* (New York: Praeger Publishers, 1982), pp. 66–71.

3. The revolutionary movements that followed the Cuban Revolution came in two basically distinct waves. The first was a series of attempts at rural guerrilla warfare; this wave lasted from approximately 1960 to 1967. The second wave was a series of urban guerrilla movements; these movements enjoyed their high point in the earlier 1970s but were for the most part destroyed by the late 1970s. Roughly, therefore, one can say that the time frame of the earlier generation of revolutionary movements was 1960–1977.

4. For histories of several of these rural guerrilla movements, see Richard

Gott, *Guerrilla Movements in Latin America* (Garden City, N.Y.: Doubleday, 1971).

5. For Guevara's personal account of the Bolivian campaign, see Ernesto Che Guevara, *The Diary of Che Guevara* (New York: Bantam Books, 1968).

6. For a discussion of some of the most important of the urban guerrilla movements in Latin America, see James Kohl and John Litt, *Urban Guerrilla Warfare in Latin America* (Cambridge, Mass.: M.I.T. Press, 1974).

7. Douglas S. Blaufarb, *The Counter-Insurgency Era: U.S. Doctrine and Performance, 1950 to the Present* (New York: Free Press, 1977), pp. 279–86.

8. Gott, *Guerrilla Movements*, p. 163.

9. Ibid., p. 316.

10. Ibid., p. 369.

11. Ibid., p. 497.

12. Ernesto Che Guevara, *Guerrilla Warfare* (New York: Vintage Books, 1961), pp. 1–2.

13. Carlos Marighella, "Minimanual of the Urban Guerrilla," appendix in Robert Moss, *Urban Guerrilla Warfare* (London: International Institute for Strategic Studies, 1971), p. 40.

14. Gott, *Guerrilla Movements*, pp. 369–70.

15. Marighella, "Minimanual," p. 23.

16. Gott, *Guerrilla Movements*, pp. 275–92.

17. Ibid., p. 286.

18. Régis Debray, "Revolution in the Revolution?" in Walter Laqueur, ed., *The Guerrilla Reader* (New York: Meridian Books, 1977), pp. 214–18.

19. Guevara, *Diary*, p. 57.

20. Guevara, *Guerrilla Warfare*, pp. 8–12.

21. Guevara, *Diary*, pp. 150, 164–65, 185–86.

22. V. I. Lenin, "Why the Social Democrats Must Declare Determined and Relentless War on the Socialist Revolutionaries" (1902), in Stefan Possony, ed., *Lenin Reader* (Chicago: Henry Regnery, 1966), pp. 470–71.

23. Guevara, *Guerrilla Warfare*, p. 15.

24. Abraham Guillen, "Strategy of the Urban Guerrilla," in Laqueur, *Guerrilla Reader*, pp. 229–37.

25. Gott, *Guerrilla Movements*, pp. 149–50.

26. Kohl and Litt, *Urban Guerrilla Warfare*, pp. 48–50.

27. James A. Miller, "Urban Terrorism in Uruguay: The Tupamaros," in Bard O'Neill, William R. Heaton, and Donald J. Alberts, eds., *Insurgency in the Modern World* (Boulder, Colo.: Westview Press, 1980), pp. 171–74.

28. For an account of the German army's innovations in armored warfare between the two world wars, see the memoirs of Heinz Guderian, *Panzer Leader* (New York: Ballantine Books, 1965), pp. 7–27.

29. Gordon A. Craig, *The Politics of the Prussian Army* (New York: Oxford University Press, 1964), pp. 354–82.

30. Blaufarb, *The Counter-Insurgency Era*, pp. 40–49.

31. Y. Harkabi, *Fedayeen Action and Arab Strategy* (London: International Institute for Strategic Studies, 1969), pp. 18–19.

32. Blaufarb, *The Counter-Insurgency Era*, pp. 2–11.

33. Don Mansfield, "The Irish Republican Army and Northern Ireland," in O'Neill et al., *Insurgency in the Modern World*, pp. 64–71.

34. Cole Blasier, *The Hovering Giant: U.S. Responses to Revolutionary Change in Latin America* (Pittsburgh, Pa.: University of Pittsburgh Press, 1976), pp. 177-78.

35. Neill Macaulay, *The Sandino Affair* (Chicago: Quadrangle Books, 1967), pp. 74, 214, 226, 265.

36. Harry E. Vanden, "The Ideology of the Insurrection," in Walker, ed., *Nicaragua in Revolution*, pp. 50–54. The El Salvadoran rebels also learned from Guevara's defeat, as the following quotation shows:". . . most of the Salvadorian revolutionaries had learned an important lesson from Che Guevara's disatrous experience in Bolivia. Guevara and his band of followers made little or no effort to build support among the population. Thus when U.S. Special Forces went looking for Che in the jungle there was no network to warn him and no one to hide him." Tommie Sue Montgomery, *Revolution in El Salvador: Origins and Evolution* (Boulder, Colo.: Westview Press, 1982), pp. 142–43.

37. Ibid., p. 50.

38. Thomas W. Walker, *Nicaragua: The Land of Sandino* (Boulder, Colo.: Westview Press, 1981), pp. 37–39.

39. John A. Booth, *The End and the Beginning: The Nicaraguan Revolution* (Boulder, Colo.: Westview Press, 1982), pp. 145–47.

40. Ibid., pp. 133–34.

41. Ibid., pp. 130–34, 165–68, 175–80.

42. LeoGrande, "The United States and the Nicaraguan Revolution," pp. 63, 66–67; Booth, *The End and the Beginning*, pp. 128–30.

43. LeoGrande, "The United States and the Nicaraguan Revolution," pp. 69–70.

44. Ibid., p. 67.

45. Enrique Baloyra, *El Salvador in Transition* (Chapel Hill: University of North Carolina Press, 1982), p. 161; idem, *El Salvador: Beyond Elections* (New York: North American Congress on Latin America, 1982), p. 28.

46. Baloyra, *El Salvador in Transition*, pp. 154, 161–62.

47. Daniel Premo, "Guatemala," in Robert Wesson, ed., *Communism in Central America and the Caribbean* (Stanford, Calif.: Hoover Institution Press, 1982), p. 83.

48. Americas Watch Committee and American Civil Liberties Union, *Report on Human Rights in El Salvador, January 26, 1982* (New York: Random House, 1982), and Americas Watch Committee and the American Civil Liberties Union, *July 20, 1982, Supplement to the Report on Human Rights in El Salvador* (Washington, D.C.: Americas Watch Committee, 1982); Laurence R. Simon and James C. Stephens, Jr., *El Salvador Land Reform 1980–1981: Impact Audit* (Boston, Mass.: Oxfam-America, 1981); for a sample of the criticisms made by Amnesty International of the governments of El Salvador and Guatemala see *Amnesty International Reports for 1979, 1980, 1981, 1982* (London: Amnesty International Publications), sections on El Salvador and Guatemala. These reports are an annual summary of the human rights situation in each of the countries of the world.

49. Carmelo Mesa-Lago, *Cuba in the 1970's: Pragmatism and Institutionalization* (Albuquerque: University of New Mexico Press, 1978), pp. 117–18.

50. The Kurdish revolt in Iraq in 1974–1975 is an example of what can happen to a revolutionary movement that is dependent on only one or two outside sources of aid. When the United States and the Iranians cut off aid to the Kurd rebels in early 1975, they were quickly defeated by the Iraqi army. Paul Viotti, "Iraq: The Kurdish Rebellion," in O'Neill et al., *Insurgency in the Modern World*, p. 202.

51. Gott, *Guerrilla Movements*, pp. 321–29.

52. Walter Laqueur, *Terrorism* (Boston: Little, Brown, 1977), pp. 203–4.

53. In the Algerian war, a major reason for the Soviet coolness toward the Algerian revolutionaries was that both the French Communist party (PCF) and the Algerian Communist party (PCA) had ambivalent attitudes toward the Algerian revolution. The ambivalence of the French Communists was due to the fact that the PCF realized that the French working class was to a considerable extent hostile to the Algerian cause, whereas the ambivalence of the Algerian Communists stemmed from the commitment of the PCA to defend the interests of the workers among the French settlers in Algeria. Alistair Horne, *A Savage War of Peace: Algeria, 1954–1962* (New York: Penguin Books, 1977), p. 405.

54. Paul Sigmund, "The USSR, Cuba, and the Revolution in Cuba," in Robert Donaldson, ed., *The Soviet Union in the Third World: Successes and Failures* (Boulder, Colo.: Westview Press, 1981), pp. 37–40.

55. Joseph L. Nogee and John W. Sloan, "Allende's Chile and the Soviet Union: A Policy Lesson for Latin American Nations Seeking Autonomy," *Journal of Inter-American Studies and World Affairs*, vol. 21, no. 3 (August 1979), pp. 339–68.

56. Premo, "Guatemala," pp. 82–83; Baloyra, *El Salvador in Transition*, pp. 161–62.

57. Booth, *The End and the Beginning*, p. 212.

58. Horne, *A Savage War of Peace*, p. 559.

59. In February 1981 the State Department issued a White Paper entitled "Communist Interference in El Salvador." The White Paper argued that the Soviet Union and certain of its allies had provided military aid to the guerrillas in El Salvador. The conclusions and the documentation of the White Paper have been widely criticized. It is important, however, to understand that very few critics deny that the Soviet bloc has provided military aid to the rebels; rather, the critics maintain that the amount of aid is less than the White Paper claims and that the White Paper is wrong in claiming that the Soviet bloc created and controls the revolutionary movement in El Salvador. For the text of the White Paper, see *Department of State Bulletin*, March 1981, pp. 1–7.

60. Gott, *Guerrilla Movements*, pp. 366, 371, 379.

61. Ibid., pp. 420–22, 474–76.

62. Luis Mercier Vega, *Guerrillas in Latin America: The Technique of the Counter-State* (New York: Frederick A. Praeger, 1969), pp. 115–17.

63. Baloyra, *El Salvador in Transition*, p. 161; Premo, "Guatemala," pp. 82–83; Booth, *The End and the Beginning*, p. 139.

64. Gott, *Guerrilla Movements*, pp. 99–101, 361–62.

65. Thomas P. Anderson, *Politics in Central America* (New York: Praeger Publishers, 1982), p. 63.

66. *Department of State Bulletin*, March 1981, p. 1.

67. See Baloyra, *El Salvador in Transition*, p. 191, for some of these various estimates.

68. Carol Baumann, *The Diplomatic Kidnappings* (The Hague: Martinas Nijhoff, 1973), pp. 99–100.

69. Baloyra, *El Salvador in Transition*, pp. 64–65.

70. Gott, *Guerrilla Movements*, pp. 450–51, 474–76.

71. Guevara, *Diary*, pp. 92–93, 120–21, 181–82, 186.

72. Brian Jenkins and Caesar D. Sereseres, "U.S. Military Assistance and the Guatemalan Armed Forces," *Armed Forces and Society* (Summer 1977), p. 578.

73. Ibid., p. 588.

74. Montgomery, *Revolution in El Salvador*, p. 221; Baloyra, *El Salvador in Transition*, p. 166.

75. Richard K. Betts, *Soldiers, Statesmen and Cold War Crises* (Cambridge, Mass.: Harvard University Press, 1977), pp. 130–31.

76. Brian M. Jenkins, *The Unchangeable War* (Santa Monica, Calif.: Rand Corporation, 1970), p. v; Blaufarb, *The Counter-Insurgency Era*, pp. 55–56, 78–79.

77. Robert Thompson, "Squaring the Error," *Foreign Affairs* (April 1968), p. 449.

78. Booth, *The End and the Beginning*, pp. 132–33, 211–13.

7
Bishop's Cuba, Castro's Grenada: Notes toward an Inner History

Mark Falcoff

The capture of several thousand documents pertaining to the brief rule of the New Jewel Movement (NJM) in Grenada (1979–1983) is without doubt one of the most important scholarly events since World War II. For apart from the fact that these papers afford us an intimate view of a Leninist state in the making, they allow us to chart clearly those currents of Soviet, Eastern bloc, Cuban, and third world influence of which Grenada was for more than three years a peculiar and in many ways improbable point of convergence. They are of particular interest for students of the Cuban role in the circum-Caribbean, for Cuba was—by the frequent admission of the NJM leadership—the most important country for the Grenadian revolutionary process.[1] This chapter attempts to draw upon those sources to measure the dimensions of that relationship, to characterize the nature of Soviet-Cuban strategic cooperation in Grenada, and finally to identify some of the implications for the future that the Grenadian episode poses for Cuba, Cuban-Soviet relations, and U.S. policy makers who must respond to both.

Cuba's Revolutionary Foreign Policy

Almost from its inception the Castro regime has been actively engaged in the export of revolution, as a means of historical and ideological self-justification, as a substitute for economic success at home, and as an extension of Castro's outsized ego. But the theaters of opportunity—both real and perceived—have shifted several times since 1959. In the beginning the Cubans sought to replicate their own experience of rural guerrilla warfare in other Latin American countries, convinced that—whether dictatorships or democracies—they were ripe for overthrow. Such efforts did not, however, include the English Caribbean. After several failures, including a particularly grievous setback in Bolivia, Havana shifted course and sought normal state-to-state relations with the proximate governments it had formerly sought to overthrow. This policy eventually led three of them—Colombia, Venezuela, and Costa Rica—to propose to the Organization of American States in 1975 that members be permitted to lift the embargo on Cuba on which they had commonly agreed a decade before.

At the same time, however, Cuba folded into its policy of "ideological pluralism" yet another: the pragmatic search for targets of opportunity—whether in Africa, the Middle East, or the Caribbean region. By the end of that decade, Cuban "advisers" were at work in an astonishing variety of nations, not all of whose governments could, strictly speaking, qualify as Marxist. Moreover, in the English-speaking Caribbean, the Cubans finally succeeded in surmounting linguistic and cultural barriers to become an important presence in Jamaica and Guyana, with diplomatic missions that presided over "an ever-increasing network of . . . activities in health, education, construction, agriculture, tourism, sports, and some would maintain, politics."[2] These activities did not significantly alter the nature of the recipient governments, whose Cuban policies were very clearly—if cynically—conceived: to outflank their domestic left and to put the fear of God into reluctant sources of economic largesse in Washington, London, and elsewhere. They did, however, indicate the degree of flexibility the Cubans were now prepared to bring to their international policies, still officially denominated by the quaint sobriquet "proletarian internationalism."

Cuba and the New Jewel Revolution

Cuba's relationship to the English Caribbean entered an entirely new phase in 1979, when the NJM seized power in Grenada through a *coup d'état*—the first in West Indian history. From Havana's perspective what was particularly significant about this event was the emergence—again, for the first time in that region—of a Marxist-Leninist regime, committed to restructuring society along classical Eastern bloc lines and to becoming a full partner in the Soviet international alliance. The Cubans were called upon almost immediately to provide Maurice Bishop's People's Revolutionary Government (PRG) with the economic and political assistance to make this possible, and they did so in amounts that belied the small size of the island, its limited resources, and its allegedly doubtful strategic value.

As in Guyana, Suriname, and Jamaica (during the rule of Michael

Manley), the Cuban presence in Grenada was most visible in the area of economic cooperation and assistance. This took the form of outright donations of equipment (ten fishing boats that almost immediately became inoperative), skilled construction labor, construction materials, and some technical and engineering expertise.[3] The Cubans also reportedly provided "tremendous and invaluable assistance" in agriculture, education, and health projects.[4] The largest focus of Cuban activity was at Port Salines, the site of a new international airport, where there were so many Cuban workers (living in a special compound) as to lead to serious tension and several incidents between them and their Grenadian counterparts.[5]

The ostensible purpose of the airport was to generate additional foreign exchange by developing a new source of tourism from Western Europe. Although doubtless it would have lent itself to such use, just enough evidence has surfaced to suggest that its construction might serve other ends as well. The project was originally conceived for the same reasons by Eric Gairy and opposed by the NJM (then, of course, in opposition) on the grounds that a massive wave of affluent tourists would corrupt the morals and cultural integrity of the Grenadian people. After 1979, however, it suddenly became—as Maurice Bishop explained to Libyan dictator Muhammar Quaddafi—"of extreme importance to our revolutionary process."[6] The Cubans apparently shared this view, as evidenced by the high priority they assigned to it in their own assistance program. And one of the documents—excerpted from the notebook of an NJM Central Committee member—does explicitly note, "airport to be used by Cuban and Soviet military."[7] This was certainly the perception of local laborers at the site; as the Special Branch (assigned to look into tensions there) reported, the Grenadian workers in Port Salines regarded "the Cubans as building a military base for their own benefit."[8]

Thus far, however, nothing about the Cuban relationship with Grenada set it radically apart from Castro's links to other English Caribbean governments that by no stretch of the imagination could be regarded as Marxist-Leninist.[9] In Grenada, however, the interpenetration of ruling parties and indeed of governments went far beyond what existed elsewhere in the region (with the possible exception of Nicaragua). For example, a secret agreement between the Cuban Communist party and the NJM, projecting joint plans for 1983, called for the exchange of delegations for "mutual consultation and study." By the same accord the Cubans offered to share the experience and expertise of such organizations as the Workers' Central Union, the Cuban Women's Federation (FMC), the Association of

Small Farmers, and the Young Communists. The Cubans also promised to send over technical advisers skilled at organizing public meetings and propaganda.[10]

The Cubans were active in assisting the Grenadian government to achieve what in other contexts has been called *Gleichschaltung*—that is, the subordination of all elements of society to the purposes of the state. The NJM seriously studied the possibility of copying one version of Cuba's Labor Army for its system of national service;[11] the Cubans agreed to maintain military specialists in Grenada; and they granted Grenadian soldiers and officers scholarships at Cuban military institutions.[12]

Of particular interest were Cuban efforts to assist the Bishop government in its efforts to counteract the opposition of the churches in Grenada. For example, the joint party agreement cited above called for the Grenadians to receive in 1983 a "specialist in the work with the religious people for exchange of experiences in the work of the Party in this sector."[13] The churches must have posed a problem almost from the beginning, for as early as 1981 the NJM leaders were conferring with the Cubans on the subject.[14] Eventually, in the fall of 1982 a special delegation from the Americas Department of the Cuban party was sent to Grenada to survey the situation and render a full report. It concluded by recommending (1) the need for a full-time NJM member to deal with the religious question; (2) collation and consolidation of factual information on Grenada's religious institutions and their activities; (3) promotion of contacts among clergy and laity from Nicaragua and other Latin American circles linked to the theology of liberation; (4) familiarization visits by selected Grenadian Protestant pastors to the Matanzas Evangelical Seminary; and (5) establishment of "a reciprocal information link and an exchange of criteria on the strategy and tactics of the Church and the mechanisms of prevention and response."[15]

The Cubans' most valuable contribution to the Bishop regime lay, however, in the international sphere. In the first place, they acted as a guide to world politics, particularly the labyrinth of third world and Soviet international front organizations. For example, when three Grenadian women were scheduled to attend the World Conference of Women in Prague in 1981, they stopped first in Havana to receive a briefing from Esther Véliz, the international secretary of the FMC. The discussion reportedly centered on "what Cuba sees as a difference in emphasis between the European organizations and those of the underdeveloped world. . . . The FMC felt that the European organizations emphasize peace at the expense of National Liberation Struggles."[16] When Don Rojas of the NJM went to Angola on an orientation visit, he stopped in Cuba to coordinate with the Casa de las Américas on a forthcoming conference on the Caribbean Committee of Intellectual Workers.[17]

Both parties also worked closely within the context of the Socialist International, where the NJM had the status of an observer party. The Cubans provided the Grenadians with their own confidential assessment of socialist leaders, some of which makes quite piquant reading;[18] for their part, the Grenadians agreed in the 1983 joint party accord to provide the Cubans with "two comrades linked to the work of the Socialist International for exchanging experiences and criteria on this aspect."[19]

The American wife of the Cuban ambassador to Grenada was invited to coach Bishop on how he should conduct a coming visit to the United States. "On the subject of specific meetings," she wrote, "[Ramón Sánchez] Parodi from the Cuban Interests Section [of the Czech Embassy in Washington] will be the single most clear person on this whole question."[20] Apparently the Cubans were also prepared to assist the Grenadians in financing a meeting there of the Non-Aligned Movement.[21]

Second, Cuba became an international entrepôt through which the Soviets and other members of the Eastern bloc funneled both economic and military aid. For example, at a meeting between Bishop and the Soviet ambassador in May 1983, the ambassador promised BTR armored carriers, 14.5-mm shells, and spare parts, all to be transshipped through Havana. At the same time the Soviets promised Bishop a plane (apparently to be used on the Havana–St. George's run), which would be shipped in parts and assembled in Cuba. ("They will prefer Cuban pilots use it.")[22] The Cubans were also used as a conduit by the German Democratic Republic; it was from the Ministry of Interior in Havana, thus, that Colonel Liam James, Grenadian director of security and internal order, learned of a grant of military equipment and small arms for his country from that source.[23]

The choice of Cuba was doubtless determined largely by the fact that the port and storage facilities of Havana harbor were far superior to anything in Grenada itself, but in all probability it also responded to a deeply felt Soviet need to maintain a low profile in the Caribbean, a region where—according to the Grenadian ambassador in Moscow—they were interested "in reducing areas of conflict with the USA."[24] On another occasion the same Grenadian diplomat wrote:

> If we meet at too high a level [in the context of party-to-party contacts between the NJM and the CPSU], the USA would use this as an excuse to further squeeze Grenada. (This is

one of the explanations as to why the Prime Minister did not meet with Andropov in April.)[25]

Third, the Cubans became the most important source of guidance for the NJM in its dealings with the Soviet Union. This was true on matters both large and small. When Bishop decided to send a military delegation to Moscow to request additional assistance, he first sent its leader, General Hudson Austin (together with the Cuban military attaché) to Havana. As Bishop explained in a letter to Raúl Castro, chief of the Cuban armed forces (FAR), "I hope that during this period you or Cde. Senen Casas may be able to find time to hold discussions with him, and offer your advice and suggestions on the best ways to present this document to the Soviets."[26] When the Grenadian government was exploring the possibilities of installing a satellite dish to link the island to InterSputnik, the Soviet international telecommunications organization, they met with officials of the Cuban Ministry of Communications, who explained the capabilities of the system and offered to provide technicians familiar with the equipment to install telephonic centrals manufactured in East Germany.[27]

Most of all, Cuba acted as an advocate for the Grenadians in the highest circles in Moscow. From the lengthy reports sent back by W. Richard Jacobs, Bishop's ambassador in the Soviet Union, it is clear that the Soviets were reluctant to make commitments to Grenada beyond their power to fulfill them ("and, if necessary, defend those commitments"). They had only responded as far as they had, he wrote, "because Cuba has strongly championed our case."[28] It would appear, in fact, that the Soviets regarded Grenada as Cuba's "project," to which they would lend assistance provisionally, pending additional evidence of (1) the stability of its government, (2) its relative immunity from U.S. intervention, and (3) above all, the durability of its professed "socialist orientation," that is, pro-Soviet orientation. In other words Grenada's relationship to Cuba was roughly congruent with Cuba's relationship to the Soviet Union. This suggests a kind of subcontracting of Soviet influence in certain areas of the third world where Moscow lacks experience, knowledge, and geographical proximity but possesses a reliable surrogate. It is a tactic designed to explore fully the possibilities for expanded influence without risking future Egypts (or Somalias, or Ghanas, or Perus).

This was a frustrating situation for the Bishop government, all the more because, as Jacobs reported, "the comrades responsible for Grenada in the International Division [of the CPSU] have told me that they operate on the basis that the NJM is a 'communist party.'"[29] The ambassador gave some thought as to how Grenada might coax the Soviets into a higher profile and thus qualitatively modify the relationship. In one particularly interesting dispatch in mid-1983, he speculated that Grenada could assume a position of "increasingly greater importance" only if "seen as influencing regional events. We have to establish ourselves as the authority on events at least in the English-speaking Caribbean, and be the sponsor of revolutionary activities and progressive developments in this region at least."

To this end he proposed semiannual meetings with "progressive and revolutionary" parties of the region "critical to the development of closer relations with the USSR." Perhaps, he suggested, someone on the Central Committee of the NJM could "pay a visit to the USSR after one of these meetings [for information purposes]. We must be sure, though, that we become the principal point of access to the USSR even to the point of having our Embassy serve as their representative while in the USSR." This was a formula for hiving off pro-Soviet activities in the Caribbean along racial-cultural and linguistic lines, in which Grenada would stand to the ministates of the region as Cuba to the revolutionary left in the Dominican Republic, Puerto Rico, or Central America. It would also raise Grenada's stature in the Soviet Union and allow the NJM eventually to bypass somewhat their Cuban sponsors.

Implications for Future Cuban Policy

The PRG of Grenada is now history. What impact is that history likely to have on its principal foreign sponsor? In the first place, it seems doubtful that Cuba will again so unreservedly support a revolutionary government in the English Caribbean purely on the basis of a personal friendship with its leader. That this was the operative consideration in Grenada lies beyond all doubt. A Central Committee document drafted after the palace coup that deposed Bishop referred to "the deep personal friendship between Fidel and Maurice which," it noted with some irritation, "caused the Cuban leadership to take a *personal* and not a *class* approach to developments in Grenada."[30] For his part, Castro told Bishop's successors, "in our country, the Grenadian revolution and Cde. Bishop as its central figure were the object of great sympathy and respect. Even explaining the event to our own people will not be easy."[31] Of course, the PRG dissolved in much the same fashion as it had formed in the first place. This raises further questions—for the Cubans at least—about the viability of fundamentally personalistic, self-styled vanguards in the eastern Caribbean behind whom rests no substantial, organized popular movement. In this unique sense, Grenada could be seen as Cuba's "Egypt" or "Peru."

Second, the joint rescue operation undertaken by the Organization of Eastern Caribbean States (OECS) and the United States has forced the Cuban regime to revise its views on the political feasibility of U.S. military operations in the Caribbean Basin. In Cuba as in the United States itself, conventional wisdom before the event was that the use of force to depose Marxist regimes in the area would meet with such overwhelming congressional and public opposition as to be effectively discarded as an option. It is now clear that that will not be the case where military force can be marshaled effectively and *quickly*. In particular, the ministates of the eastern Caribbean offer far more vulnerable targets than the countries on the mainland or even Cuba itself. They also operate within a different cultural world from the Hispanic-American left and for that reason may prove less amenable to reshaping from the top. All of this may well presage a long period of "malign neglect" in the English-speaking islands, as Cuba rededicates its efforts on behalf of revolutionary forces in El Salvador and Guatemala and toward shoring up the Sandinista regime in Nicaragua.

Third, the capacity of the Cubans to leverage aid from the Soviet Union for its own clients, at least in the Caribbean Basin, may have been seriously damaged. Not that it appears that such leverage was very great in the first place: the Soviets were sending the Grenadians just about everywhere else to find the resources to complete the international airport;[32] virtually steered them into the arms of the International Monetary Fund;[33] and apart from arms transfers and scholarships to CPSU party schools and Soviet military institutions, were remarkably unresponsive to pleas for wide-scale assistance. This—to October 1983. What must Cuban leverage be now? As in the wake of Allende's fall in Chile, Cuba's failure to impose its purposes within its own region may well lead Soviet strategists to rethink the reliability of Havana's intelligence and the perspicacity of its political planners.

Implications for Future U.S. Policy

The most significant contribution that the Grenada documents make to our strategic understanding is to illuminate further the nature of the Cuban-Soviet alliance. Therein we find confirmation of what is gradually becoming something of a scholarly consensus: namely, that while the Cubans cannot—and therefore do not—differ from the Soviets on any major international issue, they have considerable freedom to pursue their own goals, particularly within the Caribbean.[34] Moreover, in the service of these objectives they can draw on a wide range of Soviet-bloc contacts and sources of assistance. Hence, except on issues that directly affect U.S.-Soviet relations (such as the placement of offensive missiles in Cuba), the United States cannot logically expect to negotiate the dimensions of Cuban international conduct with Moscow, especially in areas that, though of minor interest to the Soviet Union, are of major interest to both Cuba and the United States.

Second, the collapse of the New Jewel regime in Grenada and the subsequent willingness of the United States (along with the OECS states) to reestablish order and expel the Cuban mission there have inflicted serious damage on Castro's credibility throughout the eastern Caribbean. Before 1983 it was widely assumed among parties and forces of the left in that part of the world that Cubans rode "the wave of the future" or represented "the forces of history." It is now clear that the future can be canceled; history can be turned around. Conversely, the credibility of the United States as a regional hegemon has been significantly advanced. It is difficult to exaggerate the importance of such symbolism, which becomes almost an independent variable in relations between great powers and small states on their immediate periphery.

Finally, the case of Grenada illustrates once more the willingness of the Soviets (and in their turn, the Cubans) to allow client states to draw on Western sources of aid. Although one school of foreign policy thought holds that such aid can be used to "wean" Marxist regimes away from the Soviet Union, this is not what the Soviets seem to think. Both they and the Cubans regard the political order as utterly fundamental to the ideological identity of a regime—hence the disproportionate attention in Grenada to the training of party cadres and military personnel and the dispatch of intelligence and police operatives. Economic assistance was to be obtained where it could be found, even if this required the anomaly of quasi-membership in such apparently incompatible organizations as the Socialist International. Such terms as "normalization of relations" and "ideological pluralism" mask a careful understanding of the sources of political power. This holds out a lesson for U.S.-Cuban relations as important as any that could be derived from the brief episode of Leninism in Grenada.

Notes

1. Document 000123, (minutes of the) extraordinary meeting of the Central Committee, September 14–16, 1983.
2. Anthony Maingot, "Cuba and the Commonwealth Caribbean: Playing the Cuban Card," in Barry B. Levine, ed., *The New Cuban Presence in the Caribbean* (Boulder, Colo.: Westview Press, 1983).

3. Document GG1, minutes of the Political Bureau meeting, Wednesday, September 15, 1982.

4. Document 1057?? (number illegible), "Foreign Relations Report," Central Committee document on Grenadian foreign policy (no date but probably 1981).

5. Document 105657, minutes of the Political Bureau meeting, Wednesday, April 7, 1982; Document 103890, report from head, special branch, to minister of national security, July 14, 1981; Document 100282, minutes of the Political/Economic Bureau, August 10, 1983.

6. Document R1/100, letter from Maurice Bishop to Muhammar Quaddafi, September 26, 1983.

7. Document Y1, excerpt from Liam James's notebook.

8. Document 103890, cited in note 5.

9. Maingot, "Cuba and the Commonwealth Caribbean."

10. Document 100016, Cooperation and Exchange Plan between the Communist party of Cuba and the New Jewel Movement for 1983.

11. Document 102602, Progress Report on Commission No. 5.

12. Document 000194, Protocol of Military Cooperation between the Government of the Republic of Cuba and the People's Revolutionary Government of Grenada.

13. Document 100016, cited in note 10.

14. Document H48, minutes of the Political Bureau meeting, Wednesday, May 20, 1981.

15. Document II-1 [restricted], report of the delegation sent to Grenada by the Americas Department with the aim of starting the gathering of sources for the characterization of the religious situation in the country, and the contacts for further cooperation between the Cuban Communist party and the New Jewel Movement regarding the question (October 14, 1982).

16. Document 105656, report to the Political Bureau, NJM, "World Conference of Women and WDIF Congress, Prague, and Visit to Bulgaria by Sisters P. Coard, R. Joseph, and E. Calliste," October 3–30, 1981.

17. Document EE1, report to Prime Minister Maurice Bishop on trip to Angola, February 10, 1983.

18. Document PP1, report of Manuel Pinero Losada of the Americas Department of the Cuban Communist party on the meeting of the SI Committee for the Defense of the Nicaraguan Revolution; Document NN1, unsigned, undated report of the Bonn meeting of the SI.

19. Document 100016, cited in note 10.

20. Document DD1, holograph letter from Gail Reed to Maurice Bishop. See also Document L51, minutes of the Political Bureau meeting, Wednesday, June 17, 1981, in which George Louison was sent to get a briefing from the Cubans before taking an official delegation to Mexico.

21. Document 100270, minutes of the Political Bureau meeting, January 5, 1983; and Document 103448, minutes of the Political Bureau meeting, December 29, 1982.

22. Document 103913, summary of the prime minister's meeting with the Soviet ambassador, May 24, 1983.

23. Document 102644, letter from the Cuban minister of interior to Colonel Liam James, director of security and internal order, no date.

24. Document 102329, [confidential] report from the Embassy of Grenada, Moscow, on relations with the CPSU, no date, but sometime after December 1981.

25. Document W1, report from the Embassy of Grenada, Moscow, on relations with the USSR, July 11, 1983.

26. Document 102647, letter from Maurice Bishop to Raúl Castro, November 14, 1981.

27. Document 102517, minutes of the meeting at the Ministry of Communications in Havana, November 9, 1982.

28. Document W1, cited in note 25.

29. Ibid.

30. Document 000015, "On Cuba's Response to the Issue."

31. Document T1, letter from Fidel Castro to the Central Committee of the New Jewel Movement, October 15, 1983.

32. Document 103861, letter from Bishop to President Hussein of Iraq, asking, *inter alia*, for funds to help complete the airport; Document 103680 chronicles an agreement for such assistance from Libya.

33. Document 103448, minutes of the Political Bureau meeting, May 27, 1981.

34. Robert Pastor, "Cuba and the Soviet Union: Does Cuba Act Alone?" in Levine, *New Cuban Presence in the Caribbean*.

8
The Impact of Grenada in Central America
Howard J. Wiarda

There seem to be two senses in which the Grenada intervention of October 1983 has not yet faded, or has not been permitted to fade, from our television screens and consciousness. The first, most apparent, and probably most ephemeral reason is that Grenada became a campaign issue in the 1984 election, with the Democrats charging the intervention was another sign of the Reagan administration's "reckless adventurism" in foreign affairs, and the Republicans using films from the intervention to demonstrate administration firmness, decisiveness, and willingness to employ force to prevent Soviet-Cuban expansionism in the American sphere of influence.

The second, more lasting reason for Grenada's continuing importance is the treasure trove of documents captured on Grenada by U.S.–Organization of Eastern Caribbean States (OECS) forces. These documents, which are so extensive they can be measured most easily in cubic feet and whose authenticity cannot be doubted, show in excruciating detail a Marxist-Leninist revolution in progress. They are crucial to our understanding of the internal dynamics of the Grenadian revolution and its external ties and relations with Cuba, Czechoslovakia, the Soviet Union, Bulgaria, East Germany, Nicaragua, the Salvadoran rebels, European socialist parties and governments, as well as the Socialist International, and various support groups in the United States. The Grenada documents provide the first clear mapping of a revolution *en marche* in both its domestic and, now all-important, international relations. Without hyperbole it may be said that they do for our understanding of these international links what the documents made available to Harvard Professor Merle Fainsod after World War II did for our understanding of the internal dynamics of Soviet rule.[1]

The purposes of this paper are to comment on the rising Soviet-Cuban presence in Central America and the Caribbean Basin, to discuss preliminarily what the Grenada documents reveal about the international aspects of the revolutionary process in the area, to focus on the impact of the U.S. intervention on revolutionary prospects in Central America and Suriname, and to offer some conclusions concerning the impact of Grenada on changing Soviet-Cuban strategy in the region and what this implies for U.S. policy.

The Rising Soviet-Cuban Presence in Central America and the Caribbean Basin

In another paper,[2] the author has analyzed the rising presence of the Soviet Union and Cuba in Central America and the Caribbean Basin. Overall, the Soviets have considerably increased their presence and capabilities in the region during the past two decades—diplomatically, politically, commercially, militarily, culturally, and in terms of Soviet prestige and power. Moreover, the strategies and tactics pursued by the Soviet Union and its allies are now considerably more sophisticated than they were twenty years ago. Nevertheless, the paper also emphasized the severe constraints—having to do with distance, logistics, the difficulties the Soviets face operating in the Latin American context, and the domestic conditions of the Soviet Union itself—that serve to limit the Soviet role and presence in the area.

Hence, while Soviet capabilities in Latin America have increased, and while its tactics and strategy have become more sophisticated, there are also severe restraints operating on Soviet initiatives in the Western Hemisphere. It seems unlikely that we shall soon see a much larger and direct Soviet presence in Latin America. Rather what we will probably see is the Soviet Union attempting to continue to take advantage of revolutionary situations and anti-American sentiments that already exist in the area to gain advantage for itself and to frustrate and embarrass the United States. That is what Soviet machinations with regard to Cuba, Nicaragua, and Grenada—the three Marxist-Leninist regimes that have come to power in Latin America—are all about.

What the Grenada Documents Reveal

In light of recent events in Central America and Grenada, the question arises as to whether the Soviet Union has a timetable for expansion in Latin America.[3] Is there a master plan or a blueprint for the conquest of the Western Hemisphere, like Hitler's plan to build a European empire?[4]

The information we have points toward negative answers to these questions. There appears to be no timetable, no master plan, no blueprint. But perhaps we are asking the wrong set of questions. If we ask instead, does the Soviet Union have a set of global goals, strategies, and tactics, the answer is yes. To date, these goals include protecting the Soviet strategic superstructure, expanding Soviet influence and prestige worldwide, embarrassing and weakening the United States, and strengthening the Soviet state and military. The tactics are to take advantage of opportunities as they present themselves, even to hurry them along if possible. This implies that Soviet foreign policy focusing on the third world, and more specifically on Central America and the Caribbean Basin, is driven more by opportunities than by a master plan. This is true of Soviet policy in general, and the Grenada documents seem to confirm the assertion.

Under Khrushchev, the Soviet Union sought to expand its ties with the third world left in general, not just with orthodox Communist regimes and parties as under Stalin. But these early tactics produced a mixed set of results. Arms transfers did not seem to gain the Soviets much mileage. Sometimes overly close relations were established with charismatic leaders (Sadat, for example), and when they changed their minds the Soviets sometimes lost all. The Soviets posited these regimes would gradually evolve toward Marxism-Leninism, but it seldom worked out that way, and few orthodox Communists were produced. Growing disillusionment set in within the Soviet leadership regarding the third world, and in the late 1960s and early 1970s there was a certain retreat from several third world commitments.

More recently, the Soviets have reassessed their attitudes toward the third world. When Nicaragua, rather like Cuba, gravitated unexpectedly into the Soviet camp, the conclusion became obvious that with relatively little commitment, opportunities could be seized upon and important gains could be made. Soviet strategy became a matter of focusing on long-term possibilities rather than scoring short-term advantages.[5] This is a formula for assistance to broad-based popular-front and "anti-imperialist" forces in revolutionary contexts, and even in some democratic countries. But there are currently more "quality controls" built into Soviet foreign policy in Latin America than during earlier Soviet forays into the third world. These include the following:

- greater selectivity regarding the quality and reliability of the client
- greater willingness by the Soviets to involve themselves in the internal affairs of their clients
- greater use of proxy forces (for example, the Cubans)

- greater use of local intermediaries who presumably know more about local conditions than the Soviets (again the Cubans)
- greater control over local internal policy and security forces, with special assistance provided by the East Germans
- greater support for local Communist parties in directing and leading more broadly based revolutions
- greater centralization of political control over revolutionary insurrections, including the forging of unity among otherwise disparate groups as in Nicaragua and El Salvador
- greater concern for third world collective security arrangements for mutual support of revolutionary regimes using the GDR for security training, Bulgaria for intelligence work, and Cuba for the direct supply of troops when necessary

Planning, Coordination, and Tactics. The above background discussion provides us with a sense of the general orientation and strategies pursued by the Soviets in dealing with the third world. However, with regard to more specific tactics and orientations, the Grenada documents are most revealing. What follows is a listing of some of the important points that stand out in the documents. Other investigators might well be impressed by additional features or give different emphases to the same points.

1. From 1979 onward, the Soviet Union appeared to keep a certain distance from the Grenadian revolution and the New Jewel Movement (NJM). The NJM was considered a "fraternal party," but it was not treated on the same level as other Communist parties. The Grenadian ambassador in Moscow labored to increase the Soviet involvement in Grenada, but the Soviets were often reluctant. There was not a high degree of Soviet attention to day-to-day events in Grenada. The Soviets were involved in and supportive of the Grenadian revolution, but they appeared to refrain from "micro-managing" Grenadian affairs. Thus the Soviet role in Grenada was limited.[6]

Perhaps two dozen Grenadians were given training in the Soviet Union, but they were unhappy in the "American" division in Moscow where they were in the same study group as the *gringos* and the Canadians. The documents also show that the Soviets wanted the Grenadians to serve as intermediaries to other English-speaking groups in the Caribbean and to bring another country into the Communist fold. Moscow suggested either Suriname or Belize, but it recognized the latter might take some time. The documents further show that Cuba, Nicaragua, and Grenada were already thought of as securely ensconced in the Soviet camp and that El Salvador would be the next battleground. But the Soviets did not press too hard, and apparently they had modest expectations of the Grenadian revolution. One senses from the documents a certain skepticism on the part of the Soviets as to the stability and the trustworthiness of their Grenadian client. The coup against Bishop might in fact demonstrate a Soviet willingness to dump unorthodox Marxist leaders of whom it disapproves, but Soviet complicity in Bishop's overthrow and violent death is not indicated in the documents.

2. Instead of becoming directly involved in everyday Grenadian affairs, the Soviet Union chose to operate through Cuba. A fascinating question, not fully resolved by the documents, is the degree to which there is a central direction from Moscow versus autonomy on the part of Soviet proxies. The documents seem to show that the Cubans had considerable autonomy, though ultimate authority was lodged in Moscow.[7] In this sense, the Soviets had the best of all possible worlds. They could claim credit for all successes, wash their hands of failures and blame them on the Cubans, and embarrass the United States in its own backyard without actually provoking the United States by becoming directly involved in its backyard.

3. This analysis, however, does not do full justice to the Cuban role in Grenada. The documents show the Cubans were pivotal to a degree not realized before. They were involved in all aspects of the Grenadian revolution. Grenada was Cuba's "project" or "client," just as Cuba is a client of the Soviet Union. Cuba was the go-between in the Soviet-Grenadian relationship. Cuban technicians not only helped build the famous Port Salines airport, but also provided doctors, medical assistance, and several teachers. Cubans sometimes sat in on meetings of the Central Committee and Politburo of the NJM. Grenadian leaders were frequently shuttled to Havana for advice and counsel. There was a cooperation and exchange agreement between the Cuban Communist party and the NJM, as well as between the NJM and the Communist party of the Soviet Union (CPSU). One gets the impression that the Grenadians did practically nothing without consulting with the Cubans first, certainly on important matters.[8]

4. The Grenadian revolution was much more planned, sophisticated, and serious than commonly believed. In the Western media, Grenada has been generally pictured as "comic opera." A revolution on a small island whose population is only 100,000 and whose chief export is nutmeg is not taken seriously. But in fact the Grenadian revolution was very serious. It had its comic opera aspects, and these sometimes have been seized upon even by those who have examined the documents (which are full of misspellings, amusing anecdotes,

personal foibles, amateurism, and misbegotten encounters of various sorts); but a closer reading reveals a serious revolution, with serious leaders, serious issues, serious debates, wrenching decisions, and finally, a horrendous dénouement in the events leading to the murder of Maurice Bishop and his followers. This is serious business, not the stuff of *opéra bouffe*.

5. Related to the seriousness of the Grenadian revolution is the fact that it was considerably more Marxist-Leninist than previously thought. Reading only the popular press accounts prior to the intervention, one had the image of a carefree and relaxed revolution, led by romantic Socialists, a merry band of Robin Hoods, and a revolution calmed by cool island breezes and shaded by lazy palm trees. On the contrary, the detailed minutes of Politburo meetings show a dedicated Marxist-Leninist leadership unequivocally committed to embarrassing the United States and strengthening its ties with Cuba and the Soviet Union. This was not a group of somewhat fuzzy-headed reformers, but a dedicated cadre of Marxist-Leninists with clear aims and goals.[9]

6. Equally impressive is the degree of coordination among the international actors involved in the Grenadian revolution. Again, Cuba provided the key. But the East Germans, Czechoslovakians, Bulgarians, and Soviets were also intimately involved. Jamaican Prime Minister Michael Manley lent support and occasionally was useful to the above revolutionary coalition. The division of labor among the Communist countries aiding Grenada was quite impressive. The Soviet Union provided overall guidance and direction; the East Germans were involved in security and police training; Czechoslovakia sent weapons; and Cuba provided trainers, construction crews, and technicians. Not all Eastern European nations were involved in or even interested in Grenada, but among those Communist states involved in the Caribbean, the planning and coordination have increased markedly over the years.[10] The popular image of the Grenadian revolution is one of haphazardness, disorganization, and general sloppiness. But the reality revealed in the Grenada documents is one of coordination, a rather efficient and quite rational division of labor, and a level of sophistication and Communist cooperation both unexpected and impressive.

7. Some of the most revealing documents deal with the Socialist International (SI). The Grenadians and their allies made strenuous efforts to manipulate the SI—to turn it into an anti-American organ and use it to gain support and legitimacy for the revolution.[11] The documents reveal a sophisticated understanding of the SI and its

divisions. Particularly singled out for disapproval by the Grenadians and Cubans were former Venezuelan President Carlos Andres Pérez, Portuguese Prime Minister Mario Soares, and Spanish Prime Minister Felipe González—all of whom had reservations about the Nicaraguan revolution and the purity of purpose of the Salvadoran guerrillas and insisted on coupling condemnations of U.S. military machinations in Central America with a call for the removal of "all" (presumably Cuban as well as American) military forces from the area. Particularly singled out for praise were former West German Chancellor Willy Brandt and Dutch and Scandinavian Socialist and Social-Democratic parties who were more sympathetic to Cuban, Nicaraguan, and Grenadian points of view. The SI has long been a major worldwide voice in support of democracy and human rights, but that should not blind us to the divisions within its ranks that are being manipulated by elements whose agendas are not at all democratic. The Grenada documents even suggest that certain revolutionary states were planning a secret coalition within the Socialist Intenational.

8. Finally, the Grenada documents indicate an effort by the Soviets, Cubans, Nicaraguans, and Grenadians to influence domestic opinion in the United States (and also Canada).[12] Various church groups, human rights agencies, newspapers, university groups, and congressmen are singled out as avenues for spreading propaganda, disinformation, and favorable publicity about the Grenadian revolution. One of the more extraordinary documents in the collection is a letter from Gail Reed, the American wife of the Cuban Ambassador to Grenada Julian Torres Rizo, to Maurice Bishop prior to his visit to the United States. Among other things, Bishop is advised on how to deal with the American media: "In the absence of violence . . . controversy will do."[13]

Grenada's Ties with Nicaragua Prior to the U.S. Intervention. Other authors in this volume have focused their analyses on Grenada's ties with revolutionary Cuba. As the documents reveal, Cuba is the linchpin in revolutionary operations in the Caribbean—the essential hub from which other activities radiate. In a manner of speaking, Nicaragua is one of the "spokes" in the Cuban "wheel," and Grenada was yet another. Cuba was the center, but there were also direct ties between Grenada and Nicaragua. These ties were not extensive, and the barriers of language, political culture, and the absence of direct transportation further added to the difficulty of maintaining close relations. Nevertheless, the documents reveal some interesting ties.

Grenada signed a mutual health assistance pact with Nicaragua.

Two Grenadian teachers (out of twelve originally scheduled to go) were sent to Nicaragua to assist in its literacy program. Indicative of the limited ties between the two countries, and also the way in which relations among revolutionary countries in the Caribbean were coordinated, travel arrangements for these teachers had to be made through the Nicaraguan ambassador to Havana.[14]

Grenadian representatives were sent to a secret regional caucus held in Managua to plan strategy for influencing the Socialist International.[15] This was not a meeting of the SI itself, but only of revolutionary countries making plans for an upcoming meeting. Grenada professed its solidarity with the Nicaraguan revolution and with the Salvadoran guerrillas on many occasions. It registered its protest against the U.S.-supported *contras* in Nicaragua, but there are documents that speak of Grenadians being sent to the Nicaraguan-Honduran front as a symbol of solidarity with the Nicaraguan militia.[16] There are also letters from Nicaraguan commanders to their Grenadian counterparts wishing their revolution well. So far as material aid, however, the documents only reveal that Nicaragua sent 2,000 militia uniforms to Grenada and the material for 2,000 more.[17]

Grenada and Nicaragua had virtually no relations whatsoever prior to 1979, and, even after their respective revolutions, Grenadian-Nicaraguan relations remained quite limited. Relations were confined for the most part to symbolic expressions of sympathy and solidarity. The real impact of Grenada on Nicaragua came in the wake of the U.S.-OECS intervention, not before.

The U.S. Intervention and its Effects

The U.S.-OECS intervention in Grenada in October 1983 may have been a watershed. From the point of view of the Reagan administration, the Grenada intervention showed both the efficiency of U.S. military actions and, perhaps more important, a willingness to use force in defense of American interests, thus demonstrating that the United States had finally overcome its guilt complex over Vietnam. Perhaps the major effect of the intervention, however, was felt by Grenada's revolutionary neighbors: Suriname, the rebels in El Salvador, and Nicaragua.

The impact of the intervention in Grenada was felt most immediately in Suriname. On the night of October 25, only hours after the U.S. intervention in Grenada, Lt. Colonel Daysie Bouterse, chief of the Surinamese army and head of the government since February 1980, announced on national television that Cuban Ambassador Oscar Osvaldo Cárdenas had been given six days to leave the country. Cuba was asked to reduce its diplomatic relations to the *chargé d'affaires* level. Bouterse announced further that a cultural and economic agreement with Havana had been suspended. In addition, twenty-five Cuban diplomats and eighty advisers were asked to leave the country, leaving the Cuban Embassy in Paramaribo with only minimum personnel.[18]

Bouterse's rule in Suriname had become increasingly brutal over the years. His relations with Cuba had once been warm, and the Cubans had been energetically cultivating ties with Suriname at several levels. They had given training to the leaders of Suriname's 3,000-man militia. The Cubans were suspected of being behind some of the moves toward greater totalitarianism that characterized Bouterse's rule, and they had sought to increase their influence within the army.[19]

The expulsion of the Cuban ambassador and other actions to reduce Cuban influence in Suriname were directly related to the events in Grenada, albeit not entirely in sequence and for the precise reasons that one might expect. Bouterse had become increasingly resentful of the Cubans' interference in his country. In 1983, he sought to mend relations with the United States. Suriname army officials felt the Cubans were partly responsible for the bloody developments in Grenada and feared the same might happen in their country. Some military officers were also resentful of Cuban efforts to interfere in army affairs, and hence they put pressure on Bouterse to remove the Cubans. Bouterse apparently feared he might meet the same fate as Maurice Bishop. Finally, there are reports that Brazil, which lies on Suriname's southern border and is fearful of any Cuban or leftist presence nearby, exercised pressure on Paramaribo.[20]

Although Bouterse's actions coincided with the U.S. intervention and were doubtless influenced by it, the decision to reduce the Cuban presence was actually made before the invasion. The intervention accelerated the process and gave it particular immediacy, but the process was already under way. Partly for economic reasons, the Surinamese had been trying to improve ties with Washington so as to qualify for economic assistance and better trade relations. Apparently, the Cubans had been trying to influence key Surinamese groups to oppose this policy—a strategy that produced resentment toward the Cubans, especially from inside the army. Suriname also tried to obtain aid from the Dutch to improve its failing economy, but the Dutch said there would be no renewed assistance until progress had been made to restore democracy and improve human rights.[21] Thus a considerable variety of motives lay behind Suriname's strong actions against the Cubans. But while the Grenada intervention was not the sole cause of Suriname's change of policy, it certainly helped accelerate the decision.

The impact of the U.S.-OECS intervention was also felt strongly but somewhat ambiguously by the guerrillas in El Salvador. In general, the U.S. action was seen as a blow to revolutionary hopes and aspirations throughout the hemisphere.[22] For the Salvadoran guerrillas, it meant that the United States was willing to use force to prevent their coming to power. With the strong U.S. military buildup in Central America over the past four years, this did not come entirely as a surprise. Rather than representing a break with the past, the Salvadoran guerrilla leadership saw the invasion of Grenada as merely one more, albeit dramatic, military escalation in a process that had been long under way. Nevertheless, the invasion forced a major reassessment of guerrilla policies.

For the rank-and-file in the Salvadoran guerrilla movement, there were now additional calls for patriotism, heroism, and the need for a long struggle. Whether such admonitions would be acceptable to the peasants who make up the guerrilla ranks was questionable. Fighting a corrupt and incompetent El Salvadoran army is one thing, but the prospect of fighting the well-equipped Americans is quite another. The possibility of defeat or death began to loom large, and the guerrillas began to have trouble filling their ranks. The election of a legitimate, democratic president in 1984 added further to these fears, and the guerrillas increasingly turned to forced impressment to fill their ranks.[23]

One conclusion reached by the guerrilla leadership was that the Reagan administration was willing to employ any means, including armed intervention, to prevent a guerrilla victory. Thus, in contrast to the high expectations of some guerrilla leaders for a quick victory, others began to feel that final victory might be a long way off. A second conclusion, flowing from the logic of the first, was that the guerrillas should try to remove President Reagan from office. If Mr. Reagan was willing to go so far as to use force in the region, perhaps a Democratic president would not be so inclined. With the Soviet Union similarly disinclined to see a second Reagan term and Cubans providing the arms, the guerrillas began preparing for a fall offensive. Rather like the Tet offensive in Vietnam, the guerrillas hoped to raise the costs of continuing American support for El Salvador by launching a bloody offensive just prior to the U.S. election. Aimed chiefly at influencing U.S. voters, the offensive was designed (1) to raise the level of carnage and violence seen on U.S. television screens and kill as many as possible in the process (which might have an effect similar to the October 1983 killing of the 241 servicemen in Lebanon that led to an American withdrawal); (2) to provoke right-wing death squads into further undisciplined and indiscriminate slaughters (thus stimulating U.S. outcries similar to those that followed the killing of the four church women in December 1980); and (3) to make the cost of "staying the course" in El Salvador so high that the American public—notoriously impatient with murky and protracted guerrilla wars—would force the administration to withdraw or elect a new administration. The wheels and mechanisms were thus put in place to affect the U.S. elections.[24] But the offensive was never launched, and President Reagan was reelected.

An alternative conclusion, also stemming from the logic of the first, was that the guerrillas should increase pressures for a negotiated solution while simultaneously continuing the guerrilla struggle. Some guerrilla leaders feel that because the United States will not let them win, it is prudent to opt for a negotiated settlement that brings them into a position of power and gives them the opportunity to regroup and continue their struggle by other means. Indeed, it is current guerrilla strategy to increase pressure in El Salvador and the United States for a negotiated settlement, and the guerrillas are presently engaged in talks with the El Salvadoran government. Among some guerrilla leaders, a negotiated settlement is now viewed as preferable to a guerrilla victory because the latter, à la Grenada, will only invite U.S. armed intervention.[25]

Once again, it is Cuba at least as much as the Salvadoran guerrillas who have formulated these plans. But the high level of coordination and centralization of tactics among revolutionary groups and countries is a phenomenon that was well under way before the invasion of Grenada. It is Cuba (and obviously by extension the Soviet Union) that insisted on a Tet-like offensive to affect U.S. public opinion. Deputy Foreign Minister Ricardo Alarcon set forth the logic for such an offensive, and Vice President Carlos Rafael Rodríguez, plainly speaking for Fidel Castro, has provided the logic for a negotiated settlement. According to Mr. Rodríguez, "A military victory by the guerrillas now in El Salvador could provoke an immediate U.S. reaction. We of course believe the guerrillas can win but that through negotiations we can avoid what might occur if they do."[26]

Such "advice" has not been always appreciated by the guerrillas in El Salvador. Some guerrilla leaders still believe they can win the war and that the threat of U.S. intervention is exaggerated. Having struggled in the bush for so long, they harbor a certain resentment toward the Cubans for trying to run their revolution. They remain convinced, perhaps rightly, that the United States will eventually tire of the war, pack its bags, and go home. Then their moment of triumph will have arrived.

The impact of the Grenada intervention on El Salvador therefore might have been temporary. There was much soul-searching among the guerrillas, but now they have a new strategy. They know that the present heavy U.S. commitment to Central America will not allow a quick victory. They hope that a new offensive can affect U.S. public opinion. Guerrilla leader Joaquín Villalobos has a long history of sacrificing his men for the sake of affecting U.S. elections. But even if this strategy fails, the guerrillas are prepared for a long struggle.

Initially, the strongest effects of the invasion of Grenada were felt in Nicaragua. To the point of paranoia, the Nicaraguans were absolutely convinced that they were next. Of course the Sandinistas have long felt that a U.S. invasion was imminent. Even while fighting during 1977–1979, they kept looking up at the sky waiting for the 82nd Airborne to drop down upon them. They were surprised when the expected invasion never occurred and the revolution succeeded. Some analysts believe that this partially explains the chaos and confusion in the present Nicaraguan regime. It is possible that the Sandinistas never expected to win and that they still don't know what to do with the power they have gained.

The Grenada intervention unquestionably added to the paranoia of the Sandinista regime. In the first blush of the intervention, the Sandinistas were absolutely certain they would be invaded. These fears were fanned further by the American media's reaction to the intervention, which suggested that Grenada was a "dress rehearsal" or "warm-up" for invading Nicaragua. Even columnists such as Tom Wicker of the *New York Times* and Mary McGrory of the *Washington Post* made these claims.[27] They attempted to sway U.S. public opinion against such an invasion, but the effect of their columns was to fan the flames of paranoia in Managua.

The Reagan administration was not averse to seeing the Sandinistas squirm and added further pressures with its studied ambiguity. When asked if Grenada was a prelude to Nicaragua, President Reagan refused to say that it was not, and he dropped several strong hints that it might be. The Nicaraguans had long been fearful that the "cowboy" in the White House might be "crazy" enough to consider invading them, but now they were certain of his intentions. Other administration officials were equally vague when asked similar questions about an invasion of Nicaragua. Meanwhile, adding further to the Sandinistas' fears, the U.S. military buildup in the Caribbean and

Central America continued; the U.S.-sponsored *contras* stepped up their raids; and the Central American Defense Council (CONDECA), which like the Organization of East Caribbean States (OECS) might help legitimize and provide multilateral cover for a U.S. intervention, was revived.

Nicaragua's erstwhile allies were not always helpful. The Soviet Union advised the Sandinistas that in the event of an invasion, they could not count on Soviet military assistance. The Soviets said plainly they would write no blank checks for economic assistance and that Soviet military involvement was out of the question. The Cubans also told the Nicaraguans that Cuba would not be able to defend them in the event of an American invasion. This left Nicaragua alone and isolated to face the "Colossus of the North." In addition, it was known that Cuban "workers" in Grenada had been instructed to "fight to the death" to show the United States how bloody and difficult it would be if the United States invaded Nicaragua or Cuba. However, the Cubans did not fight to the death for Grenada—a fact that was not lost on the Sandinista leadership. Playing the "Cuba card" was looking less and less attractive to the revolutionary governments of Suriname and Nicaragua. The already powerful sense of paranoia in Managua was strengthened when the Cubans announced plans to pull some of their advisers out of Nicaragua and to reduce their military presence and training programs. This partially removed one of the possible provocations for an American intervention, but left Nicaragua to fend for itself.[28]

These feelings of defeatism, impending doom, and paranoia on the part of the Nicaraguan leadership eventually gave way to more reasoned assessments. The fear of a U.S. invasion was (and is) still present, but paralysis was replaced by preparations. The elements in the Sandinista plans to resist an American invasion include the following:[29]

• Use the American threat as a means to rally Nicaraguan public opinion, unify the population behind the revolution, and call for greater popular efforts and sacrifices to repel a possible invasion.

• Build up Nicaragua's defense forces by further increasing the size of the armed forces and the militia (which are already the largest and best equipped in Central America) and strengthen centralized and concentrated political controls.

• Let the United States know how costly an intervention would be by stressing how stiff the resistance will be. To this end, the Nicaraguans revealed some of their defensive strategies. In addition, they emphasized their intention to fight to the bitter end, the fact that

Nicaragua is much stronger and more heavily armed than Grenada had been, and that U.S. intervention would be bloody and prolonged—as opposed to the quick, surgical strike in Grenada. Their intention was to convince the United States that an invasion of Nicaragua would require far more patience and commitment on the part of American public opinion than are likely to be forthcoming.

- Step up the propaganda war internationally with special emphasis on the United States. This includes reestablishing good relations with the Socialist International (which had become disillusioned with Nicaragua) and activating the revolution's friends and supporters in the United States to write letters, sway public opinion, and support alternative peace plans which, if adopted, would at least allow the revolution to survive.
- Avoid antagonizing the United States. This message was conveyed forcefully to the Sandinistas by Castro himself, that is, maintain a low profile for the time being. As a result, a substantial number of Cubans were removed from Nicaragua. Such a strategy would seem to indicate that the Sandinistas should become more conciliatory and allow a certain degree of domestic liberalization. The problem, as both the Sandinistas and the Americans know, is that these steps might produce an independent dynamic of their own that could undermine the revolution and its leadership—and still not satisfy the Americans.

There can be no doubt that the Grenada intervention greatly increased U.S. pressure on Nicaragua. It gave the United States an immense amount of renewed leverage in determining the fate and ultimate direction of the Nicaraguan revolution. Essentially, the Nicaraguan response has been to augment preparations for a possible invasion and to step up its propaganda war while seeking to avoid provocation. The Nicaraguans have reassessed their situation. The early effect of the intervention was very sobering, but the shock has worn off. There is still fear of a U.S.-sponsored invasion in one of several forms—directly, by the *contras*, with CONDECA, or a combination of all three—but several members of the Sandinista leadership are no longer certain of an intervention. They are perfectly aware that U.S. public opinion will not support a foreign quagmire such as Vietnam or Lebanon for a long period of time (as distinct from the "quick and clean" operation in Grenada). They know that Congress and U.S. foreign policy agencies are divided, and they know that the U.S. Department of Defense is extremely reluctant to become involved in another imbroglio where goals are not clearly defined, the public is not supportive, and becoming bogged down would reflect adversely on the military itself.

211

Nevertheless, a certain sense of fatalism and despair has set in among the Nicaraguan leadership. The revolution has not produced the glorious results expected. The economy is a disaster; the country is beginning to fragment and polarize; the opposition is growing; and the Americans might well strangle the revolution. Policy has reached a dead end. Many Sandinistas have decided they were far happier as triumphant guerrillas than with the far more complex, less glorious, even boring task of governing. No matter what they do, the revolution does not seem to be working. They are damned if they liberalize and open up the country, and damned if they go further toward full-fledged Marxism-Leninism of the Cuban variety. Tomás Borge of the Sandanista junta has said privately that no matter what they do, the Americans will not allow their revolution to survive. In short, the Sandinistas are convinced that their revolution is in grave trouble.[30]

Conclusions and Implications

The fact that Grenada has faded from the American news and public consciousness does not mean it has been forgotten by foreign policy analysts. Throughout the world—particularly in Central America and the Caribbean, the Soviet bloc, and the United States—analyses of the implications of Grenada are ongoing. My own assessment is that the Grenada intervention had far greater implications internationally than the small size or importance of that particular island would seem to indicate.

However, it is not likely that Grenada was a watershed in the sense that some enthusiasts have written. I do not believe that Grenada shows that the United States has definitely overcome the Vietnam syndrome, that it has surmounted its foreign policy divisions, or that it will now be prepared to act decisively in other areas where its basic interests are affected. There is some truth in these claims, but it is not likely that things have changed all that much.

Similarly, we must distinguish between interventions in small islands and interventions in mainland countries. These might be designated as "models." The first is the "Santo Domingo model," and the second is the "Vietnam model" (after the two major U.S. military interventions of the 1960s). In the first paradigm, of which Grenada is a recent illustration, it is possible to move in quickly, isolate and defeat the resistance, form a provisional government, and withdraw quickly, all of which are elements of a "successful" intervention. But in a mainland country such as Vietnam or Nicaragua, matters are not so easy. Guerrilla forces cannot be isolated and pinned down so easily. Rather than face defeat they may flee into a neighboring country, and the invading forces would then have to bomb their sanctuaries, etc. In this event, the United States would have a "second Vietnam" on its hands. The distinction between Santo Domingo and Vietnam, or between Grenada and Nicaragua, is carefully kept in mind in Department of Defense contingency planning. This is why we should not expect Grenada-like invasions on the mainland of Central America—although that possibility cannot be ruled out entirely.

We must further distinguish between countries. In Nicaragua, which displayed an acute sense of paranoia and had long expected a U.S. invasion, the effect of Grenada was electric. In Cuba, which has been living with the threat of American intervention for a full quarter century, the invasion of Grenada undoubtedly caused fears, but the Cuban leadership probably does not believe it will be invaded in the foreseeable future. The Grenada intervention had a galvanizing effect on Suriname, and while it had little immediate effect on the guerrillas in El Salvador, it did prompt a change in tactics.

Nevertheless, there are considerable clues that the Grenada intervention had significant long-term implications for guerrilla and revolutionary forces in Central America and the Caribbean Basin. The evidence is still fragmentary, but it seems to point to the following implications which add up in an especially significant manner.

1. Though the immediate effects on El Salvador were not marked, the Grenada intervention appears to have prompted the guerrillas into a long-term reassessment. The guerrillas now appear to realize that they underestimated the strength of the Salvadoran army, underestimated the resiliency of Salvadoran society, overestimated the degree of support for their cause by the Salvadoran people, underestimated the will and staying power of the United States, underestimated Mr. Duarte and the importance of elections and a legitimated Salvadoran government, and overestimated their own possibilities. Hence they are "hunkered" in for a long struggle, which they may not win and which might lead to a certain atrophy and isolation of their struggle.[31]

2. Cuba is also taking stock. Although there is much rhetorical flourish to the contrary, some reports indicate that Castro has concluded that socialism will not soon triumph anywhere else in Central America and that he has already begun to pull back his forces.[32] If this is so, Cuba might begin to look elsewhere for the furtherance of "proletarian internationalism."

3. The Nicaraguan revolution has become somewhat immobilized in a bunker mentality and is facing frustration or defeat on all sides. This might well lead to diminished Nicaraguan (and Cuban) support for the guerrillas in El Salvador and significantly reduced efforts to spread the Nicaraguan revolution to other countries.[33]

4. There are signs that the Soviet Union is reassessing its options as well. Historically, Latin America has not been a high-priority area for the Soviets. At little or no cost, they have made gains by catching plums that fall into their lap. But aside from their close relationship with Cuba, they have not been willing to commit major resources to the region. The Soviets are not looking for a major confrontation with the United States in the Caribbean. The invasion of Grenada coupled with the U.S. military buildup in the area might influence the Soviets to look elsewhere for targets of opportunity. This would be consistent with Leninist principles concerning the need to probe constantly for soft spots, a long history of cautious Soviet involvement in the third world, and a quiet assessment of what they can reasonably expect to accomplish.[34]

It is not entirely clear that the Grenada intervention was an unadulterated defeat for the Soviet Union. The Soviets and Cubans have reaped some propaganda advantages from the invasion. Moreover, the Soviets do not suffer long from pique or guilt. They will reassess and try again. In this sense, Grenada might be seen as only a temporary setback for the Soviets. It also might lead the Soviets to conclude that the United States has raised the costs of Soviet adventurism in Central America and the Caribbean to a level they are unwilling to pay. Hence they might opt to look to other areas for opportunities to expand their influence. The Grenada intervention might have been a significant triumph for American foreign policy in the Western Hemisphere, but it did not in any significant way reduce the overall strength and reach of the Soviet Union or its capacity to look for advantages in other areas where the United States seems less heavily committed.

Notes

1. Merle Fainsod, *Smolensk Under Soviet Rule* (Cambridge: Harvard University Press, 1958); Fainsod, *How Russia is Ruled* (Cambridge: Harvard University Press, 1953).

2. Howard Wiarda, "Soviet Policy in the Caribbean and Central America: Opportunities and Constraints," Paper presented at a conference on Soviet Foreign Policy, The Kennan Institute of Advanced Russian Studies, Woodrow Wilson International Center for Scholars, and the United States Information Agency, Washington, D.C., March 2, 1984; forthcoming in a volume entitled *Soviet Foreign Policy,* edited by Helmut Sonnenfeldt. This paper contains considerably greater detail on each of the themes mentioned—Soviet capabilities, tactics, and constraints.

3. As of April 1984, the U.S. government had released several series of documents captured in Grenada cited here as the Grenada Documents. The documents consist of New Jewel Movement Politburo and Central Committee

minutes, secret agreements with communist countries, letters, diaries, personal papers, and letters from the Grenadian embassies in Moscow and Havana, etc. Most of the documents have been logged but not necessarily properly sorted. Some are unnumbered and others are illegible; others have yet to be released. (Chap. 3 in this book.)

A preliminary evaluation was published by the Departments of State and Defense on December 16, 1983 entitled *Grenada: A Preliminary Report*. Michael Ledeen of the Center for Strategic and International Studies is editing another volume of documents soon to be published.

4. The information in this part of the paper derives from a conference on "The Orchestration of Soviet Proxy Assets: The Case of Latin America and the Caribbean," The Hoover Institution, Washington, D.C., June 13, 1984, the presentations and papers of which are forthcoming in a book to be published by the Hoover Institution.

5. The best analysis is Ernest Evans, "Revolutionary Movements in Central America: The Development of a New Strategy," in Howard J. Wiarda, ed., *Rift and Revolution: The Central American Imbroglio* (Washington, D.C.: American Enterprise Institute, 1984), pp. 167–93. (Chap. 6 in this book.)

6. Jiri and Virginia Valenta, "Leninism in Grenada," *Problems of Communism* (July–August 1984); *see also* Confidential report on Grenada's Relations with the USSR, July 11, 1983, Grenada Documents, Log No. W.

7. Memo from Bernard Bourne [Minister-Counsellor of the Grenadian Embassy in Moscow] to Comrade Maurice Bishop, Chairman of the Central Committee of the New Jewel Movement, June 30, 1982, Grenada Documents, Log No. 104262; *see also* Jorge Dominguez, "Cuba's Relations with Caribbean and Central American Countries" in Alan Adelman and Reid Reading, eds., *Confrontation in the Caribbean Basin* (Pittsburgh: Center for Latin American Studies, University of Pittsburgh, 1984), pp. 165–202.

8. The full impact of Cuba's role can only be appreciated by a full reading of the Grenada documents. See especially the minutes of NJM Politburo and Central Committee meetings.

9. *See*, for example, Top Secret Agreement on Cooperation between the New Jewel Movement of Grenada and the Communist Party of the Soviet Union, July 27, 1982, Grenada Documents, Log No. 102318; and Henry Feuer, "Was Bishop a Social Democrat?" *Caribbean Review* (March 1974), pp. 37–39.

10. Confidential report from the Grenadian Embassy in Moscow on the NJM's relations with the CPSU, undated (but sometime after December 1981), Grenada Documents, Log No. 012329; handwritten notes from meeting between Hudson Austin and the Cuban Minister of Construction, ibid., Log No. 10003; Secret Cooperation and Exchange Plan between the Communist party of Cuba and the New Jewel Movement of Grenada for the 1983 Period, ibid., Log No. 100016; and Meeting with [East German] Deputy Minister of Foreign Affairs (Latin America and Caribbean) V. Neugebanck, May 18, 1983, ibid., Log No. 102855.

11. Emergency SI [Socialist International] Meeting in Panama, memo from Unison Whiteman to NJM leadership of March 3, 1981, ibid., Log No. NM; unsigned analysis of SI Presidium Meetings in Bonn, April 1–2, 1982, ibid.,

Log No. NN; and Report on Meeting of SI held in Bonn, April 1–2, 1982, by Ferris Augustine, High Commissioner, to Foreign Minister Unison Whiteman, ibid., Log No. OO.

12. Report to the Politburo Meeting, March 29, 1983, from Unison Whiteman on attempts to influence U.S., British, and Canadian public opinion, ibid., Log No. 2.

13. Letter headed "Dear Maurice" from Gail Reed advising Bishop on tactics to use with the press and other organizations during his visit to the United States, ibid., Log No. DD.

14. Minutes of the Politburo meeting of October 21, 1981, ibid., Log No. B.

15. Unsigned, untitled report on the SI from a Leninist perspective, ibid., Log No. UU. Report on Meeting of Secret Regional Caucus of SI [Socialist International] Held in Managua, January 6–7, 1983, ibid., Log No. 100446.

16. Portion of a handwritten note from Major Roberts concerning observers to be sent to the Nicaraguan war, ibid., undated, Log No. 000084.

17. Letter from Nicaraguan Minister of Defense Humberto Ortega Savadera to Comrade Maurice Bishop, February 19, 1981, ibid., Log No. X.

18. *Foreign Broadcast Information Service* (hereafter FBIS), October 28, 1983; and *The New York Times*, October 27, 1983.

19. FBIS, *Defense and Foreign Affairs Daily,* October 28, 1983, 46–47.

20. FBIS, *Defense and Foreign Affairs Daily,* October 21, 1983. Note that this report is dated *before* the Grenada intervention.

21. FBIS, *Latin American Index,* July 15, 1984; and FBIS, October 28, 1983.

22. *The Washington Post,* March 31, 1984; and the *Los Angeles Times,* October 28, 1983.

23. The material in this section was based in part on interviews with U.S. intelligence officials; also see the papers prepared as part of the Hoover Institution study mentioned in note 4.

24. Based on press accounts of interviews with the guerrillas, for example, *Washington Post,* October 31, 1983, and May 14, 1984.

25. *See* especially the report from Havana by Edward Cody, *Washington Post,* March 18, 1984. The strongest case for a negotiated settlement is Robert Leiken's Introduction in *Central America: Anatomy of Conflict* (New York: Pergamon Press, 1984). This position was set forth by Leiken before it became, for other reasons, the strategy of the guerrillas. For the problems and traps in such a policy see the discussion in U.S. Congress, House Committee on Foreign Affairs, Foreign Assistance Legislation for Fiscal Year 1985 (Part 6): Hearings and Markup before the Committee on Foreign Affairs and its Subcommittee on Western Hemisphere Affairs. *Review of Proposed Economic and Security Assistance Requests for Latin America and the Caribbean: Recommendations of the National Bipartisan Commission on Central America* (Washington, D.C.: Government Printing Office, 1984), pp. 213–14.

26. Quoted in Cody, *Washington Post* report. The same position was set forth by Fidel Castro in his interview with Tad Szulc, *Parade,* April 1, 1984.

27. See Mary McGrory's column in the *Washington Post,* November 28, 1983.

28. *Soviet World Outlook* (November 15, 1983); *International Outlook* (November 28, 1983).

29. Based on Reports from Nicaragua in the *Washington Post*, October 27, 1983, October 31, 1983, November 12, 1983, and in *The New York Times*, November 10, 1983, November 24, 1983, and November 25, 1983.

30. Based on interviews by U.S. Department of State officials with the Sandinista leadership in April–May 1984.

31. Based on interviews by the author with U.S. intelligence officials during June–July 1984.

32. *Washington Post*, October 30, 1983 and March 18, 1984; *Economist*, January 14, 1984; *World Press Review*, March 1984; and *El Pais*, December 5, 1983.

33. This is one of the bargaining chips Nicaragua has in its renewed efforts to open negotiations with the United States.

34. W. Raymond Duncan, "Soviet Interests in Latin America: New Opportunities and Old Constraints," *Journal of Interamerican Studies and World Affairs*, May 1984; R. Osgood, "Central America in U.S. Containment Policy," in A. F. Lowenthal and S. F. Wells, eds., *Working Papers* (Washington, D.C.: Latin American Program, Wilson Center, 1983), and *Washington Post*, May 28, 1984.

9
Nicaraguan Harvest
Mark Falcoff

Nicaragua's Revolution

In 1979 Nicaraguan dictator Anastasio Somoza fled his country before the victorious onslaught of a popular revolution. This was no ordinary episode in the history of Central America, a region where governments have often disappeared abruptly and under violent circumstances. Rather, it marked the end of more than thirty years of political domination by a single family, in which local forces of revolutionary change were aided and abetted by other governments in the region and, at the very end, the United States. Although elements of the revolutionary leadership were troubling to the State Department and some members of Congress, the new regime in Nicaragua began its life with a generous legacy of optimism, hope, and good will, both at home and abroad. To some degree, this was not to be wondered at: several political generations of Nicaraguans had convinced themselves that *anything* would be better than Somoza, and sympathetic foreigners could only regard the dynasty of uniformed thugs that had governed that country since 1934 as, at best, a grotesque anachronism.

Moreover, Nicaragua was seen in July 1979 as a laboratory where all kinds of lessons learned from other places could be successfully applied. Almost immediately after the fall of Somoza, the tiny nation was almost literally overrun with foreign well-wishers bearing unsolicited advice—Spanish, Portuguese, German, and Swedish social democrats; congressmen and officials of the agency for International Development from Washington; representatives of the governments of Mexico, Venezuela, Colombia, and Panama; and a remarkable assortment of revolutionary tourists—including, but not limited to, West German Trotskyists, Maryknoll nuns, Spanish Jesuits, Italian Marxists, and North Americans of all ages, classes, and conditions. Each of these groups expected the new regime in Nicaragua to validate its own peculiar notions of social and political change, although in the euphoria of those first days no one thought to ask whether one set of agendas was compatible with another. Nor did anyone apart from the authors of the 1980 Republican platform in the United States (and, ironically, some members of the new government in Managua) seriously consider the possibility that Nicaragua might become, like Cuba, an ally and client state of the Soviet Union. Rather, it was assumed on all sides that because the past had been so bad, the future *had* to be better.

The "future" is now here, and by the reckoning of all but the most inflexible apologists for the Nicaraguan regime, it is perceptibly and measurably worse. Nicaragua is not a wealthy country, but it has always been reasonably self-sufficient in basic foodstuffs and also capable of producing or importing most basic consumer items. Indeed, over the past thirty-odd years, the living standards of the Nicaraguan people (like those in other Central American countries) had steadily risen, and the overall rates of economic growth had been, historically, quite impressive compared with those in most regions of the third world. Since 1979, however, the indicators of Nicaragua's economic performance have pointed unswervingly downward. With 1978 as a base year, by 1982 agriculture, the country's principal source of foreign exchange, had declined 17 percent, industry 18 percent, and commerce 27 percent. The only sector, in fact, that showed significant growth during that four-year period was the government, which tripled in size after the current regime took power.

These stark figures reflect a steady drop in living standards for the ordinary Nicaraguan. Private consumption fell in real terms by 12 percent in 1983 (the latest figures available), and official sources concede a 20 percent rate of unemployment. Salary levels have been frozen since 1981, and the annual rate of inflation has been higher than 25 percent (according to Nicaraguan government figures). In spite of government subsidies for basic foodstuffs, for the first time in the nation's history there are serious shortages of staple items.

It is true, as spokesmen for the regime often point out, that the Nicaraguan revolution occurred a mere seven years after a devastating earthquake that leveled Managua, the capital, and visited untold millions' worth of destruction on housing stocks, physical plant, and infractructure. It is also true that, like other Central American countries, Nicaragua is suffering from a depression in the prices of its primary exports and from increases in interest rates and in the cost of imported oil. Unlike its neighbors, however, it has been the recipient of almost unlimited foreign assistance. Since 1979 the country has received some $3 billion in new foreign loans and $250 million in outright donations (including $118 million from the United States authorized during the administration of Jimmy Carter). At the same time, like other Central American countries, Nicaragua has been able to purchase oil from Mexico and Venezuela under preferential terms and was permitted to "roll over" the old (Somoza-contracted) foreign debt with American banks—some $582 million—under exceptionally favorable circumstances. In addition, between July 1979 and November 1981 Nicaragua received an average of $12 million in new lines of credit *per month* from the World Bank and the Inter-American Development Bank.

To put matters in some perspective, during the past six years democratic Costa Rica, Nicaragua's immediate neighbor to the south, has received a mere $250 million in international assistance from the United States and Western Europe. Thus, if Nicaragua has economic problems, they cannot be due to a lack of comprehension or even solidarity on the part of the outside world.

Nicaragua's Problems

Nicaragua's problems are, however, not primarily economic but political. They arise from the disarmingly simple fact that control of what was a political revolution against Somoza has been effectively seized by a cabal of Marxist-Leninists—the Sandinista front—who believe themselves in exclusive possession of historical truth and authorized to impose it on a largely unwilling populace. In some ways what has happened in Nicaragua is not much different from what occurred in Cuba some twenty years earlier. In both cases a hated dictator was overthrown by an extremely broad coalition of forces, including business, students, labor, the traditional political class, and even the U.S. embassy. But the coalition's numerical preponderance was not sufficient in the immediate postrevolutionary period to counterbalance another group—heavily armed, better organized, more ruthless, and committed to a single, unambiguous goal.

In Nicaragua, however, there were two crucial differences. The precedent of Cuba having been clearly established, no one could plead ignorance of the process whereby a democratic revolution in the Caribbean could be derailed into a totalitarian police state. Hence the Sandinista front had to take special care to reassure its democratic allies in the struggle against Somoza, as well as the United States and other Latin American governments. This also meant that the actual *rate* at which the regime moved from control of the "commanding heights" to the institutions of daily life was bound to be much slower.

More remarkable still was the fact that precisely because of the Cuban experience, Nicaragua's well-wishers at home and abroad were desperately anxious to accept the Sandinistas' stated commitments to pluralism, a mixed economy, and a nonaligned foreign policy. This was so because they shared the view that the tragic course of the Cuban revolution had been determined by the United States, whose alleged insensitivity to Castro's needs presumably "drove" or "forced" him into the arms of the Soviet Union. By the time it had become clear that a policy of conciliation and even appeasement was having no effect whatsoever on the conduct of the Nicaraguan government, these well-wishers were rescued by the advent of a conservative Republican administration in Washington. This allowed them to avert their gaze from the unbecoming spectacle of the Sandinistas asphyxiating Nicaragua's infant democracy in, as it were, the cradle and to concentrate on the allegedly intemperate rhetoric of the White House and later the iniquities, real or imagined, of the rebel force that arose to challenge the new dictatorship.

In retrospect it seems remarkable that so many otherwise well-informed people could believe that the Sandinistas were—or could come to be—a broadly representative political force responsive even in the most general way to the wishes of the Nicaraguan people. Their world view, their ideological commitments, even their strategies for achieving power were a matter of abundant historical record long before 1979. This much is clear from an important new monograph by David Nolan,[1] which examines in considerable detail what its author calls the "internal logic" of Sandinista ideology.

Founded in 1961, the Sandinista National Liberation Front (FSLN) took its name from a guerrilla leader who had fought the American Marines in the 1920s and was subsequently murdered by the first Somoza. General Sandino was not, however, a Marxist, so that the link between his reflexively nationalist movement and the FSLN is purely metaphoric and folkloric. As Nolan shows, the Sandinistas have always been Marxist-Leninist and, beyond that, conspicuously loyal to the Soviet position in world affairs. At no time have they seriously contemplated an "independent" form of Marxism such as we are repeatedly told they might assume were the United States to alter its own policies toward them. (They have even gone so far as to continue diplomatic relations with Taiwan rather than recognize the anti-Soviet government in Beijing, even though Taipei had strongly supported Somoza and had continued to provision him with weaponry to the very end of his rule.)

Moreover, although the leadership of the FSLN has split periodically, their differences have been purely methodological, pertaining only to the question of how to achieve power, not to what to do with it once it has been attained. At times this has even meant temporarily shelving Marxist-Leninist rhetoric to reassure potential allies and, in the final phase of the struggle against Somoza, to persuade other countries to assist them with arms, base areas, and international recognition. Once in control of the army and police, the Sandinistas could afford to be more candid. To this effect, Nolan quotes Henry Ruiz, one of the nine members of the ruling National Directorate, who by June 1982 thought events sufficiently advanced to admit openly that

> the reveolution's honeymoon is coming to an end. By this I mean the romantic idea among those who believed that the Sandinista peoples' revolution was an idyllic revolution in which the interests of a group of traitors and the interests of the real working people could be fused; a shortsighted point of view, from which our revolutionary directorate never suffered.

If this was so, it was only because the National Directorate, almost unique among observers of or other participants in the Nicaraguan revolution, had no desire to deceive itself. In that sense the footnotes in Nolan's book are perhaps more dramatic than the text, for they demonstrate that Sandinista notions of power and its purpose have long been readily available—not in the secret files of Somoza's police or the computers of the Central Intelligence Agency but to literate Nicaraguans in dozens of books, pamphlets, and periodicals and to American policy makers in the unclassfied translations regularly circulated by the *Joint Publications Research Service (JPRS)* and the Latin American series of the *Foreign Broadcast Information Service (FBIS)*.

At this point the Sandinistas have clearly won control of the guns, the ministries, the media, and the largest portion of the foreign liberal public. They have demobilized most of the other political parties and forces active in the struggle against Somoza and driven most of their leaders into exile. The Sandinistas' problem, however, remains how to extend their grip on the institutions of civil society—the private sector, the peasantry, the labor movement, the Indian minorities on the Atlantic coast, and above all the Roman Catholic church. As long as these groups exist as entities separate and apart from the Nicaraguan state, they will continue to resist Sandinista rule. The cost of this struggle in economic and human terms has already been very high although, if the resistance is defeated, it will be higher still.

The best account of how the Sandinistas grew from a small group of Cuban-trained guerrillas to their present eminence is that of Shirley Christian, formerly Central American correspondent of the *Miami Herald*, and now with the *New York Times*.[2] While her book in many ways adds immeasurably to our knowledge of Nicaragua and the

Sandinistas, her narrative of events between 1979 and 1981 tells us little that we could not have anticipated from a reading of Claire Sterling's book on the communist coup in Czechoslovakia.[3] That is, the Sandinistas used the classic techniques of political domination first developed by Lenin in 1918–1923—the organization of "broad fronts" under whose ostensible banner a vanguard seizes power; the consolidation of that power through control of the organs of state security; the elimination, one by one, of quondam allies ("salami tactics"); and the creation of parallel organs (trade unions, peasant organizations, legislative bodies) to replace those that the vanguard cannot dominate. To these must be added a new Nicaraguan contribution to the repertoire—a plebiscite cleverly disguised as a competitive election.

One of the virtues of Christian's book is that many chapters are subdivided chronologically. This allows us to see how little the growth of a totalitarian state in Nicaragua could have been a response to pressure from the U.S. government or the counterrevolutionary force that (until recently) it supported. Specifically, by the end of 1979—which is to say long before the Republican party had nominated Ronald Reagan and at a time when the Carter administration was actively courting the new Nicaraguan regime with money, technical assistance, and huge quantities of food and medicine—the Sandinistas had already imposed press censorship, established neighborhood surveillance committees to monitor the lives of ordinary citizens, and begun to establish, with Cuban assistance, the largest army and the most elaborate domestic police apparatus in Central America.

In 1980, again before the change of administrations in Washington, the Sandinista front had peremptorily increased the size of the Council of State to forty-seven members and reapportioned the seats in its favor, postponed promised elections indefinitely, signed a party-to-party agreement with the Communist party of the Soviet Union, and begun to harass the leaders of Nicaragua's Permanent Commission on Human Rights.

In March 1981, two months after the Reagan administration took office, the *contras* were organized. For most of that year they were a force of negligible military significance, a few hundred men recruited mainly from the ranks of Somoza's National Guard by the U.S. Central Intelligence Agency and rather inexpertly advised by Argentine military officers and counterintelligence agents. At the time it was common for the Sandinistas themselves to poke fun at the *contras*—calling attention to their impotence and extremely limited political appeal.

Then in June 1981 the chief of the new Popular Sandinista Army, Comandante Humberto Ortega, made a secret speech to a gathering of military officers avowing that "without *sandinismo* we cannot be Marxist-Leninist, and *sandinismo* without Marxism-Leninism cannot be revolutionary" and admitting that the existing pacts with other, more moderate political forces had been mere expedients to get rid of Somoza, hold off U.S. military intervention, and keep the economy intact. This did not mean, he assured his audience, that the Sandinista front had any intention of caving in to a "bourgeois" political program; indeed, all non-Marxists who had been allies in the struggle against the dictatorship were now declared to be the enemy.

A few weeks later Assistant Secretary of State Thomas Enders visited Managua to discuss a possible démarche in relations. Enders made four demands of the Sandinistas—that they withdraw from arms trafficking into El Salvador; that they slow or cease their own military buildup, which was upsetting the regional arms balance; that they take steps to fulfill their promises of economic and political pluralism at home; and that they temper their association with Cuba and the Soviet bloc. In exchange he offered a resumption of U.S. economic aid (which had actually been suspended in the last days of the *Carter* administration) and stern measures to prevent any exile force from attacking Nicaragua from U.S. territory or with U.S. assistance. His offer was categorically turned aside. Since the Enders mission in August 1981, relations between the Nicaraguan government and the United States have continued to deteriorate.

The real conflict, however, has not been the one between Managua and Washington; it has been the growing antagonism between the Sandinista front and the people in whose name it presumes to speak. This conflict was, in a sense, inevitable, because a society can be organized effortlessly along Marxist lines only if the vast majority of the population has absolutely nothing to lose. Of course no such society has ever existed, and Nicaragua is no exception. By one authoritative estimate, in 1978 the number of Nicaraguan families that possessed property in one form or another was some 180,000,[4] which when increased conservatively by a multiplier of five amounts to 900,000 people, or just short of one-third of the population. Whether such people qualify for the term "middle class" (or even "bourgeoisie") is a matter of sociological judgment or of one's political vocabulary. But so numerous a stratum would normally give pause to any government intent on restructuring society—unless, of course, the government believed that even an extremely modest stake in the existing system of private property automatically rendered one morally deficient.

In the United States and elsewhere there is considerable confusion about the private sector in Nicaragua because the regime continues to insist that it favors a mixed economy and because it can point to the fact that slightly more than half the means of production formally remains in private hands. Shortly after the fall of Somoza, however, all banks, shipping, and export-marketing firms were taken over by the state, so that from the beginning the government was in a position to control the disbursement of credit and foreign exchange. By 1983 the public sector was receiving more than six times as much credit as the private, at far more favorable rates of interest. This, in conjunction with high taxes and price controls, has allowed the Sandinistas quietly to absorb private business through what appear to be perfectly legal procedures—first bankruptcy, then the takeover of defunct enterprises by their creditors (that is, the state).

This process has been slower than the Sandinistas' ideological predilections would normally dictate, because they understand that the apparent survival of a private sector in Nicaragua is a political fact that strongly influences their credibility in Western Europe and the United States. Then, too, some industries, like cotton, are highly centralized and capital-intensive and require annual reinfusions of capital. This explains why cotton planters have been favored with relatively higher prices for their crop than producers of coffee, who tend to be small farmers without the kinds of skills, education, and capital that would allow them to emigrate and whose fixed investment—in this case, the plants—is not readily transferable.[5]

The most important indicator of the Sandinistas' ultimate intentions toward the private sector is that they have deprived its umbrella organization, the Supreme Council of Private Enterprise (COSEP), of the political representation it originally received in the Council of State. As serious Marxists they understand that economic power cannot be artificially separated from political participation: if the one is to be abolished, the other must eventually also be liquidated. In this instance, they are working both ends against the middle. Properly interpreting the signs of the times, leaders of the private sector have declined to accept periodic assurances of good will in place of concrete acts. Instead, over the past six years there has been a catastrophic flight of capital and managerial skills.

Because they are privileged beings in a society where most people are poor, businessmen in Nicaragua cannot expect to command much sympathy abroad. But for a variety of reasons the Sandinistas' treatment of COSEP has actually been somewhat gentle compared with that doled out to smaller entrepreneurs. One such group, which Shirley Christian singles out for special attention, is the market vendors. These are penny capitalists, many of them women, who rise at dawn to set up makeshift stalls in open-air markets, where they sell everything from rice and beans to articles of clothing and children's toys. In the Department of Managua alone, there are some 30,000 such people; she estimates that there may be another 30,000 scattered throughout the provincial market towns.

The problem began in early 1982, when the government suddenly declared that for the foreseeable future sugar would be rationed. Consumers were told that to obtain this most basic of items they would have to get a ration card from their local block (surveillance) committee; they were assigned stores according to the neighborhood in which they lived and specific days on which they could buy their allotment. The stores were either "popular" groceries established by the government or supermarkets expropriated from Somoza or his cronies. The market vendors were not supplied. During the next three years similar measures were enacted for many other basic consumer items, all of which were removed from the normal channels of supply and demand.

To ask why sugar (and later rice, beans, corn, milk, bananas, cooking oil, and a dozen other articles) came to be rationed in Nicaragua when the country had never before suffered a shortage of foodstuffs is to ask the wrong question. It presupposes that the purpose of the Sandinista government is to encourage agricultural production and widespread consumption, whereas in fact its intention is to use food as a means of political control. It is in line with this intention that priorities are organized. Immediately after the revolution, the FSLN created a new agricultural marketing agency, National Enterprise for Basic Foodstuffs (ENABAS), to purchase the harvest from farmers and to provision the urban consumer. This effectively disfranchised two groups that the government could not control: the vendors themselves and private middlemen, some of whom were simply independent cooperatives. The market vendors have fought back—with demonstrations, passive resistance, participation in the nation's growing underground economy, even at times with rough justice before sunrise when local Sandinista officials display an excess of zeal. But precisely because the government is willing to subordinate the normal imperatives of the market economy to its political agendas, in the end, other things being equal, it will win.

Rising Totalitarianism

The creation of ENABAS also put the regime in a position to discipline the farmers, since it was now the only customer for their produce. At first there was no problem because ENABAS paid the farmers more than they would otherwise have received and sold their output at artificially low prices. As time went on, the ordinary rules of economics reasserted themselves, and the agency began to quarrel with producers over prices and also over access to certain essential inputs, such as fertilizer and chemicals. Eventually farmers saw no reason to produce beyond their immediate needs, and there was a dramatic drop in several basic foodstuffs, notably corn and beans. One cannot assume, however, that the Sandinistas found the shortages wholly disconcerting. Shortages, after all, justify the introduction of ration cards, which in turn enhance the importance and power of the block committees and also apparently underscore the need for agencies like ENABAS, which ostensibly address what is, in fact, a very serious national crisis.

The Sandinistas have also had their problems with the peasantry. Although historically much of the productive agricultural land in Nicaragua has been concentrated in large agribusiness combines, the country has always had a fairly numerous smallholder class and an even larger group of tenant farmers who worked subsistence plots. Unlike El Salvador, moreover, Nicaragua also has plenty of vacant land, and in the days of Somoza there was even a small and poorly funded program to encourage homesteading in virgin territories. There was, then, a "land question" in Nicaragua, but it was far less pressing then in many Central American countries. Further, the immediate expropriation in 1979 of 2.75 million acres formerly belonging to Somoza, his associates, or simply people whom the FSLN decided to call *somocistas* in order to take their land presumably equipped the government with a large store of rural properties with which it could abundantly satisfy peasant aspirations to ownership.

The difficulty has been, of course, that, like Marxist revolutionaries everywhere, the Sandinistas do not look with favor on private property in land, even on a very modest scale. Consequently, all the larger properties were converted into "state farms" or government-run cooperatives, and in many respects—though not all—the condition of peasants on these lands is not very different from what it was under Somoza. Peasants now receive training in literacy, to which, however, are attached ceaseless political indoctrination and what must be enormously boring classes in "anti-imperialism." Peasants are also encouraged to offer their sons for service in the Popular Sandinista Army.

All this, but especially the failure of the Sandinistas to award individual titles of ownership (as they often quite uninhibitedly promised to do before 1979), has provided the *contras* with a ready source of food, recruits, and intelligence, particularly in the northern provinces bordering on Honduras. But the *contras* draw as well from smallholders who fear that they will be next in the sequence of expropriations or at any rate forced to sell their produce at whatever prices ENABAS deems politically expedient. In some areas matters have become so serious that the Sandinistas have had to evacuate communities forcibly to areas far from military operations or even to grant a limited number of deeds.

Before the revolution Nicaragua possessed a small labor movement not notable for its political militance. This is not surprising: industrial workers received wages that put them considerably above other manual workers, and, as Shirley Christian acutely observes, "people who would be working in factories in more developed countries were, in Nicaragua, making their livings as small entrepreneurs"—market vendors, taxi drivers, and so forth. Again, not surprisingly, the labor federation that represented most industrial workers was closely tied to the Somoza regime. Almost immediately after their victory the Sandinistas essentially took over this trade union movement and renamed it the Central Sandinistas de Trabajadores (CST), placing at its head a small group of activists from the underground days. By mid-1981 the CST accounted for roughly half the union membership; the other half was divided between the Federation of Nicaraguan Workers (FTN), affiliated with the Christian Democratic International, and the Federation of United Workers (FTU), with links to the AFL-CIO.

As with the peasantry, political indoctrination rather than the advancement of group interests has become the most important object of the CST. Wage increases and strikes have been prohibited, and when some workers have dared to contravene the orders of their putative leaders, they have been threatened with conscription into the army. Independent labor federations have found it increasingly difficult to operate, and as they face a state that will, in time, be the employer of sole resort, their future existence is in serious doubt.

The Nicaraguans who have suffered most from Sandinista rule are the Indians of the Atlantic coast—the Miskito, Rama, and Sumo peoples. Separated from "Spanish" Nicaragua by geography, language, culture, and religion, they were neglected by all governments before 1979. For many years the only outsiders interested in their welfare were Moravian missionaries (which perhaps explains why so many of their leaders are ordained pastors of that denomination). Although the Miskitos did not participate in the uprising against Somoza, several of their younger leaders studying at the time at the National University in Managua were persuaded to offer public support to the new regime in exchange for promises of autonomy and communal control of forest lands.

Almost immediately difficulties ensued. The Atlantic coast is the region of Nicaragua closest to Cuba and also the route of U.S. Marine landings in the 1920s. The Sandinistas' principal interest in the region was military, and by 1981 some 7,000 troops were stationed there, disrupting the peace of the inhabitants by constant maneuvers, target practice, and the careless use of tracked vehicles. Nor did the Miskitos take kindly to the Cuban doctors and teachers who poured into the area and who seemed more interested in raising the Indians' "political consciousness" than in teaching or healing. It was difficult, too, for people in the care of two or three generations of Moravian pastors to repose much confidence in leaders who boasted of being "scientific atheists."

The real difficulty, however, was the condescending attitude of the Sandinista leadership toward indigenous peoples. Luis Carrión Cruz, the member of the National Directorate delegated to handle Indian affairs, spoke openly of the Miskitos' "very large ideological backwardness" and refused any serious discussion of communal control of forest lands. The problem was not, of course, collective ownership as such but the desire of the Sandinistas not to allow the emergence of new forms of property that did not in some way depend on the state.

These developments led to violent incidents, the jailing of Miskito leaders, and a massive flight of younger Miskitos to Honduras, where they provided fresh troops for the tiny insurgency launched by former National Guardsmen. The Sandinistas responded by forcibly relocating some 15,000 Miskitos and Sumos from their ancestral villages; soldiers burned their homes, churches, and crops as they left. By 1984 it was estimated that at least 25,000 Miskitos, Ramas, and Sumos were in exile in Honduras; another 20,000 had been involuntarily resettled in other parts of the country. The Sandinistas often charm foreign innocents with the frank admission that they have committed "errors" with respect to the Indian communities. But as Christian notes, they did so with their eyes open: "The priorities were military security and political control. Past promises aside, these things were not negotiable."

The rapid decline of open political institutions in Sandinista Nicaragua has led to a transformation in the role of the Roman Catholic church. As in Poland, the church has become an opposition party *manqué;* though unable to overthrow the regime, it is the most important instrument of serious resistance within the country. A generation or two ago it would have been possible to dismiss this phenomenon as a reactionary holdover from the old regime; efforts to do so have, indeed, been made, but they do not stand up well in the light of recent history. The spiritual leader of Nicaragua, Cardinal Miguel Obando y Bravo, has long been noted for his liberal views on social and economic issues and was always one of the most courageous and outspoken opponents of the Somoza dictatorship.

The spectacle of a liberal cleric opposing the Sandinistas is especially discomfiting to well-wishers of the regime in Catholic circles abroad, for the Nicaraguan revolution has become one of the two or three most important repositories of hope for those clergy and laity broadly identified with the movement known as "liberation theology." For these people, ideologically speaking, there can be no disjunction between a church committed to the interests of the poor and a government that formally embraces and practices Marxism. This notion dovetails with another held by the government—namely, that since (according to a 1981 poll) 80 percent of the Nicaraguans identify "religion" as the most important value in their lives, the regime cannot afford a direct confrontation with the church. Rather, the church must be absorbed and controlled. Hence the creation of a "People's Church"—a caucus (to use conventional political terminology) within the Body of Christ that either is declared to be, or at any rate soon will become, coterminous with it.

Nicaragua's revolutionary Christians have set about this application of Leninist principles to religious organization with some very distinct advantages. They have received generous donations from overseas, particularly from the World Council of Churches ($176,000), the National Council of Churches ($365,329), the Methodists ($100,000), the Presbyterian Program to Fight World Hunger ($10,000), and the United Methodists ($25,000). All this money has allowed them to maintain a full-time staff, mostly foreigners, who operate out of the Valdivieso Center in Managua. They are viewed with distinct benevolence by the regime, which periodically supplies them with access to controlled media, transportation, and other facilities (in exchange for which they periodically appear to give witness to visiting coreligionists).

More important still has been the way that the Sandinista *turbas*, or mobs, have attacked bishops and priests loyal to Cardinal Obando, including, most spectacularly, the pope himself on the occasion of his visit to Managua in March 1983. The government or its dependencies have also harassed or expelled leaders of Protestant denominations insufficiently *aggiornado*, including Jehovah's Witnesses, Moravians, Seventh-Day Adventists, and some evangelicals. And it has shut down Radio Católica, the property of the Roman Catholic archdiocese, the country's sole remaining independent station. Moreover, a person's religious views have become a crucial factor of survival in an increasingly difficult (and government-controlled) job market.

Under these circumstances one would have the right to expect the church in Nicaragua to be, at the very least, deeply divided, and this is the way many left-wing Christians in the United States and elsewhere have described it. Yet after a conscientious effort to determine the relative strength of the traditional and "people's" churches, Shirley Christian found that most parish priests, including a majority of the foreign-born, usually support their bishops. Further, she discovered that "generally . . . the liberation priests did not attract big crowds to their masses." Cardinal Obando's dispute with the Sandinistas has made him the most popular man in the country, and the only reason the regime has not attacked him more strongly is out of fear of increasing his stature even further. She closes her survey with an interesting question: If the Sandinistas ever do succeed in subverting the church hierarchy, will they continue to feel the need for their revolutionary Christian friends?

The Opposition and the Future

A regime that seeks to impose Marxist patterns of social control on an unwilling population and is willing to sacrifice its economy in the process is bound to find an uncommon need for instruments of force and violence. This explains why, among other things, the Sandinistas have raised an army larger than that of all other Central American nations combined. It accounts for the need for massive foreign assistance from countries like Cuba, the Soviet Union, East Germany, and Bulgaria, whose major, perhaps only, real contribution to the armature of modern life is the art of domestic surveillance. It also explains the steady pattern of Soviet deliveries of military materiel to Nicaragua, including (until 1983) smaller transport planes, helicopters, and tankers, as well as heavy weapons like tanks, armored personnel carriers, artillery, and aircraft. Thus what at first glance appears to be an exclusively internal affair of the Nicaraguans—how to organize their own society—becomes a matter of legitimate security concern to their neighbors and to the United States.

Such efforts at the Marxist reorganization of society will also lead opponents—when their patience and good will are finally exhausted—to grasp at whatever violent alternatives are available. In Nicaragua this has meant a veritable flowering and transformation of the *contras*. In a mere five years the *contras* have grown from perhaps 300 to 15,000 men, which is precisely three times the number of men who fought Somoza at the height of the civil war in 1979. There have been some qualitative changes as well: the preponderance of former National Guardsmen has dwindled, so that today only nine of the fifty-four commanders can be so described; as for the soldiers themselves, they now consist largely of peasants, shopkeepers, Miskito Indians, and, on the southern front, even former Sandinistas.

At the same time, there has been a dramatic change in the political leadership of the resistance. It now includes not merely conservatives with good anti-Somoza credentials like Adolfo Calero and Fernando Chamorro but social democrats and liberals who collaborated with the Sandinistas during their initial period of power—Arturo Cruz, former president of the Central Bank and ambassador to the United States; Alfonso Robelo, former member of the Council of State; and Edén Pastora Gómez, who as "Comandante Zero" was the most important combat hero of the revolution and later served it as deputy minister of defense. The fact that so many commentators in the United States continue to talk about the *contras* in terms appropriate to five years ago says far more about the state of affairs in this country than about the situation in Nicaragua or its immediate environs.

Partly as a result of such talk, Congress voted in May 1985 to cut off all aid to the *contras*. The day after the vote, Nicaraguan President Daniel Ortega went off to Moscow to confer with his allies—much to the horror and consternation of Congress. Precisely why so many congressmen were in such an uproar over Ortega's trip—which was far from his first—is something of a mystery. Perhaps it was because in one single act Ortega had eloquently demonstrated something many Nicaraguans have known for six years: that the course of events in their country is following a logic of its own, not reacting to provocations from the United States. Members of Congress could have known this long ago had they simply focused on the way the Sandinistas have treated their own people, instead of trying to squeeze the entire contents of Nicaraguan reality into the narrow tube of bilateral relations or, worse still, into the tiny prism of partisan politics. There is still time for them to reverse course, but they must act quickly, or all of us—Nicaraguans, Hondurans, Costa Ricans, and ultimately Americans—will reap a very bitter harvest indeed.

Notes

1. David Nolan, *FSLN: The Ideology of the Sandinistas and the Nicaraguan Revolution* (Miami: Graduate School of International Studies, University of Miami).

2. Shirley Christian, *Nicaragua: A Revolution in the Family* (New York: Random House, 1985).
3. Claire Sterling, *The Masaryk Case,* new ed. (Boston: David R. Godine, 1982).
4. Arturo Cruz Sequeira, "Introducción," in José Luis Velásquez and Arturo Cruz Sequeira, eds., *Nicaragua: regresión en la revolución* [Regression in the revolution] (San José, Costa Rica: El Libro Libre, 1986).
5. Forest Colburn and Silvio de Franco, "Elite agraria en la revolución nicaragüense" [The agrarian elite in the Nicaraguan revolution], in Velásquez and Sequeira, Nicaragua, pp. 167–88.

10
Afterword
Mark Falcoff

As frustrated foreigners frequently remark, American foreign policy is almost wholly *reflexive:* it reacts to events rather than shapes them or plans for their eventuality. When a crisis finally comes, the full weight of U.S. military, diplomatic, and policy energies is ruthlessly thrust at a problem, typically too late to rectify the error of past neglect. This is the way almost all our foreign policy disasters have been explained since at least Pearl Harbor, and it raises serious questions about the capacity of American democracy to deal with the great power status and the international responsibilities that it has fallen heir to (or has sought) since 1945.

If this is so for major issues, it applies even more to problems of middle- or longer-range import, such as the Communist challenge in the Western Hemisphere. On one hand, as the papers collected here make clear, the Soviet Union is still very much a secondary power in the region, restricted by geography, logistics, culture, and other, more pressing international priorities. On the other, it is clearly in the ascendant, and the vectors of its growing influence can be seen in many areas—trade, scholarships, intelligence, a naval and military presence in the Caribbean, and the presence of two client-states, one now on the Latin American mainland. As Howard Wiarda points out in chapter 1, separating out the strands of the Soviet threat and possibility would be a daunting intellectual exercise under the best of circumstances. But more daunting still is the task of forging a policy consensus on the problem in Washington and in the country at large.

First, it must be accepted that in a certain way the Soviet Union benefits simply from being the "other"—the alternative pole of influence, the point of reference for those disenchanted with the status quo in their countries, which they attribute to the hegemony, real or imagined, of the United States. In some ways Moscow's role is thus not very different from that of Great Britain in the nineteenth century or imperial or Nazi Germany in part of the twentieth. There is, however, an important qualitative distinction: the Soviet Union hides its great power aspirations behind an ideological mask of presumptive universality—one that, as Wiarda points out in chapter 3, seems to mesh at least superficially with some aspects of the intellectual and political culture of many Latin American countries. Of course, not everyone who is a Marxist or who sympathizes with or unconsciously absorbs Marxist ideas is necessarily a Communist or an advocate of Soviet interests, but the pervasiveness of such notions means that all but the most conservative governments profess a very different view of the Soviet Union from that of their counterparts in the United States and Western Europe.

At the same time the need to place some distance between themselves and the United States to justify their nationalist *bona fides* leads many otherwise responsible Latin American leaders to tilt diplomatically toward Soviet positions, particularly in large international bodies like the United Nations and the Non-Aligned Movement. This creates special problems of assessment for the United States: To what degree is the Soviet Union being used simply to obtain greater benefits from Washington? To what degree does the policy respond to a genuine support (quid pro quo) of Soviet international aspirations?

Second, although some aspects of the social and economic picture in Latin America, particularly in the poorer countries of the Caribbean Basin, would seem to *justify* the professed political agendas of Marxist parties and movements, I show in chapter 2 that in the three cases to date—Cuba, Nicaragua, and Grenada—the accession to power of a Marxist-Leninist regime occurred not as a response to widespread economic deprivation but as a consequence of purely political revolution. This means that massive aid programs—whatever their intrinsic value—may be irrelevant to the prevention of "other Cubas" or "other Nicaraguas": in fact, one could make almost the opposite case. The Alliance for Progress, launched by the Kennedy administration in 1961 as a response to the Cuban revolution, arguably introduced into the region new elements of instability and even of class conflict.[1] At a minimum, it is surely a subject for further thought.

Finally, once revolutionary governments come to power, it is by no means clear that the United States possesses the means to moderate their course. Because the evidence on Cuba is just sufficiently ambiguous,[2] the Carter administration was convinced that a more comprehending and generous attitude toward the victorious Sandinistas would produce a more desirable result. As chapter 9 carefully documents, the new rulers in Managua were not "forced" into the arms of the Soviet Union—they were already there even before taking power, and nothing the United States did thereafter was capable of wrenching (or coaxing) them free.

Policy makers might well reflect on why this is so. Had the Sandinistas agreed to a more pragmatic policy toward the United States, they could have counted on very considerable economic assistance and probably also support for their continued political hegemony within Nicaraguan society. But an alliance with the Soviet Union was evidently more attractive: it raised their international importance, guaranteed them a wider range of financial assistance, and made their revolution an international "cause," not merely in Western Europe and Latin America but even in the United States, by tying it directly to opposition to the United States and all its works. Probably also the willingness of the Soviet Union to provide the new Nicaraguan government with unlimited arms and the technology of surveillance (through East Germany and Bulgaria) addressed agendas more urgent—for the Sandinista directorate—than mere economic development.

This brings us to the third point: what the Soviet Union has to offer revolutionary governments is really a praxis for dictatorial rule, not a formula for economic development. This has been the source of no small amount of confusion both in Latin America and in the United States: the Latin left, of course, imagines that the "anti-Communism" of the United States is some sort of conspiracy to prevent it from developing; establishment politicians in the region often talk as if Communism were simply a more ruthless version of social reform ("progressives in a hurry"); some conservative and reactionary elements—notably in Guatemala, El Salvador, and Chile—inadvertently reinforce this notion by bracketing all genuine social and economic change with "Communism," sometimes killing and torturing to make their point. Republicans and Democrats in the United States act as if the Communist challenge were primarily economic and therefore propose to curb it through the export of American notions of free enterprise or massive infusions of foreign aid or, more likely, both.

Fourth and finally, American policy makers can never agree on exactly where Latin America fits into the overall Soviet strategic picture. As I suggest in chapter 2, perhaps even the Soviets themselves are unsure whether their own interests are better served by new client-states like Cuba and Nicaragua or merely by permanent unrest throughout the Caribbean Basin, which diverts the resources and attention of the United States from Western Europe and elsewhere.[3] Ernest Evans shows how a native tradition of political violence meshes with the latter; the Valentas in chapter 4 show us how the

Soviets have diversified their policy goals over the past fifteen years. The growing sophistication of Soviet assessments, the willingness to pursue pragmatic policies with non-Communist Latin American governments, and the capacity to exploit local unrest when and where it occurs constitute a hydra-headed problem for which U.S. policy makers will find no immediate solution.

Perhaps the most important policy recommendation that follows from this is the need to avoid overheated rhetoric and exaggerated descriptions of the challenge that faces us. For example, the single most grievous wound inflicted on the Reagan administration's Central American policy was the assertion by Secretary of State Alexander M. Haig, Jr., at his first press conference, that El Salvador was a decisive, perhaps *the* decisive, theater of U.S.-Soviet confrontation, at which he proposed to "draw the line."[4] This unfortunate incident caused many to lose sight of the real issue—the prospect of another government in Central America allied militarily and politically to Cuba and the Soviet Union—which was serious enough, and doubled the cost in policy energy of what was, in the end, a very sound approach to the problem, namely, military assistance combined with effective social reform.

Second, the United States must clarify the nature of the Communist challenge. Abolishing poverty may be a worthy goal in itself, but so far in history no Communist government has come to power as a result of a massive uprising of the oppressed and exploited. Where armed insurgencies exist, they can only be defeated by counterforce, and this may require—in addition to land reform—the dispatch of advisers and the sale of helicopters, machine guns, and other uncongenial instruments. Conversely, military victories on the ground will not be consolidated without the evolution of more representative political institutions. As the Guatemalan experience has demonstrated, killing Communists is not sufficient to establish genuine political stability. Conversely, stable democracies do not require a perfect pattern of income distribution—merely the capacity to compete openly for the allocation of scarce resources.

Third, the United States should make clear to the Latin American nations precisely what it is that it finds objectionable about Soviet expansion in the region. The growth of trade poses no serious threat, partly because, as the Argentines have learned, the Soviets really have very little to offer except hard currency (and not always that). Even the vast number of Latin American students receiving scholarships for training in the Soviet Union may constitute an unanticipated blessing for the United States, since the Soviet model, observed at close range, often produces convinced anti-Communists. The real issue is the role of intelligence and espionage, often through embassies of the Soviet bloc or through Nicaraguan and Cuban surrogates. Even quite conservative Latin American governments are still reluctant to see the Soviet-Hungarian, the Soviet-Czech, much less the Soviet-Cuban or Soviet-Nicaraguan, relationship for what it is.[5] This is a point on which U.S. diplomacy must insist, publicly and privately, as frequently as possible.

Finally, there is a need to rethink U.S. approaches to public diplomacy in Latin America. Unfortunately, a very large part of the political community in most countries regards Communism as some sort of advanced form of liberalism or social democracy, which the United States opposes because it favors the preservation of the status quo. Part of this misconception arises out of past errors of policy, part from the conduct of the most reactionary elements of society, which gives anti-Communism an undeserved bad name. At the same time, professedly liberal elements are often quite irresponsible in their attitude toward Communism and toward the United States.[6] There is really no reason why others should define this challenge for us: through the Voice of America, Radio Martí, World Net, and its many print outlets, the United States Information Agency possesses the means to tell the truth. That is, in the final analysis, our strongest instrument in meeting and besting the Communist challenge, not only in the Caribbean but elsewhere throughout the world.

Notes

1. One could even make the case that the election of a Marxist president (Salvador Allende) in Chile in 1970 was a direct outgrowth of the Alliance for Progress, since by pressing for tax and land reforms, the Kennedy administration (and its successor) introduced a schism between the ruling Christian Democrats and the conservative parties, through which it was possible for the Socialist-Communist alliance (Unidad Popular) to squeeze into power in subsequent balloting.

2. For the best expression of this view, see Paul Sigmund, *Multinationals in Latin America: The Politics of Nationalization* (Madison: University of Wisconsin Press, 1980), pp. 84–130.

3. Of course, the choices are not always so simple. To preserve the minimum agenda, it is something necessary to make a far larger commitment than was originally contemplated. This is the case with Cuba and may well become the case with Nicaragua.

4. Rereading the text of his statement makes clear that General Haig was slightly less inflammatory than the press chose to represent in relating the story to the American people. It is still the responsibility of major public officials in the United States, however, especially in a conservative admin-

istration, to measure their remarks about Communism so as to minimize the opportunities for distortion by the media.

5. As the captured documents summarized in the El Salvador white paper show, the Hungarian—not the Soviet—embassy in Mexico City was the site of important meetings of the FDR-FMLN guerrilla leadership, and in the journey of Salvadoran Communist leader Shafik Handal around the world in search of aid, the most important venues were East Germany, Vietnam, and Ethiopia. See Mark Falcoff, "The El Salvador White Paper and Its Critics," *AEI Foreign Policy and Defense Review*, vol. 4, no. 2 (1982).

6. One example is the vilification to which the poet and anthropologist Octavio Paz has been subject in Mexico for taking a firmly anti-Communist and liberal democratic stand in his magazine *Vuelta*. Paz is now regarded by the Mexican intelligentsia as a traitor to his country.

Acknowledgments

CHAPTER 2, "Communism in Central America and the Caribbean," is reprinted courtesy of Pergamon-Brassey's, © Pergamon-Brassey's.

CHAPTER 3, "Soviet Policy in the Caribbean and Central America: Opportunities and Constraints," was first presented at the conference "Soviet Policy in the Third World," sponsored by the Tinker Foundation and the Institute for the Study of the Soviet Union and East Europe of the University of Arizona, Tucson, January 7–11, 1987. An earlier version of this paper was presented at the Kennan Institute for Advanced Russian Studies, Woodrow Wilson International Center for Scholars and the U.S. Information Agency, Washington, D.C., March 2, 1984. A somewhat different version of this chapter is forthcoming in John Garrard and S. Neil MacFarlane, eds., *Soviet Policy in the Third World*.

CHAPTER 4, "Soviet Strategies and Policies in the Caribbean Basin" first appeared in Howard J. Wiarda, ed., *Rift and Revolution: The Central American Imbroglio* (Washington, D.C.: American Enterprise Institute, 1984).

CHAPTER 5, "Cuba's Strategies in Exporting Revolution," first appeared in Dennis L. Bark, *The Red Orchestra: Instruments of Soviet Policy in Latin America and the Caribbean* (Stanford, Calif.: Hoover Institution Press, 1985). © by the Board of Trustees of the Leland Stanford Jr. University.

CHAPTER 6, "Revolutionary Movements in Central America: The Development of a New Strategy," first appeared in Howard J. Wiarda, ed., *Rift and Revolution: The Central American Imbroglio* (Washington, D.C.: American Enterprise Institute, 1984).

CHAPTER 7, "Bishop's Cuba, Castro's Grenada," first appeared in an earlier version in Jiri Valenta and Herbert Ellison, eds., *Grenada and Soviet/Cuban Policy* (Boulder, Colo.: Westview Press, 1986).

CHAPTER 8, "The Impact of Grenada in Central America," first appeared in Jiri Valenta and Herbert J. Ellison, eds., *Grenada and Soviet/Cuban Policy* (Boulder, Colo.: Westview Press, 1986). The author would like to acknowledge the assistance of Janine T. Perfit, who aided enormously with the research. Dr. Iêda Siqueira Wiarda and Professor Richard M. Millett offered useful comments on an earlier version. Some of the analyses in this paper were based on classified materials made available on a not-for-direct-attribution basis and on interviews with U.S. intelligence officers, also on a not-for-attribution basis.

CHAPTER 9, "Nicaraguan Harvest," was first published in *Commentary* (July 1985).

Index

Afanasiev, Victor, 87
Afghanistan, 6, 9, 82, 90, 96, 100, 131, 132, 134
Africa, 146, 152
Alarcon, Ricardo, 208
Algeria, 124
Algerian National Liberation Front (FLN), 169, 173–74, 177
Allende, Salvador, 82, 86, 88, 176
Alliance for Progress, 235
American Civil Liberties Union, 175
Americas Watch Committee, 175
Amnesty International, 175
Anderson, Thomas, 32
Angola, 23, 29, 82, 96, 99, 100, 127, 130, 132, 134
Anti-American sentiments, 60, 62
Arbatov, Georgi, 90
Arbenz, Jacobo, 1, 121, 170
Arditto Barletta, Nicolás, 112, 129
Argentina, 97, 125, 135, 145, 223
    Cuban policy, 133, 146, 149
    early revolutionary movements, 162, 176, 178
    Soviet relations, 56, 60, 145
    Soviet trade, 7, 57, 92, 237
Arias, Oscar, 116
Armed Forces of National Liberation, 163
Armed Forces of National Resistance, 150
Austin, Hudson, 192
Australia, 15
Austria, 175

Barbados, 137
Barco, Virgilio, 117
Bay of Pigs invasion, 85
Belenko, Viktor, 91
Belize, 123–24, 201
Bermúdez, Enrique, 38
Betancourt, Rómulo, 161
Betancur, Belisario, 117
Bishop, Maurice, 43–44, 46, 102, 108, 189, 191–93, 202
Blanco, Hugo, 163, 176
Blasier, Cole, 70

Bolãnos Hunter, Miguel, 154
Bolivia, 64
    guerrilla insurrection, 4, 59, 82, 149, 162, 165, 178, 180, 188
    Soviet relations, 57, 145
Bonaparte, Napoleon, 168, 169
Borge, Tomás, 31, 97, 98, 128, 171, 212
Bouterse, D., 135, 205–6
Brandt, Willy, 37, 204
Bravo, Douglas, 167–68
Brazil, 64, 94, 135, 177
    early revolutionary movements, 162, 168
    Soviet relations, 60, 92, 146
    Suriname relations, 128, 206
Brinton, Crane, 63
Brutents, K., 119
Bulgaria, 98, 99, 103, 106, 107, 153, 201, 203, 231
Burnham, Forbes, 136

Calero, Adolfo, 38, 232
Canada, 107, 204
Cañas Jerez Treaty of 1858, 123
Cárdenas, Oscar Osvaldo, 205–6
Caribbean Basin
    cultural diversity, 13–14
    political environment, 17–20, 128
    Soviet strategy and tactics, 16–17
    strategic importance, 14–16, 134
    See also specific countries and issues
Caribbean Basin Initiative, 137
Carrión Cruz, Luis, 229
Carter administration, 41, 132, 136, 219, 224, 235
Castro, Fidel, 4, 31, 83, 95–96, 147, 170, 193
Castro, Raúl, 31, 96, 131, 148, 192
Central America
    economic development, 18–19
    regional conflict, 123–26
    revolutionary potential, 19–20, 128–30
    See also specific countries and issues

INDEX

Central American Defense Council (CONDECA), 210, 211
Central American Democratic Community, 126
Central American Project, 137
Central Intelligence Agency (CIA), 124, 223
Central Sandinista de Trabajadores (CST), 36–37, 228
Cerezo, Vinicio, 122
Chamorro, Fernando, 39, 232
Chernishov, Vladimir, 115
Chile, 82, 86, 88, 135, 145, 176
China, People's Republic of, 32, 135, 169–70
Christian Democratic trade union international, 36
Christian, Shirley, 222, 225, 228, 229, 231
Church opposition
    Grenada, 45–46, 190
    Nicaragua, 35–36, 229–31
Clausewitz, Karl von, 169
Coard, Bernard, 44, 46, 102, 108, 139
Colombia
    Central American relations, 39, 123, 188
    Cuban policy, 129, 132, 146
    guerrilla activity in, 79, 97, 125, 162
    Soviet policy, 60, 82, 87, 89, 116–17
Committee for Solidarity with the Struggle of the Central American Peoples, 123
Communist parties in Latin America
    characteristics, 66
    Costa Rica, 114
    El Salvador, 118–21, 150
    Guatemala, 122
    Honduras, 123
    Panama, 112
Confederación de Trabajadores Nicaragüenses, 36
Confederación de Unificación Sindical, 36
Contadora group, 111
Costa Rica, 175, 220
    arms buildup, 124–25
    Central American relations, 123, 126, 130, 172
    Cuban policy, 146, 188
    revolutionary activity, 97, 129
    Soviet policy, 60, 87, 89, 92, 114–16
Council for Mutual Economic Assistance (COMECON), 93, 110
Counterrevolutionary insurrection
    Nicaragua, 38–39, 100–101, 125, 210, 211, 223, 227–28, 231–32
Cruz Porras, Arturo, 37, 232
Cuba, 14, 172, 231
    effects of U.S. intervention in Grenada, 127–28, 193–95, 213
    Grenada, role in New Jewel Movement, 187–93
    internal stresses, 21–24
    military capability, 153
    normalization of U.S.-Cuban relations, 29–30
    oil suppliers to, 26–27, 92, 93, 113
    regime characteristics, 20–21
    Soviet economic relations, 26–27, 67, 92, 93, 146
    Soviet military links, 94–95, 147–49
    Soviet policies, 17, 81, 92–96, 145, 202
    strategic importance to U.S.S.R., 8, 56–57, 91, 95–96
    Suriname relations, 206–7
    U.S. invasion scenario, 16
    U.S. policies and options, 24–30, 132, 138, 139
Cuban and Soviet activities, 79–82
    Colombia, 116–17
    Costa Rica, 114–16
    Cuban contributions to Soviet expansionism, 151–54, 156–57, 201
    El Salvador, 118–21, 151, 208
    future strategies, 126–33
    Grenada, 101–9, 155
    Guatemala, 121–22
    Honduras, 123
    Mexico, 109–11
    Nicaragua, 96–101, 150–51, 154–55, 210, 211
    Panama, 111–13
    strategic objectives, 82–83, 85–92, 144–47, 149–51, 187–88
    support to contemporary revolutionary movements, 175–77
    U.S. counter-strategies, 133–40
    Venezuela, 113–14
Cuban missile crisis, 5, 82
Cuban revolution
    characteristics of, 19, 31, 220, 235
    rationale for, 24–25
    Soviet response to, 4, 15–16
    U.S. response to, 4–5, 15, 87
Cultural differences, 65
Cultural exchanges, 57–58
Czechoslovakia, 99, 106, 146, 153, 203, 223

Debray, Régis, 165
De Gaulle, Charles, 169
de la Espriella, Ricardo, 112
De la Madrid, Miguel, 111
del Valle, Erick Arturo, 112

INDEX

Democratic Coordinator, 35, 37–38
Democratic Revolutionary Action (ARDE), 38, 39
Democratic Revolutionary Front (FDR), 111, 120, 151, 174
Domínguez, Jorge, 119
Dominica, 127, 137
Dominican Republic, 56, 60, 85, 116, 128, 175
Duarte, José Napoleón, 120, 213
Duvalier, Jean-Claude, 128

East European politics, 83–84, 131–32, 138
Economic aid, 67–68
    assessment of, 235
    to Costa Rica, 220
    to Cuba, 26–27, 67, 93–94, 146
    to Grenada, 44–45, 107
    to Mexico, 110
    to Nicaragua, 34–35, 42, 67, 99, 219–20
    U.S. policy options, 137
Economic conditions
    Costa Rica, 114
    Cuba, 21–22, 24, 26
    Nicaragua, 33–35, 219–20
    Soviet tactics exploiting, 63, 82
    within Soviet Union, 69
Ecuador, 146
El Salvador, 124, 126
    Cuban policy, 130, 132, 146, 150, 151, 153–54
    death statistics, 178–79
    effect of U.S. intervention in Grenada, 207–9, 213
    guerrilla activities, 79, 82, 86, 97, 125
    population density, 178
    revolutionary potential, 129
    revolutionary strategy, 172–75, 178
    Soviet policy, 6, 59, 61, 87, 89, 118–21, 134, 201, 202
    terrorism against foreigners, 179
    U.S. military aid, 180
    U.S. policy options, 29, 135, 139, 237
Emigration
    from Cuba, 28–29
    Nicaragua, Indian migrations, 38–39, 125, 228–29
Enders, Thomas, 224
Ethiopia, 23, 24, 82, 96, 99, 100, 127, 130, 132, 134, 154
European Economic Community, 44, 107
Evans, Ernest, 160–86

Falcoff, Mark, 13–50, 144–59, 187–97, 218–39

Falklands Islands war, 133
Farabundo Martí National Liberation Front (FMLN), 97, 111, 118, 120–21, 146, 153, 173, 174
Federation of Nicaraguan Workers, 228
Federation of United Workers, 228
Financial aid. *See* Economic aid
Foco theory, 161, 165
Foreign policy. *See* Policy options, U.S.
France, 7, 14, 111, 124, 168, 169, 173, 175
Frente Sandinista de Liberación Nacional (FSLN), 30. *See also* Nicaragua

Gairy, Eric, 136, 189
Garcia, Aníbal, 122
Geostrategic considerations, 67, 68
    Caribbean Basin, 14–17, 90–92, 134
    Cuba, 8, 56–57, 91, 95–96
    Panama, 111
Germany, 14, 168–69
Germany, Democratic Republic of (East), 98, 99, 103, 106, 107, 153, 191, 201, 203, 231
Germany, Federal Republic of (West), 7, 9, 42, 179
González, Felipe, 204
González Videla, Gabriel, 145
Gorbachev, Mikhail, 132
Great Britain, 18, 123, 133
Greece, 175
Grenada, 79, 88, 99, 136
    church opposition, 45–46, 190
    Cuban policy and activity, 146, 148, 152, 154, 155, 187–94, 202–4
    New Jewel Movement, 19, 43–47, 96, 202–3, 235
    Nicaraguan ties, 204–5
    Soviet policy, 17, 86, 88, 91, 92, 97, 99, 101–9, 134, 199–204
    U.S. intervention, 6, 82, 107–9, 127–28, 133, 198–99, 205–14
    U.S. policy options, 47–48, 138, 139, 194–95
Grenada Peace Council, 103
Guatemala, 1, 56, 170, 237
    Central American relations, 123–24, 126
    early revolutionary movements, 161–63
    guerrilla activities in, 79, 97
    revolutionary potential, 129
    revolutionary strategy, 172–75, 178, 179
    Soviet policy, 59, 61, 82, 87, 89, 121–22, 145
    U.S. military aid, 180

245

INDEX

Guatemalan Labor (Communist) party, 122
Guatemalan Nationalist Revolutionary Union, 122
Guerra Popular Prolongada, 171
Guerrilla Army of the Poor, 97
Guerrilla strategy. *See* Revolutionary strategy
Guerrilla Warfare (Guevara), 163, 164, 167
Guevara, Ernesto (Che), 4, 31, 59, 83, 162–67, 175, 178, 180
Guillen, Abraham, 167
Guyana, 123, 136, 156, 188

Haig, Alexander M., Jr., 132, 237
Haiti, 14, 128
Handal, Shafik Jorge, 118, 119, 139
Herrera, Luis, 113
Honduras, 123–26, 129, 130, 229
Horowitz, Irving Louis, 148
Human rights concerns, 175

India, 6, 9
Indian migrations, 38–39, 125, 228–29
Indochina, 173, 180–81
Intelligence activities, 15, 56–57, 91, 136, 238
International Confederation of Free Trade Unions, 36
International support, 61, 172, 174–75
Iran, 44
Iraq, 44, 107
Irish Republican Army, 170
Israel, 39, 126
Italy, 135

Jacobs, W. Richard, 155, 192–93
Jamaica, 87, 102, 108, 127, 128, 156, 188
James, Liam, 106, 191
Japan, 7, 15
John Paul II (pope), 36, 230
Jorge, Antonio, 155, 156

Katushev, Konstantin, 93
Kazimirov, Vladimir, 116
Kennedy administration, 85, 235
Kissinger, Henry, 134
Korolev, Yu. N., 88
Kudachkin, M., 119

Labor movement
 El Salvador, 121
 Grenada, 46
 Nicaragua, 36–37, 228
 overall weakness, 66–67
Lenin, V. I., 166
Libya, 24, 44, 97, 107, 138, 154
López Portillo, José, 80, 110

Louison, Einstein, 103
Lucas, Romeo, 121
Luers, William, 53, 54, 59
Lusinchi, Jaime, 113

M-19 guerrillas, 97, 116, 117
McGrory, Mary, 209
Malaya, 169
Manley, Michael, 87, 127, 203
Mao Tse-tung, 169
Marighella, Carlos, 163–64, 168
Marxist model of change, 63–64
Mejia Victores, Oscar Humberto, 122
Mesa-Lago, Carmelo, 29
Methodist church, 230
Mexico, 153
 Central American relations, 34, 126, 172, 177, 182, 220
 revolutionary potential, 129, 135
 Soviet policy, 17, 56, 87, 88, 92, 109–11, 133, 145
Military issues
 Central American arms buildup, 124–25, 130
 Costa Rica, arms transfers through, 114–15
 Cuban military adventurism, 23–24, 29
 Cuban military capability, 94–95, 147–49, 153
 Grenada, Cuban and Soviet assistance to, 103–7
 Mexico, Cuban and Soviet relations with, 110–11
 Nicaragua, Cuban and Soviet assistance to, 97–99
 Soviet presence in Latin America, 7–8, 56
 U.S. assistance, 137, 180
Millett, Richard, 38
"Minimanual of the Urban Guerrilla" (Marighella), 163–64
Miskito Indians, 38–39, 125, 228–29, 232
Mondale, Walter F., 42
Monge, Luis Alberto, 115
Monroe Doctrine, 87, 90
Montaner, Carlos Alberto, 23, 28
Montero, Renán, 154
Montoneros movement, 97
Morse, Richard, 64
Movement of the Revolutionary Left (MIR), 163, 164, 176
Mozambique, 100

Naipaul, V. S., 18
National Bipartisan Commission on Central America, 134, 139
National Council of Churches, 230

246

INDEX

National Endowment for Democracy, 136
National Enterprise for Basic Foodstuffs (ENABAS), 226
National Revolutionary Movement, 174
Nationalism factors, 62
Netherlands, 42, 206–7
New Jewel Movement. *See* Grenada
New Zealand, 15
Nicaragua, 6, 123, 127
    arms buildup, 124
    church opposition, 35–36, 229–31
    counterrevolutionary activity, 38–39, 100, 125, 210, 211, 223, 227–28, 231–32
    Cuban activity in, 23–24, 150, 152, 154–55
    Cuban and Soviet military assistance, 97–99, 134, 148
    domestic political opposition, 35–38
    economic problems, 33–35, 219–20
    effects of U.S. intervention in Grenada, 128, 209–13
    elections in, 40
    Grenadian ties, 204–5
    Indian migrations, 38–39, 125, 228–29
    international activities, 80, 97, 117, 126
    international support for, 111, 113, 153, 154, 177, 218–19
    regime characteristics, 30–33, 39–40, 79, 86, 221–29, 231, 235–36
    Soviet economic relations, 90, 92, 99, 132, 157
    Soviet policy, 17, 57, 82, 87, 88, 91, 96–101, 200–2
    U.S. policy options, 5, 40–43, 138–39, 212–13
Nicaraguan Armed Revolutionary Force (FARN), 38, 39
Nicaraguan Democratic Force (FDN), 38–39, 42, 125
Nicaraguan revolution, 82, 88, 146, 151
    characteristics of, 19, 61, 129, 220–21, 235
    revolutionary strategy, 170–72, 178
    U.S. policy response, 161
Nolan, David, 221, 222
Noriega, Manuel, 112
North Korea, 106, 107, 138, 153
Northern Ireland, 170

Obando y Bravo, Miguel, 35, 36, 230, 231
Ogarkov, Nikolay, 98, 103, 105
Organization of East Caribbean States (OECS), 82, 210
Organization of Petroleum Exporting Countries (OPEC), 107

Ortega, Daniel, 98, 232
Ortega, Humberto, 31, 97, 98, 224
Oxfam-America, 175

Pakistan, 6, 9
Palestine Liberation Organization (PLO), 97, 98, 154, 169
Panama, 116, 129, 172
    Soviet policy, 17, 60, 87, 88, 90, 111–13
Panama Canal, 15, 90
Pastora Gómez, Eden, 31, 39, 125, 232
Pavlov, Yuri, 115
People's Liberation Army, 116
People's Revolutionary Army, 176
Pérez, Carlos Andres, 204
Peru, 64, 135, 146, 149
    early revolutionary movements, 161–64, 176, 178
    Soviet policy, 57, 60, 82
Petroleum sales and shipments
    to Cuba, 26–27, 92, 93, 113
    to Nicaragua, 34, 35, 157, 220
Petroleum transport, 15, 90
Piñeiro Losada, Manuel, 152
Poland, 82, 90, 131
Policy options, U.S., 133–40, 234–39
    differing perspectives on, 51–55
    effect of intervention in Grenada, 194–95, 212–13
    toward Cuba, 24–30
    toward Grenada, 47–48
    toward Nicaragua, 40–43, 161
    toward revolutionary strategies, 160–61, 179–82
Political conditions. *See* Sociopolitical factors
Ponomarev, Boris, 96
Popular Liberation Forces, 150
Popular Vanguard party, 114, 115
Portugal, 64
Prensa, La (Nicaragua), 30–32
Presbyterian Program to Fight World Hunger, 230
Propaganda, 204
Providencia island, 123
Prussia, 168, 169
Puerto Rico, 14

Quaddafi, Muhammar, 189
Quitasueño island, 123

Radio broadcasting, 25–26, 31, 238
Rama Indians, 125, 228, 229
Rastafarians, 46
Reagan administration, 41–42, 47–48, 132, 209
Reed, Gail, 204

247

INDEX

Revolution in the Revolution? (Debray), 165
Revolutionary Armed Forces of Colombia, 116
Revolutionary Movement of November 13, 163
Revolutionary Movement of the People, 115
Revolutionary potential, 63, 68, 128–30
Revolutionary strategy
    contemporary movements, 168–77
    early movements, 161–68
    patterns of violence, 177–79
    Soviet–Cuban dynamics, 82–83, 85–92, 144–47, 149–51, 187–88
    U.S. response to, 160–61, 179–82
Ríos Montt, Efraím, 122
Robelo, Alfonso, 39, 232
Rodríguez, Carlos Rafael, 96, 208
Rojas, Don, 190–91
Romero, Carlos Humberto, 151
Roncador Cay island, 123
Royo, Aristides, 112
Ruiz, Henry, 222

Sadat, Anwar, 138, 200
Saint Dominique, 14
Saint Kitts-Nevis, 127
Saint Lucia, 127
Saint Vincent, 127
San Andrés island, 123
Sánchez Parodi, Ramón, 191
Sandino, Augusto, 170–71, 221
Santo Domingo, 212, 213
Seaga, Edward, 14, 127
Security issues. *See* Geostrategic considerations; Military issues
Sergeiev, Rostislav, 111
Serrana Keys, 123
Soares, Mario, 204
Soccer War, 124
Socialist International (SI), 174–75, 179, 191, 203, 205, 211
Sociopolitical factors
    changes within Latin America, 63, 64, 79–80
    cultural exchanges, 57–58
    Latin American attitudes toward Soviet Union, 65–66
    Soviet ideological preconceptions, 68–69
    U.S. perspectives, 51–55
Somoza Debayle, Anastasio, 30, 218
South Yemen, 134
Soviet-American relations, 84–85, 132–33
Soviet military buildup, 7–8
Soviet policy and strategy
    capabilities, 55–58

    effect of U.S. intervention in Grenada, 214
    host country factors affecting expanded Soviet influence, 62–69
    presence in Latin America, 1–10, 70–72, 199
    shifts, 1960–1986, 81–85
    strategies and tactics, 58–62, 200–201, 234, 236–37
    See also Cuban and Soviet activities; specific countries and issues
Soviet trade, 7, 57, 92, 114. *See also* Economic aid
Spain, 7, 14, 42, 175
Spanish Basque separatist organization ETA, 98
Sterling, Claire, 223
Strategy of the Urban Guerrilla, The (Guillen), 167
Sugar industry, 21–22, 93
Sumo Indians, 125, 228, 229
Suriname, 128, 129, 135, 153, 201, 205–7, 213
Sweden, 42
"Swing strategy," 16
Syria, 107

Taiwan, 221
Television networks, 31
Tendencia Proleteria, 171
Thompson, Robert, 181
Torres, Camillo, 164
Torres Rizo, Julian, 204
Torrijos, Omar, 87, 111
Trade issues
    Central American conflicts, 124
    Cuba, 27–28
    Nicaragua, 42
    Soviet trade with Latin America, 7, 57, 92, 114
Trade unions. *See* Labor movement
Tupamaro guerrillas, 162, 166–68

Ungo, Guillermo, 174
Unified Revolutionary Directorate (DRU), 151, 174
United Methodists, 230
United States Information Agency, 238
Urban terrorism. *See* Revolutionary strategy
Uruguay, 55, 135
    early revolutionary movements, 162, 166, 168
Ustinov, Dimitriy, 98

Valenta, Jiri and Virginia, 79–143
Véliz, Esther, 190

Venezuela
    Central American relations, 34, 39, 123, 172, 177, 182, 220
    Cuban policy, 82, 146, 149, 188
    early revolutionary movements, 161–63, 167
    Soviet policy, 87, 92, 113–14, 145
Vietnam, 106, 138, 154
Vietnam War, 180–81, 212, 213
Villalobos, Joaquín, 209
Visits to Cuba, 26

Wheelock, Jaime, 31

White Warriors Union, 179
Wiarda, Howard J., 1–12, 51–78, 198–217
Wicker, Tom, 209
Workers' Party of Jamaica, 102
World Confederation of Labor, 36
World Council of Churches, 230
World Federation of Trade Unions, 36
World Peace Council, 103
World War II, 168

Yugoslavia, 135

Zhurkin, V., 90

A Note on the Book

*This book was edited by Trudy Kaplan,
Dana Lane, and Janet Schilling of the
Publications Staff of the American Enterprise Institute.
The index was prepared by Patricia R. Foreman.
The text was set in Palatino, a typeface designed by Hermann Zapf.
Coghill Book Typesetting Company, of Richmond, Virginia,
set the type, and Edwards Brothers Incorporated,
of Ann Arbor, Michigan, printed and bound the book,
using permanent acid-free paper.*